POLITICAL ACTION IN EUROPE AND THE USA

Also by Alan Marsh
PROTEST AND POLITICAL CONSCIOUSNESS

Political Action in Europe and the USA

Alan Marsh
Senior Research Fellow
Social Statistics Research Unit, City University, London

The abridged edition of *Political Action: Mass Participation in Five Western Democracies* (Sage, 1979)

by

Samuel H. Barnes and Max Kaase

and

Klaus R. Allerbeck
Barbara G. Farah
Felix Heunks
Ronald Inglehart
M. Kent Jennings
Hans D. Klingemann
Alan Marsh
Leopold Rosenmayr

MACMILLAN

© Alan Marsh 1990

All rights reserved. No reproduction, copy or transmission
of this publication may be made without written permission.

No paragraph of this publication may be reproduced, copied
or transmitted save with written permission or in accordance
with the provisions of the Copyright, Designs and Patents Act
1988, or under the terms of any licence permitting limited copying
issued by the Copyright Licensing Agency, 33–4 Alfred Place,
London WC1E 7DP.

Any person who does any unauthorised act in relation to
this publication may be liable to criminal prosecution and
civil claims for damages.

First published 1990

Published by
THE MACMILLAN PRESS LTD
Houndmills, Basingstoke, Hampshire RG21 2XS
and London
Companies and representatives
throughout the world

British Library Cataloguing in Publication Data
Marsh, Alan
Political Action in Europe and the USA.
1. Western World. Democracies. Politics.
Participation of Public
I. Title   II. Barnes, Samuel H. (Samuel Henry).
Political Action
306.2
ISBN 978-0-333-51572-3   ISBN 978-1-349-20608-7 (eBook)
DOI 10.1007/978-1-349-20608-7

To Mark Abrams

Contents

List of Figures	ix
List of Tables	xi
Foreword	xiii
Preface	xv

1 The Theory and Measurement of Political Action	1
1.1 The Theory	1
1.2 Measuring Political Action	9
1.3 The Political Action Repertory	28
2 The Social Background of Political Action	33
2.1 The Baseline Model: Age, Sex and Education	35
2.2 The Political Action Repertory and the Baseline Model	52
2.3 Social Class and Other Problems	54
3 Ideology and Political Action	56
3.1 Ideology, Values and the New Politics	56
3.2 Measuring Ideological Thought	61
3.3 Ideology, Education and Political Interest	72
4 Values and Political Action	86
5 Dissatisfaction and Political Action	109
5.1 Social Stratification or the Old Politics Model	124
5.2 Value Discrepancy or the New Politics Model	126
5.3 Electoral Partisanship	126
5.4 Summary	130
6 The General Model of Political Action	131
6.1 Conventional Political Participation	136
6.2 Protest Potential	138
6.3 The Final Model of Political Action	142

6.4 Summary	146
7 Generations and Families	147
7.1 Political Evaluations	162
7.2 Conventional Political Participation	177
7.3 Protest Potential	180
7.4 Summary: Political Socialisation and Political Change	183
8 In Conclusion: The Future of Political Action in Western Democracies	184
8.1 Instrumental and Expressive Politics	189
8.2 Conclusion	193
Bibliography	195
Index	197

List of Figures

1.1	Ideal Patterns of Activity	12
1.2	Ten Examples of Protest Activity	16
1.3	Questionnaire Format	18
1.4	A Combined Scale of Approval and Intentions	22
1.5	The Political Action Repertory	30
2.1	Protest Potential by Age by Country	35
2.2	The Impact of the Baseline Model upon the Political Action Repertory	53
3.1	The Political Parties Judged by Respondents in Each Country	63
3.2	The Left-Right Self-Placement Scale	66
3.3	Levels of Ideological Thought in Politics: Definition of Types	70
3.4	Levels of Ideological Thought in Politics	71
3.5	Levels of Ideological Conceptualisation in Politics and Education (controlling for country-specific effects)	74
3.6	Relationship Between Ideological Thinking, Political Interest and Political Action	80
3.7	Political Values and Political Action	82
3.8	The Balance of Political Values among the Five Action Types, Averaged over Five Countries, by Levels of Ideological Thinking	85
4.1	The Materialist-Postmaterialist Dimension	92
4.2	Left-Right Self-Placement by Value Type	99
4.3	Value Priorities and Partisan Attitudes	100
4.4	Value Priorities and Attitudes Toward the Establishment (factor scores)	101
4.5	The Combined Influence of Age, Education, Value Priorities and Levels of Ideological Thinking upon Political Action	105
5.1	Model of Policy Dissatisfaction	125
5.2	A Linear Model of Political Policy Dissatisfaction	130
6.1	A General Model of Political Action	132
6.2	How Political Judgement is Formed	134
6.3	System Support, Political Evaluation and Political Action	137

6.4 The Revised Model of Political Action 143
7.1 Measures of Agreement and Disagreement between
    Parents and their Children 150
8.1 Four Styles of Political Orientation 191

List of Tables

1.1	The Conventional Political Participation Scale	14
1.2	Protest Potential Scale	23
1.3	The Proportion Among Those Reinterviewed in 1979–81 Who Reported Having Participated in Protest Actions Who Had Earlier Said that They Would or Would Not Participate	27
1.4	Political Action Repertory	32
2.1	Protest Potential by Age, by Sex, by Country	37
2.2	Conventional Participation by Age, by Sex, by Country	40
2.3	Conventional Political Participation by Type of Schooling Received	43
2.4	Protest Potential by Type of Schooling Received	44
3.1	The Use of Different Kinds of Ideas in Judging Political Parties	64
3.2	The Use of Different Kinds of Ideas to Recognise the 'Left' and the 'Right'	67
3.3	Distribution of Political Interest by Country	76
4.1	Distribution of Value Types	93
4.2	Value Priorities by Age Cohort, 1974: Percentage Falling into Materialist or Postmaterialist Category	94
4.3	Value Priorities by Respondent's Socio-Economic Status (by Respondent's Father's Socio-Economic Status)	96
4.4	Protest Potential by Value Type	102
4.5	Conventional Political Participation by Value Type	103
5.1	National Dissatisfaction Levels	112
5.2	Satisfaction and Action Typology	114
5.3	Changes in Expectation and Protest Potential	116
5.4	Mean Score Rankings of Issue Agendas	120
5.5	Ranking of Issue Agendas	122
7.1	Postmaterialism	154
7.2	Understanding of Left-Right Continuum	157
7.3	Placement on Left-Right Continuum	160
7.4	System Responsiveness	164
7.5	Political Trust	166

7.6	Political Efficacy	169
7.7	Overall Issue Agenda	172
7.8	Overall Policy Dissatisfaction	174
7.9	Conventional Political Participation	178
7.10	Protest Potential	181
8.1	The Balance between Styles of Political Involvement	192
8.2	Ratio of Instrumental Over Expressive Political Styles	193

Foreword

It is with pleasure that we write, on behalf of the ten authors of *Political Action*, in praise of this special edition of that volume. Alan Marsh was an original member of the international group that designed and executed the cross-national surveys that provide the data base for this and many other works on conventional and unconventional political participation. As Britain was the first country to carry out field work, Marsh had a special role in developing the final form and content of the core questionnaire that was eventually administered in eight countries. His volume on Britain, *Protest and Political Consciousness* (Sage, 1977), was the first book-length manuscript to be completed in the project. He and Kaase assumed primary responsibility for the treatment of participation in both the design of the project and in the original *Political Action*. And Marsh was, of course, one of the ten authors of that volume. For all these reasons, he is particularly qualified to rewrite *Political Action* for a non-technical audience.

The original volume is not an easy read for non-specialists. It examines the structure and sources of conventional and unconventional participation in political action in considerable detail and with extensive documentation. It explores several islands of theory, carefully develops its empirical analyses, and relates the various strands both theoretically and empirically. Today, almost ten years after the first draft of *Political Action* was completed, its authors feel that the rigour with which they approached their task of analysing the interplay between various modes of political participation and its meaning for democratic polities has had a fine pay-off. Unconventional political participation has turned out to be not a passing fancy but rather a permanent feature of the political process in our times. It is not the least because of this consideration that we so strongly welcome Alan Marsh's effort to make *Political Action* accessible to a wider, less specialised audience.

Writing the initial *Political Action*, like the entire project, was an equal-partners venture. Although individuals and small groups carried out the analyses and writing on particular topics, all of the book was subjected to the intensive and spirited criticism of the entire group. The result was a genuinely co-authored integrated volume by ten scholars from five countries. We are proud of that achievement. It is difficult for a book dealing with such complex theoretical topics and with such a rich and varied empirical data base to meet simultaneously the needs of scholarship, of students, and of the scientific community at large. The present version by Marsh admirably serves the purpose of presenting the principal findings of *Political Action* without undue emphasis on theoretical rationales and data manipulation. It explains in succinct, eloquent and authoritative language what was accomplished in the original volume. That ten authors created that book was a *tour de force*. Marsh has produced another.

Samuel H. Barnes
Ann Arbor

Max Kaase
Mannheim

Preface

This book is about mass political behaviour in five advanced industrial societies: Austria, Britain, Germany, The Netherlands and the United States of America. It is based on a large cross-national study by the Political Action Study Group that began in 1970 and continues today. This particular volume has its origins in the surveys of political behaviour among the populations of each of these five nations during the 1970s. It is an enquiry into the social and psychological basis of modern political mobilisation, into why people do the things they do when they participate in political actions.

Uniquely in its time, the study opened the field of enquiry to include unconventional as well as conventional political behaviour, political protest as well as party campaigning. During the few years preceding the start of the project, political scientists had watched puzzled as the conformity and passivity of the 1950s and early 1960s had disappeared and was replaced by waves of demonstrations, blockades, boycotts, strikes and occupations accompanied on occasion by damage, arson and violence. Such activities were not new in themselves but most had not been seen in a long while and new kinds of people seemed to be doing them: not only the oppressed but the advantaged and educated, and many in between, too. It was already clear by the early 1970s that mass unconventional political participation – doing things that went well beyond voting and canvassing for political parties – was spreading out and becoming part of the political resources of many ordinary people.

This movement, the adoption of protest techniques by local political activists, was a good deal less dramatic than the national civil rights campaigns and student 'revolutions' they copied but was of far greater political significance in the longer term. The question was: did this new and expanded repertory of political action mark no more than a passing interest soon to die away and be confined once more among only the most determined political ideologues? Or was it the start of a new kind of political citizenship of a far more active and assertive kind? If so, what would that mean for the conduct of political life in advanced industrial societies?

A popular view of politics that does not depend for its means of redress solely upon those channels provided by the official party system is a *conditional* view of democracy that makes greater and more varied demands upon the system than one in which politicians and civil servants are simply trusted to get on with it between elections. The spread of such a view in the 1970s and the direct political action that it almost daily inspired gave rise at the time to anxieties about how 'governable' such systems would become. It was feared that, by a sad irony, the economic and social freedoms associated with the dawn of a post-industrial society would be accompanied by a reduction in political freedoms as beleaguered governments reached for increasingly authoritarian methods to keep the lid on a boiling political pot.

On the other hand, this conditional view of democracy is one that places a premium on the need of citizens to exercise their civil rights directly. This is necessary both to achieve their policy aims and their demands for political redress and simply in order to preserve those same rights through frequent usage. This in turn makes heavy demands upon the citizens themselves, upon their individual skills and resourcefulness and on their willingness to join with strangers in common cause. It was this side of the equation, how and why ordinary citizens came to involve themselves in political events, that most intrigued the Political Action Study Group. Quite a lot was known about the social basis of conventional political activity, about why people got involved in parties and elections, in canvassing and propaganda. Almost nothing was known about what might be causing people to expand their repertory of political actions to include unconventional or 'protest' actions.

The key question concerned the relationship between conventional and unconventional political behaviour. Were they really opposing forms of activity? Did they have similar or quite different origins? To use a modern term, what was the extent of *skill transfer* from the conventional to the unconventional spheres of political activities?

The wisdom of the day said that skill transfer was low, that political protest arose from sources quite alien to the conventional party system. Those who favoured protest were those, mainly young people, who were turning their backs on the party system. They were bidding for a new kind of political conduct entirely, for an individualistic, almost a hedonistic political free-for-all where democracy would be exercised directly. These people were said to have quite new political skills, new motives and to come from different social locations compared with the ranks of the traditional party faithful.

Some observers were more cautious. True, the protesters of the

1970s wanted new things. Many of them wanted an expanded political agenda that included new equalities of race and sex, new concerns for the natural environment and new access to planning and decision-making, especially locally. They went about all this noisily too and so at first glance they did not sound much like politicians. But many of the skills they used looked familiar. Some of their faces looked familiar too in the sense that they came from social locations familiar to political scientists. Political leadership does not spring ready made from a social void. Leadership of any kind is shaped by familiar processes: by the established routes of access to social and economic privilege; by social class and education; by knowledge, skill and flair; by individual confidence; by the will of the young and able first to coerce and then to oust the existing élites. The social basis for political mobilisation is something that is unlikely to be reinvented anew by each succeeding generation. But it does change and the pace of that change differs from time to time. However jaundiced a view might now be taken of some of the excesses of the generation of '68, it was a time of rapid and significant political change. The Political Action Study Group set out to capture the origins of those changes.

In each of the five countries, these are the principal investigators who undertook the studies:

Austria	Leopold Rosenmayr
Britain	Alan Marsh
Germany	Klaus Allerbeck, Max Kaase and Hans Dieter Klingemann
The Netherlands	Cees de Graaf, Felix Heunks and Phillip Stouthard
United States	Samuel H. Barnes, Barbara G. Farah, Ronald Inglehart and M. Kent Jennings

Since this international team had set itself the goal of explaining the origins of mass political participation in advanced industrial societies, it follows that it was the mass of people in these five countries who should be studied. Consequently, national random samples of the population aged 16 and over were interviewed in each country ranging from a sample of 1200 in The Netherlands up to 2300 in Germany. The fieldwork was carried out between November 1973 and August 1974. *Political Action*, the first cross-national volume based on these studies, was published in 1979.

In 1975 and 1976 three more countries joined the project and similar surveys were carried out in Switzerland, Italy and Finland. Results from these studies appear fleetingly in this book but for the most part this abridged or student edition sticks closely to the main lines of explanation advanced in such careful detail in the original *Political Action* volume.

Readers of this abridged edition of *Political Action* should be aware that, even though it is a complete rewrite into easily accessible form, the original volume, all 607 pages of it, remains available for study. Serious students will want to expand their knowledge of political action through selective expeditions into the Sage Publications volume. In this book, the technical details, theoretical expansions, tables and figures, references, and so on, have all been kept to a minimum simply because all the necessary detail is available in the original. Throughout this book, signposts have been provided back to the original whenever it seemed particularly important to do so.

It is also worth pointing out that students and indeed all members of the research community can now find their way back to the original data because a full eight-nation data set, in user-friendly form, is available from most good data archives such as the ESRC Data Archive at the University of Essex, the Zentralarchiv für Empiriche Sozialforschung in Cologne and the Center for Political Research at the Institute for Social Research at the University of Michigan. Like the Civic Culture study before it, *Political Action* will keep generations of post-graduate students in thesis material for years and years.

It remains to thank those who have assisted the production of this book. Early chapters were drafted in 1985 during a three-month stay at the International Institute for Environment and Society at the Wissenschaftzentrum in Berlin, which generously provided a fellowship for this purpose. My thanks go to them for their interest and support, especially to Udo Simonis and Nicholas Watts whose guest I was. Thanks too to the Office of Population Censuses and Surveys for allowing me official leave to go. During this time, Hans Dieter and Ute Klingemann were a great source of encouragement and support, as have been all my colleagues in the Political Action Study Group. The original editors and authors of *Political Action*, Sam Barnes and Max Kaase, as well as providing the Foreword to this book, helped me stick to my task amid many distractions.

1 The Theory and Measurement of Political Action

1.1 THE THEORY

This is but a short guide to some of the reasoning that contributed to the design of the Political Action Survey. More detailed discussion will introduce special topic areas as each is dealt with in succeeding chapters.

1.1.1 The Nature of Political Action

By political action is meant those actions that citizens of a democratic country will engage in to influence political events and policy. Such actions are of two kinds: *conventional* and *unconventional* forms of political participation. These are our 'dependent measures' – the behaviour we want to explain. Conventional political participation occurs largely within the context of party politics with its meetings, campaigns, canvassing and dealings with functionaries and officials. It also includes those actions citizens more rarely take individually to influence officials, acting though always through the 'proper channels'. Conventional political participation is the kind of political behaviour that political scientists call 'élite-directed' – the legitimate pathways of citizen involvement in politics that are sanctioned and encouraged by the élites and by the rules of a democratic regime.

Unconventional political behaviour is different. It tends, in contrast to conventional forms, to be 'élite-challenging'. It has a more familiar name too: political protest. We are interested in why people involve themselves in demonstrations, boycotts, political strikes, occupations, street blockades and even violence against property and people in pursuit of political goals. More will be said about these definitions in the second part of this chapter which deals with measurement. Much more will be said about the relationship between these two forms of political action. Let us be clear for the moment only that we have a *dualistic* definition of political action:

conventional and unconventional, party and movement, conformity and protest. This idea of political dualism represented a major departure from earlier research into mass political behaviour so it is worth a paragraph or two of explanation. Why did we need a new definition of political action?

Perhaps it is better to ask why earlier studies paid such scant regard to political protest. To answer only that there was so little protest around in the 1950s (when surveys first came to dominate this kind of research) is not enough. Surely no-one had forgotten the 1920s and 1930s when dramatic manifestations of direct political action had wracked the political systems of Europe? Had Americans forgotten the hard struggles of the labour movement in the United States at the same time? Surely not; the problem was one of definition. By the 1950s political protest was thought of as a *pre*democratic form of political action. It was a non-legitimate class of political behaviours that belonged to a previous age before the electoral emancipation of the masses and universal franchise made mass protest unnecessary. It was an atavism that occurred from time to time but one that would fade under the impact of increasing prosperity, education and greater opportunity for citizen involvement in existing democratic forms. So wrote Seymour Martin Lipsett in 1961:

> . . . . the democratic class struggle will continue, but it will be a fight without ideologies, without red flags, without May Day parades.

It is said that of all human folly, prophecy is the most easily avoided. Yet at the time Lipsett's was a reasonable conjecture. Surveys had shown again and again that whilst citizens' involvement and understanding of politics was low, their trust and confidence in the political *system* was high. These findings, and the apparently growing strength of Western corporatist democracies nourished a benignly paternalistic view of mass politics. Higher levels of political activity, it was felt, were best left to well-educated liberal élites. The participation of the masses in political life was best confined to voting, to provide a check on abuses of power, and to rank-and-file service to parties and pressure groups.

From this kind of conventional perspective it is hard to see political protest in any kind of democratic light. Those few studies that did include political protest as an object of enquiry tended to make no conceptual distinction between protest and insurrection. Things as innocuous as lawful demonstrations were viewed by political scientists only as some weaker form of riot. A good example of this is Almond and Verba's classic study *The Civic Culture*. Respondents to their surveys were asked to say what they might do to oppose an unjust law. Those relatively few respondents who replied that they might join in demonstrations, protest meetings and boycotts were coded together with those, even fewer in number, who said they would resort to riot, rebellion and internal war.

It was necessary to retrieve the idea of political protest from the realm of political pathology. It is, of course, arguable how much the Study Group was helped in this task by the startling events of the 1960s. It depends on which aspects of those events are seen as most significant. In Europe, the growth of the New Left and the rise of orderly protest movements like the Campaign for Nuclear Disarmament encouraged the view of protest as a democratic but élite-challenging form of behaviour. Students hurling pavé at CS Police in Paris did not. In America, the Civil Rights Movement and direct action against the war in Vietnam also appeared to fit a model of a widening political action repertory in a democratic system. The sight of Watts, Miami and Detroit ablaze did not. It was clear that the question was essentially one of legitimacy. To what extent can political protest be viewed as a legitimate form of political behaviour in the same way as conventional political behaviour is seen as legitimate?

An important distinction must be drawn between legitimacy and legality. Many forms of political protest that are not lawful may nevertheless enjoy a degree of legitimacy. In a democracy there can be a certain nobility in going to jail for one's beliefs. It can bring some longer-term dividends of political effectiveness too. Many of the great democratic reforms of the past had their origins in extra-parliamentary movements whose behaviour frequently transgressed the law in the name of superior moral force. Perhaps the best example is the Suffragette movement. The continuing disenfranchisement of women was so clearly unjust that hastening its end merited almost any outrage short of murder and any sacrifice short of nothing at all.

To some extent the question of legitimacy is an empirical one. How many people will endorse, favour or engage in unconventional acts of political protest? Will they approve of activities like demonstrations, boycotts, strikes, occupations or street blockades? Will they join in? Do they believe such behaviour can be effective in pressing for changes in society? If the majority, or even if sizeable minorities come to embrace political protest as a legitimate means of seeking political redress then legitimate is what it is. The Study Group took the view that protest was legitimately a topic of interest of equal significance when placed alongside conventional forms of political behaviour. To say otherwise would be to deny its place in modern political history despite some of the unattractive forms it has taken and the plainly undemocratic causes it has sometimes served, particularly in the 1930s in Europe.

Some writers have maintained that violent acts of protest also have their place in the democratic process. As Tilley observes:

> Collective violence has flowed regularly out of the central processes of Western countries . . . Men seeking to sieze, hold or realign the levers of power have continually engaged in collective violence as part of their struggles. The oppressed have struck in the name of justice, the privileged in the name of order, those in between in the name of fear.

There are places in the world where even to publish such ideas is enough to cause one's arrest. Even so, it is a thought sufficiently intriguing to merit the inclusion of questions about the use of violence against people and property in an enquiry into political action. How far are people really prepared to go?

These are the questions that will occupy most of the remainder of this chapter when we tackle the problems of measuring mass political action in five advanced industrial countries and examine the results. Before that, it is necessary to introduce briefly the ideas it was hoped would contribute to a greater understanding of why some people participate in various forms of political action and others do not. Some of these ideas were drawn from diverse theoretical and research traditions current at the time and others were new. They were assembled into a string of 'micro-theories' of the origins of political action. Each will be examined in succeeding chapters, often in combination, leading to a general model of political action that is assembled and tested in chapter 6. These ideas can usefully be summarised under four headings: the baseline model, the cognitive skills model, the value model, and the dissatisfaction model. Each of these is now briefly introduced.

1.1.2 The Baseline Model

This term, borrowed with grateful acknowledgement from Verba and Nie's study of political participation in America, refers to the social location of political action. What social characteristics such as age, sex, occupational class, education, religion and so on tend to be associated with higher or lower rates of political action? Verba and Nie, as others before them, found that higher social status, in terms both of better education and material success in life was a reliable indicator of higher levels of conventional political involvement. We can expect to find the same result. Our dualistic approach to political action also compels us to consider a wider choice of styles of involvement as well as simply levels of activity. For example, it does not tax the mind for long to favour the idea that protest behaviour will be a characteristic of younger respondents. But what of social class? As mentioned in the Introduction, one of the most vexing puzzles of the late 1960s was that new protesters were not merely young but were drawn from the most privileged sectors of society. Protest actions were often carried out in the name of the oppressed, particularly the civil rights movement, but the leadership was often provided by many young men and women who could expect nothing but favour and advantage in the lives ahead of them. Given the perjorative view of protest actions accepted by most democratic theorists of the time, it was hard to apply the baseline model to forms of behaviour that were thought most characteristic of the desperate and dispossessed peoples of the Third World. What Dahrendorf calls 'the natural group' – well-educated men aged 25–40 – had always provided the vanguard of the conventional political system. This is especially true in Europe. Could they and those about to replace them also be the main source of protest behaviour too? Can you be élite-directed *and* élite-challenging at the same time? It seems that you can and the evidence for this is examined in chapter 2.

1.1.3 The Cognitive Skills Model

The clear role of higher levels of education in promoting conventional political involvement was one of the main supports of the élitist democratic theory mentioned earlier. This was elaborated into a model of participation that held that only those having an understanding of political matters at an ideological level could function consistently in political life. In particular, an understanding that included an appreciation of the main left-right, liberal-conservative dimension of Western democratic politics was the essential equipment of any recruit to political activity. Strong evidence from survey research tended to support this view.

The Study Group could not ignore this evidence and this question is examined closely in chapter 3. On the other hand, it was felt that too exclusive a view had been taken of the quality and complexity of thought that was held to be the admission ticket to the active political arena. A wider net was cast to capture more of the everyday mental skills that might admit a far larger stratum of the population to the élite company of activists. Commonsense and the wider definition of political action the study embraced demanded as much. Again one had the problem of applying a set of ideas that were known to underpin the conventional party system to the kind of behaviour formally thought to be mainly the expression of ignorant and inarticulate rage. Yet, the student movement apart, we knew that political protest was not only carried out by intellectuals. As we shall see, certain mental skills *are* important in promoting involvement in politics. All human social behaviour is grounded in learning of some kind. In the case of political behaviour, however, such learning is not always or necessarily the kind that is acquired from higher education.

1.1.4 The Value Model

These ideas are concerned with people's basic political values – those needs and goals they think society should aim to achieve before all others. The importance of such ideas to the understanding of mass politics has long been recognised. Karl Marx, who is still given too little credit for his creative use of the subjective aspects of political ideology and consciousness, paid particular attention to the set of political values that people held. He saw what he called the false consciousness of the workers, their acceptance of bourgeois values and goals, as a major obstacle to the kind of political mobilisation necessary for revolutionary action. For this reason modern Marxists took a close interest in the protest movements of the 1960s. Their problem, like ours, was that it was not the industrial workers who were leading the charge. New political values were surfacing elsewhere and found their most enthusiastic reception among the young middle class. The New Left was new in the sense that it embraced ideas that had little to do with the established Left-wing orthodoxies of industrial class conflict. The disciplined view of a workers' movement under determined leadership gave way to demands for freedom of expression, creativity, and mass participation in decision-making in the community at every level. This movement was said to be a product of the growth of post-materialist values. The rapidly growing economic security of Western economies had been expected to put an end to vigorous political conflict. Instead it had spawned a new basis for conflict.

The postwar generations had grown up relatively free of the urgent problems of physical and economic security that had beset their parents. To them, the class-based economism of Western party systems seemed increasingly redundant. They had been freed instead to develop what the psychologist Abraham Maslow called 'higher order' needs of 'belongingness' and creative expression. There grew up among the younger generations significantly larger and larger minorities of people who placed these higher order goals before those of security and economic growth. They did so, at least, in terms of the political goals they thought their country should aim for. Their discovery by political science owes everything to the work of Ronald Inglehart. He called them Postmaterialists. They, it seems, were in the vanguard of the new politics. The growth of political protest actions in the 1960s was traceable to their efforts to introduce new political goals onto the national agenda. They demanded things like racial and sexual equality, environmental improvement and, more than anything, new democratic forms of political participation and self-determination in community life. These were things the existing political systems, Right or Left, were not accustomed to providing. A postmaterialist view was by definition élite-challenging and the means to demand such goals led naturally to protest methods. The extent of the influence of value choices upon styles of political action is examined in chapter 4.

1.1.5 The Dissatisfaction Model

This area is the most complex dealt with in the study. Political action is defined as the means through which ordinary people can mobilise to seek political redress and achieve political goals. In exploring peoples' feelings of satisfaction and dissatisfaction the study edged closer to a more obvious motivational basis for explaining political mobilisation. This is especially true for understanding protest behaviour. Surely protests are always carried out by people who have some grievance? This may be broadly true but the closer one gets to individual motivation in studies of this kind, the more complicated things become. For example, the idea of relative deprivation has proved very useful. Those who feel they are not receiving the kinds of material or other rewards from society that they realistically *expected* to get or who feel they have less than is their *entitlement* ought to be moved to seek redress for their loss. If the party system cannot provide it, then the government might be coerced by the use of more vigorous forms of protest. Such disappointment, however, can lead as much to despair and apathy as it can be a spur to action. While rising levels of relative deprivation have been shown to underlie protest movements in the Third World and among severely deprived minorities like urban blacks in America, in the mature and better-provided systems of these five countries such obvious frustration-aggression reactions are less likely.

What is more likely is a process whereby various kinds of satisfaction and dissatisfaction are translated into political demands by a complex series of judgements. We call this area political evaluation. It involves measures of the way people evaluate different aspects of the political system and its performance. Following Easton and others, the study group carefully mapped out all the areas of judgement that needed to be covered if all the links in this chain of 'politicised dissatisfaction' were to be joined in the data. Some of these links concern the way people evaluate the whole system. For example, a general feeling of support for the political system is held to be an important motive for conventional political involvement. Others concern peoples' views of the authorities. Those out of sympathy with the government in power tend often to be in a higher state of readiness to be mobilised into action. Still others concern what is called the 'issue agenda'. What political issues do people find most important? Do they hold government to be responsible for achieving those goals? How do they judge the government's performance in each area of policy? What confidence do people have in the ability of the existing system to deliver the political outcomes they want? At each level, judgements of these kinds act prismatically to direct people into different kinds of political action. This process is examined in chapter 5.

1.1.6 The General Model

This chain of thought is brought together systematically in chapter 6 to form a general model of political action. The execution is complex but the basic idea linking these four areas of enquiry is a simple one. Certain social experiences lead people to form very different views of the political system and their own place within it. Social structure and different learning experiences place constraints upon the kinds of judgements people make. Mental skills combine with basic values to provide people with a basis for political judgement. The nature of these judgements cause people to make choices about their political involvement, – to favour inaction, conventional political activities, protest methods or perhaps even both.

1.2 MEASURING POLITICAL ACTION

The theory constructed in the previous section requires that we devise two measures of political behaviour: conventional political participation and unconventional participation or 'protest potential'. Taken together, they define the realm of political action that is to be explained by the survey analysis that follows. Both these kinds of behaviour were said to be essential features of the national and community life of advanced industrial societies. Without such participation by the masses, there would be little politics as we know it. Or at least 'politics' would be very differently defined. If this is true, if ordinary people do contribute to the whole political process through their involvement, then they ought to be able to answer questions about it. They ought to be able to say clearly what they do and do not do; also to say what they feel inclined or disinclined to do.

Conventional political participation offers fairly safe ground to the survey designer. Previous researchers have shown that levels of actual involvement in community and party political work are not great among the general population but are sufficiently high to merit a simple strategy. People are asked to say how often they do such things. This is usually quite enough information to enable the analyst to distinguish between quite large groups of people having higher or lower levels of conventional political activity. The Study Group saw no good reason to depart from this tradition. Consequently, respondents in each of the five national surveys were asked

> Some people do quite a lot in politics while others find they haven't the time or perhaps the interest to participate in political activities. I'll read you briefly some of the things that people do and I would like you to tell me how often you do each of them.

Seven activities were enquired about; these were:

(1) Reading about politics in the newspapers.
(2) Discussing politics with other people.
(3) Trying to convince friends to vote the same way '. . . as you do'.
(4) Working with other people in this community to try to solve some local problems.
(5) Attending a political meeting.
(6) Contacting public officials or politicians.
(7) Spending time working for a political party or candidate.

Respondents were asked to say whether they did each of these things 'often', 'sometimes', 'seldom' or 'never'.

Even at face-value, these measures have some shortcomings. 'Never' is clear enough but the remaining categories are a little subjective. Once a week might be 'often' to some people or 'sometimes' to others. The problem with a more precise calibration in events per week or month or whatever is that the ebb and flow of party political activity would itself introduce a bias. Conduct your survey at election time and you obtain a false impression. For this and other reasons, such measures, however calibrated, will tend to underestimate levels of activity in some individuals. Someone who in a ten-year period had been quite active politically may well have taken a year or two off, perhaps to raise young children.

Despite these problems, such measures have been shown to be fairly robust. Those in the habit of political activities of these kinds say that they are, those that are not generally deny it. People have little reason to misrepresent their customary behaviour in such commonplace matters as these.

Another shortcoming that may have occurred already to some readers is that there appears to be something vital missing from the list of seven activities. What about voting? Surely this is the baseline from which all conventional political behaviour proceeds? One would certainly think so, but research has shown that it is not. Voting does not have quite the same element of volition that the other activities imply. It is a rather ritualised form of behaviour, encouraged and sanctioned by lawful process. Empirically, the *failure* to vote is rarely associated in any systematic way with other forms of participation. It is highly idiosyncratic and associated with all kinds of personal reasons that have nothing to do with people's regular political inclinations. Those that doubt this should ask their local party organisers how many of their own party *members* failed to vote in the last election. They will receive a despairing reply.

The replies people gave to these questions created quite a lot of information: four categories by seven activities by five countries. That is 140 things to look at. Happily, we do not have to fill up two pages of this text with these numbers because, as will be seen in a moment, there is a very handy way of summarising them without losing too much detail. Even the original volume relegated them to the Technical Appendix where they may be found on pages 541 and 542. The distributions shown there are anyway highly skewed. That is to say, apart from reading the political pages of their newspapers, few people say they do these things often. The main distinction is between those who do them at all and those who do not. These figures too show a bias towards inactivity. For example, only about a quarter of the British and Austrians and no more than a third of the Dutch say they *ever* attend a political meeting of any kind. In the United States and Germany, these figures are higher: about half in each case. Even the excitement of campaigning for candidates fails to move many; fewer than one-in-ten of the British and Dutch ever turn out to campaign; 12% of the Austrian but again rather more of the Germans and Americans do so: 22% and 29% respectively. These broad national differences echo Almond's and Verba's 1959/60 surveys which also found much higher levels of conventional political activity in the United States and Germany compared to Britain.

The replies people gave to these seven items have an interesting statistical property. They interlock to form a single cumulative scale. Suppose we divide people's replies to each item into only two categories: 'yes' and 'no' on the simple basis of whether or not they ever do each. Let us also consider only four items: reading, discussing, contacting and campaigning and list these in Figure 1.1 in that order, from left to right, on the basis of how many people ever do each one. In Britain, for example, the ordering is: reading (84%), discussing (69%), contacting (24%) and campaigning (7%). In an ideal sample, people would fall into only five categories or 'scale types'. There would be those who do nothing (Type 1) and those who do everything (Type 5). In between are those who do one, two, or three activities (Types 2, 3 and 4) but always in the same order of precedence that is defined by the figures for the sample as a whole. Thus, all the scale-type 3's (who do two activities) read and discuss but never contact or campaign because reading and discussing occur

Do you ever	Read about politics in newspapers	Discuss politics with friends	Contact officials	Campaign for candidates
SCALE TYPE 1	no	no	no	no
2	yes	no	no	no
3	yes	yes	no	no
4	yes	yes	yes	no
5	yes	yes	yes	yes

FIGURE 1.1 *Ideal Patterns of Activity*

more often in the sample than do contacting and campaigning.

One dreams about samples such as these, but they are never found. Instead, one finds scale-type 3s, for example, who persist in campaigning or contacting but do not read or discuss. They depart from the norm defined by the overall marginal preference of their fellow sample members. On the other hand, one often finds too that ideal types are more common than the non-ideal types. Also, those that do depart from the ideal pattern tend to do so only by one or two steps. One rarely finds people who, in this simple example, discuss, contact and campaign but never read about politics in the newspapers.

One can apply a statistical test to see *to what extent* the sample conforms to this ideal pattern. It is called unidimensional or Guttman scaling. Each case is examined (now by a computer programme though there are people living who have done this by hand) to see whether or not it is an ideal type. If it is not, the number of 'errors' the individual's pattern of responses contains (say, contacting when he or she 'ought' to have been discussing) is added to a total of such errors found among all cases. This total is then divided by the total number of responses (that is, the number of items in the scale times the number of cases in the sample). The resulting number is then subtracted from 1 to provide a 'coefficient of reliability' or θRep. Thus:

$$\theta\text{Rep} = 1 - \left(\frac{\text{errors}}{\text{items \& cases}}\right)$$

If the result suggests the items in the scale do line up in this cumulative fashion (a θRep in excess of .90 is often quoted as a criterion) then one has learned something interesting about the data. In this case, it would suggest that entry into conventional politics follows a regular, almost predetermined pattern of successive steps that follow the same sequence for most people. It also means that one is entitled to reconcile all the deviations or 'errors' to the ideal pattern. A *single* score is then awarded to each respondent on the basis of the number of items he or she endorses while still labelling each point on the scale by the name of the item that each particular point represents. This is an extremely useful tool for analysis. Every respondent then has a single score representing how *far* he or she will go in conventional political activity.

Such an analysis was carried out on each of the five national samples using all seven kinds of political activity. Since we wished to identify those people who participated fairly regularly, the 'yes' and 'no' scores were created by dividing those who did each kind of activity 'often' and 'sometimes' (= yes) from those who did them only 'seldom' or 'never' (= no). Such a dichotomy also reduces the problem of subjectivity mentioned earlier. It separates doers from the non-doers fairly effectively.

The analysis showed a cumulative scale of conventional political activity was present in each of the five original countries. Subsequent analysis showed the same thing in the three countries that joined the project later: Italy, Switzerland and Finland. For the sake of interest, these countries are included in Table 1.1 though they will not feature in the analysis later in this book.

In all eight countries, the first three points on the 8-point (0 to 7) scale are defined by the same activity. These are: (0) no activity of any kind (1) reading about politics in newspapers and (2) discussing politics with friends. The next two points, (3) and (4), are usually defined either by working on community problems or attending meetings or both. The remaining three points (5), (6) and (7) are represented mostly by contacting officials, convincing friends, and campaigning, each appearing in a different sequence. These national differences in item-ordering are caused mainly by sampling variation because relatively few people venture into the higher reaches of the scale, especially so since participating 'seldom' was discounted. The scale *means* more or less the same thing in each country. It is said to be 'functionally equivalent'. Each respondent was therefore awarded a score on the Conventional Political Participation Scale (CPP) on the basis of national item-ordering. The distributions of these scores are shown in the second part of Table 1.1.

In Europe between a quarter and a third of each national sample

TABLE 1.1 The conventional political participation scale

A) Rank Order of items

The Netherlands	1 Read About Politics in Papers	2 Discuss Politics With Friends	3 Work on Community Problems	4 Contract Politicians or Public Officials	5 Convince Friends to Vote as Self	6 Participate in Election Campaign	7 Attend Political Meetings
Britain	Read	Discuss	Community	Contact	Convince	Attend	Campaign
United States	Read	Discuss	Community	Campaign	Contact	Convince	Attend
Germany	Read	Discuss	Convince	Attend	Campaign	Community	Contact
Austria	Read	Discuss	Attend	Convince	Community	Campaign	Contact
Italy	Read	Discuss	Attend	Community	Convince	Contact	Campaign
Switzerland	Read	Discuss	Campaign	Community	Attend	Contact	Convince
Finland	Read	Discuss	Community	Attend	Campaign	Contact	Convince

B) Guttman-Scale Scores

	0 (No Participation)	1	2	3	4	5	6	7 (High)	CR	Percentage of Nonscalable Respondents	N =
The Netherlands	29	21	30	8	5	2	1	4=100%	.95	1	1194
Britain	28	25	31	7	4	1	1	3	.95	2	1460
United States	16	18	24	12	9	8	7	6	.91	0	1713
Germany	23	32	17	9	5	4	4	6	.94	1	2295
Austria	34	23	22	7	4	3	2	5	.94	0	1577
Italy	52	12	13	5	4	4	3	7	NA	NA	1179
Switzerland	28	21	24	9	4	5	5	5	NA	NA	1290
Finland	27	21	26	13	5	4	3	3	NA	NA	1224

will do none of these activities, except in Italy where the figure is a remarkably high 52%. In the United States, on the other hand, the corresponding figure is only 16%. This result reinforces the earlier point about the special status of voting. Election turnout in the United States is always lower than in European countries. Recently in Italy more than 80% voted in elections to the *European* Parliament in Strasburg. Presidential elections in the United States rarely attract votes from more than 70% of the American electorate. Yet the American sample is strikingly more active; 42% of them are found in the truly active areas of the scale (point 3 onwards) compared with an average of about one quarter throughout Europe. Very high levels of activity, however, are rare everywhere. Only between 4% (in Britain) and 13% (in the United States) accumulated six or all seven of these activities done on a regular basis. The cross-national average is 8%. This may not sound very great, but in an average-sized city of, say, 100 000 adults, 8000 of them engaging in all or most of these activities at least 'sometimes' *is* a lot. They lead the active political life of the community. Twice that number tend to do between three and five of these activities at least 'sometimes' (all of them doing more than reading or discussing politics) and so they too contribute to active political life. They are, taken together, quite a sufficiently large body of people to sustain a working democratic party system.

1.2.1 Unconventional Political Participation or 'Protest Potential'

Before coming to grips with some of the quite serious measurement problems this area presents to the designer of surveys, it will be as well to establish first exactly what we are discussing. Broadly, one can define the area as '... unconventional political behaviour (which) ... does not correspond to the legal and customary regime norms regulating political participation' (Kaase, 1972). One must be careful, however, to exclude activities such as bribery, theft, and political espionage from such a definition. The activities that interest us have indispensably a mass character: the things that people do together in fairly large groups and do them in public view. Discussions on what these activities really were detained the Study Group long into the night.

Pilot surveys were carried out in which small groups of respondents were asked to think very hard about political protest activities and to make many detailed judgements about them (see Marsh, 1974). The results encouraged the view that ordinary people were familiar with

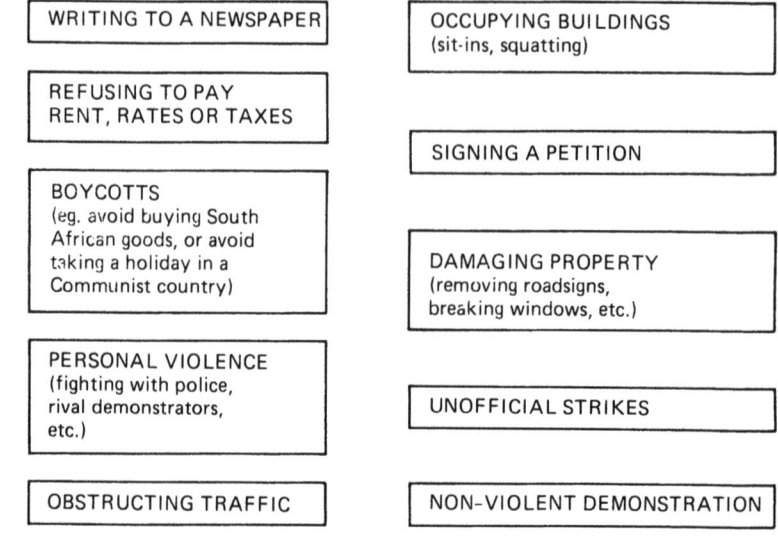

FIGURE 1.2 *Ten Examples of Protest Activity*

the idea of political protest and often had quite strong views about it, for and against. Finally, ten examples of protest activity were selected for inclusion in the main surveys and these are illustrated in Figure 1.2. All of them were activities that pilot respondents were able to recognise easily and agree that, yes, this is what they too thought of as acts of political protest.

As Figure 1.2 illustrates, each protest activity was printed on a small card. In the interview, respondents were shown all these cards and asked to say whether there were any items they did not recognise or understand. In each country, rates of recognition were very high except that about a quarter of the Austrian sample was unfamiliar with the idea of boycotts and in the later surveys, about a third of the Italian sample was puzzled by the use of both petitions and boycotts. Elsewhere nearly everyone said they were quite familiar with these activities. This simple finding is important in itself. It means that by the mid-1970s ordinary people in eight advanced industrial nations had included a wide range of political protest activities into their political vocabulary. It was not a topic dreamed up by political scientists and foisted upon obliging but uncomprehending respondents. People knew very well what we were asking them to judge.

The kinds of judgements people were asked to make about protest behaviour were also the subject of extensive discussion and exploratory research (see Marsh, 1974). There are so many things one might ask quite apart from the obvious question of whether or not people do them. For example, the pilot survey asked respondents to say whether people *approved* of each activity, found them *justified*, believed them to be *effective*, *legal*, *individual* or *mass* actions, *violent* or *non-violent* or led to *risks* for the participants and so on. These judgements or *dimensions* of attitude and belief were themselves derived from psychological testing of pre-pilot subjects using repertory-grid techniques. At each stage, we let the respondents set the pace.

Some of this pilot work was substantively valuable. For example, the extent to which people approved or disapproved of each kind of activity was not at all identical with the extent to which they believed them to be legal or illegal. As was pointed out in the previous section, legitimacy is not the same thing as legality, either theoretically or in the minds of respondents.

Another important finding from pilot work concerns context. It seemed highly likely that people's views about protest activities would be conditioned largely by the cause in which they were used. Who is protesting about what? Surprisingly, it was not so. British pilot survey respondents were asked in 1972 to judge each activity in five very different political contexts: industrial (a wage dispute), environmental (opposition to a new road), equalitarian (protesting racial discrimination), foreign policy (protesting an invasion of one country by another), and domestic policy (an anti-Common Market protest). The levels of justification, effectiveness and even people's intentions toward each activity were little changed by the context. It was the principle of their use not the political cause that dictated favourable or unfavourable judgements. From a design point of view, this result was highly encouraging. Not only do people recognise protest activities but they have formed views about their use that are independent of issues. This means that their views can be interpreted generally and not just in specific political contexts exactly in the same way as conventional political participation can be interpreted.

In the national surveys, time did not allow for all these intricate variations of judgement. There were three dimensions that seemed central to the way people viewed protest activities:

(1) *Legitimacy*: Do people approve or disapprove of their use? This is the 'affective' or 'feeling' dimension.

```
┌─────────────────────────────────────────────────────┐
│    APPROVE      APPROVE     DISAPPROVE   DISAPPROVE │
│      □            □             □            □      │
│   VERY MUCH                               VERY MUCH │
└─────────────────────────────────────────────────────┘
```

FIGURE 1.3 *Questionnaire Format*

(2) *Effectiveness*: To what extent do people believe these activities are effective '. . . in pressing for changes'? This is the 'cognitive' or 'knowledge' dimension.

(3) *Intentions*: Do people do these things or, if not, to what extent would they be inclined to do them? This is a dimension of behaviour and 'conscious behavioural intentions'.

Thirty questions (that is, three dimensions over ten items) is a lot to ask of respondents. This is why they were printed on cards. Three larger cards were then used (see Figure 1.3) and respondents placed the activity cards onto the appropriate square to indicate their view. This technique may seem a little brusque but most respondents found it helpful. It was a much more entertaining task than listening to the interviewer read out 30 very similar-sounding questions. Interviewers said that their respondents mused as they shuffled the cards about in ways that suggested serious attempts to represent their views and intentions. It is in fact a far more accurate technique than verbal questioning and it suppresses cross-national variation due to language differences.

The technique also generates a great deal of information: four categories for three dimensions for ten items in five countries is 600 things to look at. As before, this wealth of detail may remain in the Technical Appendix of the original volume. The following is a very broad summary of what was found.

Petitions are a universally acceptable means of protest, and lawful demonstrations are widely endorsed by substantial majorities. These two items appear to represent the first threshold of departure from conventional into unconventional political activity. It is important to note here that we consider petitions unconventional in the sense only that in at least three of the five countries – Britain, Germany, and Austria – there are sizeable minorities who do not approve of them and would under no circumstances sign petitions.

The use of boycotts also receives widespread support, except in Austria, and is endorsed by between 35% and 50% of the respondents. Withholding rents and taxes as a form of protest is also accepted by quite large minorities, especially in The Netherlands. These two items – boycotts and rent strikes – form a second threshold representing an unequivocal entry into the use of protest methods.

The occupation of administrative buildings or factory sit-ins receives limited support from quite significant minorities as does the practice of blocking traffic with an illegal street demonstration. Here we enter a third threshold of protest activity more commonly associated with a substantial commitment to direct action techniques or civil and political disobedience that often involves a deliberate infraction of the law. Not surprisingly, therefore, only about 15% of the people in our five-nation sample are seriously prepared to make a prior commitment to this kind of action. The obvious and remarkable exception to this are the Dutch respondents, of whom 42% approve of occupations and 22% of traffic blockades, while 25% and 14%, respectively, say they have participated in them or would definitely do so.

The position of 'unofficial strikes' is more equivocal. In terms of 'approval', such action is very unpopular, especially in Germany and, perhaps surprisingly, in Britain. Yet, in the face of their own disapproval, some people are prepared to contemplate taking such action and even more are prepared to admit that unofficial strikes can be effective.

The ultimate threshold of protest activity in these five countries is clearly signalled by the widespread condemnation heaped upon the use of personal violence, such as fighting with police or other demonstrators, and deliberate damage to property as a means of political protest. Between 94% and 98% of each national sample said they disapproved of such actions and would not contemplate their use. If further proof were needed, this result supports MacFarlane's view:

> What we are normally confronted with in constitutional democracies is action directed not at the overthrow of the social system or the government but of particular government policies. Insofar as this requires widespread public support and approval for one's aims, it places a low premium upon violence.

In view of the strong evidence that exists for very high rates of personal violence in American society and not least in American politics, compared with other countries in our study, it is perhaps surprising that the overwhelming majority who say they will never use violence is as large in the United States as it is in Europe. The level of positive support for damage and violence is so low that very little variance remains for survey analysis. Consequently, these items will play hardly any part in the analyses that follow.

One very surprising result was the similarly widespread condemnation of 'painting slogans on walls'. Superficially, this activity seems harmless enough and sometimes amusing. We believed that it might even be acceptable to the majority because putting up posters and sloganizing is a common feature of political campaigns in both the orthodox and unorthodox spheres. The only reasonable conclusion to be drawn from this result is that most people regard the activity as a defacement of visual surroundings and thereby a public nuisance and many others may associate political daubings with graffiti other than the strictly political. Political activists, on the other hand, regard slogan-painting as immature and ineffective. This item too was put aside.

There are wide differences between countries. The Netherlands has by far the highest level of approval and positive behavioural intentions toward protest, followed at some distance by the United States. Britain and Germany have similar and comparatively modest levels of protest potential, while among Austrians high protest potential is a rather rare phenomenon.

The use of the idea of thresholds to describe the acceptance by successively smaller minorities of increasingly vigourous protest activities suggests an intriguing possibility. Does entry into political protest obey the same step-by-step cumulative rules that govern entry into conventional political participation? It does. In each country strong unidimensional scales were found both for the behavioural and the approval/disapproval scores. (Such scales were not found for the effectiveness dimension and so this question will be set aside for the moment.)

The next step in the analysis was to put together the approval and intentions measures to form a single scale of protest potential. It was tempting simply to add them together but we were very keen to retain the step-by-step, explicitly labelled scale. People's responses to each activity were examined separately. In each country, approval of protest activities was strongly associated with people's intentions.

Generally speaking, people say they approve of the things they will do though not all those who approve of, for example, demonstrations also say they will demonstrate. Yet there were still significant minorities who said they would do something that they had earlier said they disapproved of. Some of these discrepancies were due to 'measurement error', which is the term political scientists use when their respondents misunderstand their questions or when the interviewers mistake the answers they are given, but many were not. Unofficial strikes, for example, attracted quite a few of these apparently inconsistent responses. They can be interpreted in two ways. Disapproval may cast doubt on the strength of intention or it may speak of true determination, that sometimes one just has to act in ways one finds distasteful.

If the second argument is true, that determined people will put aside their moral qualms and act, then it is likely that they and not others are those who believe in the effectiveness of protest activities. An item-by-item analysis showed that this was not so but rather the opposite was true; people prepared to act in the face of their own disapproval tended to believe such action was less effective compared to those who approved and would do it. The first argument was therefore accepted and positive intentions would be discounted unless accompanied by approval. The simplified 'yes' and 'no' scores were therefore constructed as shown in Figure 1.4.

This strategy appears to give pre-eminence to the attitudinal dimension over the behavioural. It appears to take us away from the 'how far are you prepared to go' measure that would be the closest possible equivalent of the wholly behavioural conventional participation scale. This is a false impression. Priority coding the disapproval responses actually strengthens the case for interpreting a 'yes' score in Figure 1.4 as potential behaviour. It says how far people are *really* prepared to go. It even discounts those few who have done something they now disapprove of. So it should; they may not do it again.

These jointly-determined 'yes' and 'no' scores were then resubmitted to the Guttman scale procedures described earlier. Very strong cumulative scales emerged in each country and these are shown in Table 1.2 together with similar results from the three subsequent surveys in Italy, Switzerland and Finland.

In each country, except Italy, where there is an unusual fondness for occupations, the first four points on the scale are defined by the same things: (0) no protest potential (of course); (1) petitions; (2) demonstrations; (3) boycotts. Rent or tax strikes define either points

	Approval				
(Potential) Participation	Approve Strongly	Approve	Disapprove	Disapprove Strongly	Don't Know
Have done	yes	yes	no	no	
Would do	yes	yes	no	no	Missing Data
Might do	yes	yes	no	no	
Would never do	no	no	no	no	
Don't know	Missing Data				

FIGURE 1.4 *A Combined Scale of Approval and Intention*

(4) or (5). The highest points (6) and (7) on the scale are usually defined by unofficial strikes (even in Britain) or occupations, although the American respondents have a particular horror of stopping the traffic. In the United States, such a tactic will endear you and your cause to no-one. Here again, though, many of these differences in item-ordering are caused by random sampling fluctuations because of the relatively small numbers venturing into the higher reaches of the scale. As before, the scale is functionally equivalent in each country and so every respondent was awarded a single protest potential score on the basis of national item-ordering.

The coefficients of reliability are higher for these protest potential scales than for the conventional political participation scales. This is, of itself, an important finding. It means that, even more so than the institutionalised pathway into party and community politics, the willingness to participate and actual participation in protest activities has a *structure*. This structure is not an artifact of measurement; people gave their views and intentions to each item separately and in random order. The structure is in the data and in people's minds. Whereas the occurrence of protest activities seems to have a spontaneous quality, people's political readiness to use protest tactics is a well-ordered dimension of increasing severity of the costs they impose on authorities and effort required from participants.

The distribution of each national sample along this dimension of protest potential is shown in the second part of Table 1.2. There are some very striking cross-national differences. Outstandingly the most protest-prone nation are the Dutch; 31% of them will go further even than demonstrations and boycotts and into more extreme forms of protest. In the United States protest potential keeps pace with the

TABLE 1.2 Protest Potential Scale

A) Rank Order of Items

	1	2	3	4	5	6	7
The Netherlands	Petitions	Demonstrations	Boycotts	Occupations	Rent Strikes	Blockades	Unofficial Strikes
Britain	Petitions	Demonstrations	Boycotts	Rent Strikes	Blockades	Occupations	Unoff. str.
United States	Petitions	Demonstrations	Boycotts	Rent Strikes	Occupations	Unoff. Str.	Blockades
Germany	Petitions	Demonstrations	Boycotts	Rent Strikes	Blockades	Unoff. Str.	Occupations
Austria	Petitions	Demonstrations	Boycotts	Blockades	Rent Strikes	Unoff. Str.	Occupations
Italy	Petitions	Demonstrations	Occupations	Rent Strikes	Boycotts	Blockades	Unoff. Str.
Switzerland	Petitions	Demonstrations	Boycotts	Occupations	Rent Strikes	Blockades	Unoff. Str.
Finland	Petitions	Demonstrations	Boycotts	Unoff. Str.	Rent Strikes	Blockades	Occupations

B) Guttman-Scale Scores

	0 (No Protest)	1	2	3	4	5	6	7 (High)	CR	Percentage of Nonscalable Respondents	N =
The Netherlands	9	20	25	15	11	7	7	6=100%	.94	4	1149
Britain	23	22	25	15	7	3	2	3	.95	6	1398
United States	9	21	24	26	8	6	3	3	.96	6	1615
Germany	19	21	29	19	5	3	2	3	.97	5	2212
Austria	21	33	26	11	5	2	1	2	.97	20	1267
Italy	17	14	37	14	9	3	3	3	NA	NA	1179
Switzerland	12	27	32	15	7	3	2	2	NA	NA	1290
Finland	25	19	24	14	8	5	2	3	NA	NA	1224

distribution found in The Netherlands up to the point of boycotts but fewer Americans than Dutch (20% compared to 31%) say they will venture beyond this point. Britain and Germany (and later Switzerland and Finland) have lower and quite similar national levels of protest potential. Between 40% and 45% will do nothing or will sign a petition from time to time compared to about 30% in The Netherlands, the United States and Italy. Twelve percent in Germany, 14% in Switzerland, 15% in Britain and 18% in Italy and Finland will enter the higher points on the scale beyond demonstrations; on average, this is half the Dutch figure. The Austrians, on the other hand, have a low protest potential. More than half will go no further than signing petitions and only 9% will go past the point of demonstrations.

Too great a stress should not be laid on the higher reaches of the scale. Going on a demonstration is a serious commitment to most ordinary people and a majority in each country except Austria say they approve and would do this, signing petitions as they go. Even in Austria this figure is 46%. It was surprising to find just how many people *were* prepared to go beyond demonstrations and boycotts. A cross-national average of 17% implies huge numbers of people who say they are ready to be mobilised in strong acts of protest, some of which are illegal. One does not need to mobilise very many of them to create a dramatic political event.

1.2.2 The Effectiveness of Protest

People's judgements about the effectiveness of these protest actions are quite closely related to their level of protest potential, but the data do not quite conform to the same step-by-step law of accumulation that applies to the approval and behavioural dimensions. People at different points on the protest scale take subtly different views. Those at the bottom of the scale say that, except petitions, all these things are quite ineffective '. . . in pressing for changes'. Those near the top of the scale tend to believe all acts of protest are effective though they tend to be more sceptical than average about the effectiveness of petitions. A certain contempt for the effectiveness of moderation is a characteristic of militants. Those in the middle of the scale (demonstrations and boycotts) believe that petitions are effective. Oddly though, they are less likely to believe, compared to those scoring higher than themselves, that demonstrations are effective even though they accept their use for themselves.

Broadly speaking, though, these results seem uncontroversial. As other studies of attitudes and behaviour have repeatedly shown, people will be favourably disposed to do those things they believe will bring them rewards. This is true even if they themselves have not yet had the experience; they learn about it from news media and from other people. However obvious this may appear on the individual level, it gives rise to a paradox when viewed in the aggregate. In each country, even in The Netherlands, the majority stop at demonstrations or boycotts and eschew strikes, occupations and blockades. Since a favourable view of the effectiveness of protest is associated with its endorsement, this means that the majority think that petitions and demonstrations are effective means '. . . of pressing for changes' and that strikes, occupations and blockades are not.

Viewed objectively this result does not seem sensible. Why do between 70 and 80% believe that petitions are effective but fewer than half that number believe strikes and occupations are effective? Strikes often *are* effective in the political arena. Witness the Protestant workers' strike against power sharing in Northern Ireland in 1974. It is hard to recall when a petition last wrung changes in policy from a government. Some people may be taking a sophisticated view that more extreme forms of protest alienate public support, anger authorities and will generally destabilise political discourse without tangible gain, but this is unlikely to be the view of the majority.

What is more likely to have happened is a familiar problem in attitude measurement. It is called the 'halo effect'. The majority approve of petitions and demonstrations and they disapprove of strikes and occupations. To call the former 'effective' and the latter 'ineffective' emphasises their endorsement of one and their scorn for the other. To admit that an activity one thoroughly disapproves of and would not do is nonetheless effective when used by others is to reveal a degree of informed ruefulness that does not come easily to most people. Only demonstrations and strikes attract this kind of view among significant proportions and these are found mostly in Britain and The Netherlands.

1.2.3 The Outcome of Intention

Critics of the Political Action Study focused on the likely predictive value of the Protest Potential Scale. They pointed out that the kind of events and issues that are the occasion for political protest tend to be those that sweep up and mobilise many who would earlier not have dreamed of getting involved in that sort of thing. Likewise, all those people who trenchantly claimed a willingness to protest about almost anything will contain many who will find other things to do when the time comes to stand on the line and be counted. What then is the use of such a measure? It may be amusing to uncover the social and psychological basis for people's intentions but it would have little significance for what goes on in the real world unless action followed intention. In 1979–81 the Study Group set out to discover what had actually been going on in the real world. In The Netherlands, in Germany and in the United States the original members of the 1974–75 surveys were relocated and asked what they had been doing since they were last spoken to.

Now, let us be clear about what we ought to expect from this second meeting with respondents. We do *not* expect that everyone or even most of those who said that they would or might do any of these activities had been busy actually doing them since 1975. We know already that this is not true because if it were true the whole of Western Europe and America would have come to resemble Berlin, Paris and Berkeley in 1968. We know also that protest potential does not work like that. It is a resource and a resource remains a resource even if it is not used very often. But it must be used from time to time or belief in its credibility will wane, especially among political authorities quietly calculating what they might get away with, where they might site the next nuclear power station, the next motorway, the next small war with, say, a beligerent but incompetent South American dictatorship and so on. So what we *do* expect is two things:

(1) That only a minority of those with positive intentions toward political protest will have actually become involved in protest activities, *but*
(2) that nearly all of those who did become involved were recruited overwhelmingly from among those who had said they would or might do these things and hardly at all from among those who said that they would never do these things.

Table 1.3 examines these two questions for three key examples of protest activities from the Protest Potential Scale in each of the three countries revisited. The examples are: signing petitions, going on lawful demonstrations and joining in boycotts. The first expectation is clearly supported; only a minority of the population has been involved in political protest of these kinds, though it is intriguing to

TABLE 1.3 *The proportion among those reinterviewed in 1979–81 who reported having participated in protest actions who had earlier said that they would or would not participate.*

	Respondent's position in 1974–75					
	Have done, would do might do			Would never do		
	NL	D	USA	NL	D	USA
Did participate in signing petitions....						
a. As % of all resps.	39%	22%	68%	2%	1%	1%
(b. As % of group.)	*(43%)*	*(25%)*	*(71%)*	*(28%)*	*(9%)*	*(25%)*
in lawful demonstrations...... a:	8%	4%	12%	0	0	1%
(b)	*(11%)*	*(6%)*	*(16%)*	*(0)*	*(0)*	*(4%)*
in boycotts.......... a:	4%	1%	17%	0	0	1%
(b)	*(7%)*	*(2%)*	*(53%)*	*(0)*	*(0)*	*(3%)*

Source: Max Kaase, Table 7 in Jennings and Van Deth (1989) with kind permission.

see just how large these minorities are. For petitions, one might expect high levels of involvement and in the United States actually a two-thirds majority got to sign up at least once over a five-year period. For demonstrations and boycotts, the figures do show relatively few becoming involved in the two European countries. Even in protest-prone Netherlands, fewer than 10% went on a demonstration. But the figures for the United States are quite surprising: 13% went on a demonstration and 18% joined in boycotts, or between one-in-eight and one-in-five of the adult American population. Given the commitment these activities demand of participants and given the size and influence of social factors like old age, infirmity, the duties of child care and so on that can discourage or prevent people joining in on the day, these are huge numbers of Americans who have come to expand their regular political behaviour to include strong acts of political protest.

The second expectation, that actual protesters should earlier have expressed a positive and not a negative intention toward protest, is supported quite dramatically. Even among the larger numbers signing petitions, and decisively among the smaller numbers going on demonstrations and joining in boycotts, all but the smallest handful of them had five or six years earlier declared their willingness to do these things. In Europe, all of those demonstrating and boycotting had earlier said they might or would do these things; none had said they would not.

Now that the data are available in such clear and simple terms, the temptation is to say 'Well, that is obvious, isn't it?' Ten years ago it was not at all obvious and not even your present author would have bet on so clear a result. Given the sheer amount of measurement error present in interview surveys, especially in two surveys over several years, one is simply not accustomed to have almost unanimous confirmation of hypotheses. Protest potential is a real resource. If authorities confront a European or American community with an issue whose appropriate response from those most affected by it is political protest, political protests, other things being equal, are exactly what they will get.

1.3 THE POLITICAL ACTION REPERTORY

The two scales, conventional political participation and protest potential, define the total stock of actual and likely participation in politics that we wish to investigate. They represent two distinct pathways, each marked by incremental steps of increasing difficulty and commitment, that people may take if they seek political involvement and political redress. An important question now arises. What is the relationship between these two kinds of political involvement?

In the early 1970s this was a question of more than academic importance. It seemed to many observers that the protest movements that swept Europe and North America heralded a real discontinuity in mass politics. Adding strength to that impression was the fact that the existing party political systems and their harrassed practitioners were so often the target of protest movements. The exemplars of conventional political participation, MPs, local and district councillors, party officials and so on, were all on the inside wondering what to do about the resourceful and demanding young people on the outside who were rattling their windows. These were times before Bob Dylan was born again and they gave every impression of a-changing. The leaders of protest movements were also keen to say they stood outside the conventional political arena and spoke vividly of a whole new political order. In places like Berlin, Paris, Amsterdam and Berkeley some of this really seemed possible. The 'explosion of consciousness' among the young looked set to sweep the old conventional political system out of its path.

Of course, it was never going to happen. Powerful institutions like political parties and trades unions could quite easily defend themselves against young radicals. But the contest that occurred then and has recurred since in the form of a revived peace movement, feminism and environmental politics did give rise to a clear hypothesis: a high protest potential would be associated with a low rate of conventional political involvement. It was, at the time, perhaps the single most important finding of the Political Action Study to show that this was not so and to show that the very opposite was true. Protest potential is *positively* associated with conventional political participation. The correlations are not high, ranging from .17 in the United States to .28 in Germany but they *are* positive. This is because our respondents are not political élites. They are not conventional politicians and protest leaders locked in conflict. They are ordinary members of the public, some of whom get involved in party politics, some of whom are favourably disposed toward protest actions and some of whom are quite likely to do both. And why not? If one is drawn into a political conflict then to many people it is an obvious strategy to make representations and to mobilise support in as many ways as seem promising. People contact politicians and use influence with officials usually before they organise a demonstration or something more drastic.

If the correlations between the two scales had been found to be very high, then we should have been justified in integrating the two completely. If most people who are active in conventional politics also favour protest and vice versa then probably we would be dealing with a single dimension of all-round political involvement. But this is not the case. There is a tendency toward dual involvement but no more than that. This opened up the intriguing possibility of combining the two scales in the form of a typology. This is described in Figure 1.5

The creation of this typology of political action was the result of a great deal of experimentation, attempts at validation using associated measures like political interest and competence, and exhaustive (and exhausting) argument. It was certainly not an arbitrary choice. The people in each of the five areas in the diagram not only fall into the same space as defined by the two scales together, they tend to be rather like one another in other ways too and to be unlike the people in the adjacent categories. This point will become abundantly clear as the story of the remainder of this book unfolds. Before that, let us be clear about these five categories of political action:

		CONVENTIONAL POLITICAL PARTICIPATION	
		None, or read about politics in newspapers.	Discuss politics, work for community or political party, convince friends to vote as oneself, attend meetings, contact officials.
PROTEST POTENTIAL	None, or only sign petitions	INACTIVES	CONFORMISTS
	Demonstrate, Boycott, Refuse rents or taxes, Occupy buildings, Block traffic, Unofficial (wildcat) strikes.	PROTESTERS	REFORMISTS
			ACTIVISTS

FIGURE 1.5 *The Political Action Repertory*

(1) *The Inactives*: These are people who will do no more than read the political news in their papers and may, if pressed, sign a petition. Many of them will do neither of these things.

(2) *The Conformists*: These people are active in conventional politics. Some do no more than read about and discuss politics with their friends but the majority do more than this, some of them attend political meetings and even involve themselves in campaigns. A few will be party members. But they will have nothing to do with protest activities except perhaps the most innocuous form of signing petitions.

(3) *The Reformists*: These people have an expanded political repertory. They, as much as the conformists, will involve themselves in conventional political activity. To this they are prepared to add *lawful* forms of political protest, namely demonstrations and boycotts. They will not venture into the more drastic forms of protest like strikes and occupations.

(4) *The Activists*: These people have the most complete repertory of political action. They are two-fisted political combatants who will, they say, have recourse to whatever means of political action seems appropriate in the circumstances. They are involved in conventional politics and are prepared to use often illegal protest activities should the need arise.

(5) *The Protesters*: These people, like the reformists and activists, distribute themselves across the range of the more committed forms of protest potential. Some say they will go all the way. Yet they shun all involvement in conventional political activity. The party system to them is a closed book.

The distribution of these five political action types is described in Table 1.4. Again, for interest, the three late-joining nations are added though this is their last appearance in this book. In these nations, Italy, Switzerland and Finland, and also in Britain and Germany, Inactives are confined to between 24 and 30% of the population. This figure is lower in the United States (only 12%) and in The Netherlands (18%), the former because of high rates of conventional political activity and the latter because of high protest potential. Neither is the case in Austria where the inactive group is large: 35%.

Conformists are uncommon everywhere, ranging between 7% in Italy and 19% in Austria with a cross-national average of 15%. This is interesting because political scientists tend to write about conventional political involvement as though it was quite undiluted by other kinds of political activity. Such single-minded purity is, in fact, quite rare. The majority of conventional participants make themselves available for mobilisation in unconventional forms too. For example, the reformists number a very consistent 20 to 28% across all nations except the United States where they are the largest group (36%). The Activists are a smaller group in every nation, ranging from a mere 6% in Austria up to 19% in the protest-prone Netherlands with a cross-national average of 11%. Given the Activists' level of commitment, this is hardly surprising. Even so, one in ten of the whole population committed in this way suggests a large constituency ready to be mobilised into all kinds of political activity.

Most surprising, perhaps, is the size of the Protester category, ranging from 19% in Austria to 32% in The Netherlands and 35% in Italy. Elsewhere it is between 20 and 25%. True, they are fewer than the Reformists and the Activists put together. Thus, political versatility is more common than an inclination only to protest. Yet the Protester category is large and suggests that the spirit of '68 may yet be present in the data or, equally perhaps, something less benign.

TABLE 1.4 Political Action Repertory

Types	The Netherlands	Britain	United States	Germany	Austria	Italy	Switzerland	Finland
Inactives	17.9=%	30.1	12.3	26.6	34.9	23.9	24.1	25.4
Conformists	11.1	15.4	17.5	13.5	19.2	7.2	14.8	18.5
Reformists	19.8	21.9	36.0	24.6	20.9	22.0	27.8	23.5
Activists	19.3	10.2	14.4	8.0	5.9	12.2	9.2	11.4
Protesters	31.9	22.4	19.8	27.3	19.1	34.7	24.0	21.1
(N = 100%)	(1144)	(1389)	(1613)	(2207)	(1265)	(1427)	(1206)	(1118)
Percentage of Nonclassified Respondents (N =100%)	5 (1203)	6 (1483)	6 (1719)	4 (2304)	20* (1584)	NA	NA	NA

* The Austrians alone were provided with an 'it depends. . . .' response category. Those using it were taken out of the analysis.

2 The Social Background of Political Action

The task in this chapter is to discover to what extent political action is concentrated in some social groups and not in others. This is a mundane task but an important one. It will help us understand much that follows. If it were to be found, for example, that political activity was randomly distributed among all kinds and classes of people, that there was no baseline model after all, then all the explanation of political action would have to be sought in people's minds. Only beliefs, feelings, values and attitudes and their responses to specific events would account for their behaviour. This is unlikely. Political sociology has long established that people's age, sex, education, jobs, religion and so on have a profound effect on their political behaviour. Since political conflict between parties reflects social cleavages within society, it is hardly surprising that membership of a distinct social constituency will influence one's vote. On the other hand, rates of political involvement can be ideologically neutral. If active partisans are mobilised by all parties, why should rates of activity be reflected in social structure?

One obvious answer is availability. Regular involvement in political activities makes demands on people's time and energy that voting does not. Thus the very old, the sick, the disabled and the poor have relatively few resources to bring to political activity however strongly they may feel about the need for social change. The familiar power structures of society also impose a bias upon recruitment to political involvement. Traditionally, the social roles assigned to women, especially to working-class women, strongly inhibit political activity. This is especially true in Europe where until recently men enjoyed a near monopoly of political party management. Even in 1985, the 623 members of the British Parliament included only 19 women among them.

Social class also imposes a distortion upon recruitment to political activity. As Verba and Nie's baseline model showed so clearly, higher social and economic status eases the entry of the more advantaged members of society into regular political involvement. They share a social identity with existing political élites so officials defer to them. Most important, they, rather than manual workers have the education and training that lowers the costs to them of learning the basic skills of politics. They also have different expectations of the political system. Middle-class values stress individual competence. For them the search for political redress places a premium on individual action. In contrast, manual workers tend more to look to existing organisations like parties and trade unions for a collective expression of political ambitions. Thus, in Western democracies at least, the political organisations of the working class tend to be led and managed by middle-class ideologues.

These simple truths have been well established in previous research. Higher rates of political activity are to be found among well educated young men, lower rates among older poorly-educated women and so on. Three measures: age, sex and education provide our baseline model. They map the social location of political involvement. This is true at least for conventional political involvement. Is it also true for protest potential?

The pre-eminence of age, or rather youth, is clear. The demands upon time and energy imposed by demonstrations, occupations and so on are most easily met by the young. More than that, young people are said naturally to be given to élite-challenging behaviour. As the old proverb has it: 'He who is not a revolutionary at 20 has no heart. He who is still a revolutionary at 40 has no head'. On the other hand, it is worth remembering that recent generations of adolescents have passed up this natural opportunity to express themselves. Were those of the 1950s heartless or somehow unnatural? Throughout this chapter we must bear in mind that people are not mobilised out of a political void. When political conditions move into a period of change, when political protest surfaces to disturb continuity and passivity as it did in the 1920s and 1930s and once more in the 1960s, then it is the young who will protest the most. This is not the same thing as saying that the young protest solely because they are young.

For this reason a measure of protest potential is probably of more value than reports of behaviour. It enables the researcher to locate political resources in the community that may, for historical reasons, lie dormant at the time.

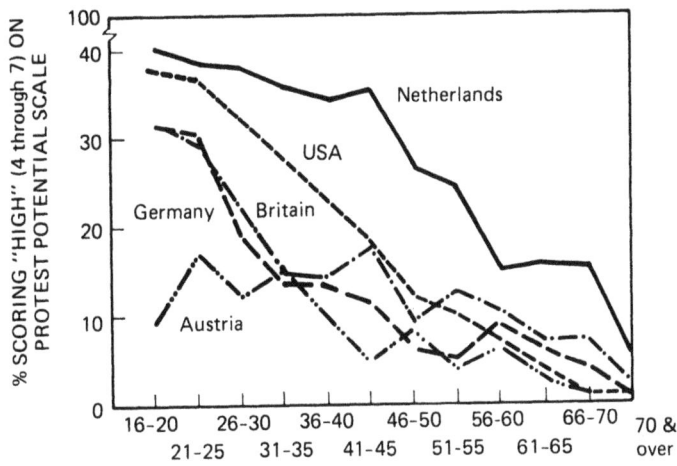

FIGURE 2.1 *Protest Potential by Age by Country*

2.1 THE BASELINE MODEL: AGE, SEX AND EDUCATION

Let us start with the relationship that is easiest to understand: age and protest potential. The graph in Figure 2.1 takes as a key indicator the proportion of people in each country who have the highest levels of protest potential. These are those who will go beyond lawful means of protest like demonstrations and boycotts and say they will engage in rent and tax strikes, unofficial strikes, occupations and street blockades. This proportion is plotted from left to right for 12 successively older age groups in five-year intervals.

In each country, though least noticeably in Austria, the proportion who will commit themselves to these more extreme forms of political protest declines steadily from the youngest to the oldest age groups. The Austrians apart, the two youngest age groups (16–20 and 21–25) have fairly similar levels of protest potential in four national samples: about 30% in Britain and Germany and about 40% in the United States and The Netherlands. In Britain and Germany these high levels of protest potential among the young decline swiftly among those over 25 to between 10 and 20% and fall below 10% among the over 60s. In the United States this decline occurs a little later in the life-cycle, among the over-40s. In The Netherlands this decline occurs later still, among those well over 50 years of age. Thus, the very large lead in protest potential among the Dutch that was noted in the previous chapter is provided not by an especially active Dutch youth (who are much like American youth) but by the middle-aged. In every age group beyond 30, even among the old, the Dutch sample contains at least twice as many people having a high protest potential as is found in the four other countries.

This apparent deviance among middle-aged Dutch men and women almost certainly has its origins in the Second World War. To resist an unreasonable authority, especially if it is wearing a uniform, is not merely an approved democratic right in the The Netherlands. It is to many a moral duty. To a moral imperative of this kind, petty considerations of lawfulness take a poor second place. The trauma of occupation without military defeat and the heroic role of the Resistance have combined with the historically strong suspicion of central authority that has always characterised Dutch politics. Anyone who has lived in Amsterdam will tell you that political protest is so much a feature of daily life there that it is hard to think of it anymore as unconventional political behaviour.

The British, German and American data behave exactly in the predicted fashion. The life-cycle effect upon people's commitment to extreme forms of protest is self-evident. The Austrian data, however, are hard to interpret. Compared with other countries, the spirit of 1968 appears to have passed by the youth of Austria unnoticed. Before writing them off entirely as potential protesters it is fair to note that more than half of the 16 to 25 year olds in Austria say they will participate in a demonstration. Austria is also a rural country lacking the large urban concentrations found in the other four countries which contain large numbers of young people and, most important, a critical mass of students who live in cities.

The next step in the analysis is to examine the influence of sex upon political action. Continuing to focus for the moment on protest potential, Table 2.1 divides each national sample into three age groups: 16–29, 30–49, and the over 50s. (We have to control for the effects of age since we know already how important it is). Within each age group in each country, the sample is further divided into men and women. For each of these age and sex groups, the distribution of protest potential is shown in a simplified form: 'low' (no further than petitions) 'medium' (demonstrations and boycotts) and 'high' (strikes, occupations and blockades).

It is clear that age remains the most important factor. Within each

TABLE 2.1 Protest Potential by Age, by Sex, by Country

	Protest Potential	16–29 Men	16–29 Women	30–49 Men	30–49 Women	50 & over Men	50 & over Women
The Netherlands	Low (0, 1)	10%	27%	22%	31%	39%	50%
	Medium (2, 3)	43	41	41	35	45	35
	High (4–7)	47	32	37	34	16	15
	(n=)	(197)	(217)	(177)	(185)	(190)	(199)
Britain	Low (0, 1)	26	30	30	47	48	65
	Medium (2, 3)	42	45	48	43	41	29
	High (4–7)	32	25	22	10	11	6
	(n=)	(133)	(165)	(215)	(212)	(290)	(362)
United States	Low (0, 1)	9	30	20	27	45	51
	Medium (2, 3)	54	30	60	51	50	43
	High (4–7)	37	40	20	22	5	5
	(n=)	(209)	(267)	(245)	(287)	(245)	(345)
Germany	Low (0, 1)	20	22	27	46	43	58
	Medium (2, 3)	47	56	58	46	50	39
	High (4–7)	33	22	15	8	7	3
	(n=)	(194)	(198)	(457)	(427)	(397)	(539)
Austria	Low (0, 1)	31	48	42	61	52	71
	Medium (2, 3)	58	41	42	32	41	25
	High (4–7)	11	11	16	7	6	4
	(n=)	(117)	(138)	(238)	(298)	(185)	(287)

of these three broad age groups, men and women have quite similar levels of protest potential. This is certainly true in The Netherlands and the United States where they are similarly high and in Austria where they are similarly low. In Britain and Germany, higher levels of protest potential tend to occur among men, especially in the 30–49 age groups, where compared with those of women they are about twice as high. Among the young (16–29) it is more a case of British and German women stopping short of unlawful forms of protest than of their shunning political protest altogether as is the case among older women.

This result was not quite what was expected. (This, remember, was still the early to mid-1970s). Given the traditional absence of large numbers of women from the conventional political scene, especially in Europe, how is it that so many appear to take a committed view of political protest methods? What happened to the availability factor? Possibly, even in 1973, the hypothesis was out of date. More and more married women remained in the labour market even if they had children. To remain at work is to remain a full member of the community at large in a way that the life of a housewife does not allow. By then the nurturant and passive aspects of a women's role in society had waned and the kind of assertiveness that a commitment to political activity requires was no longer a male prerogative. A simple test of these ideas is to turn to the data for conventional political involvement. Had women, in contrast to earlier survey evidence, now penetrated the conventional political arena too?

Table 2.2 shows that they had not. In this analysis the sample is divided in the same way as in Table 2.1 into three age groups and, within each age group in each country, by men and women. The distribution of conventional political activity within each age and sex group is similarly shown as 'low' (no further than reading about politics in newspapers) 'medium' (discussing politics or, variously in different countries, working on community problems, convincing friends to vote as oneself or attending meetings) and 'high' (contacting officials, campaigning and so on.)

In each group in each country men have a clear lead over women in their rates of conventional political involvement. Not that women do nothing, but men do more. This is especially true in Germany where men appear to have a stranglehold upon the party system and its management. In the three successive age groups, German men compared with women are twice, three times and nearly four times more likely to have a high involvement in conventional political activities. The Austrians show a similar pattern, the Dutch and

Americans less so. In the American case, older women retain very high levels of conventional political activity compared with women elsewhere: 26% among women over 50 compared with between 11% in Austria and only 5% in The Netherlands. It is they alone who account for the overall lead in the levels of conventional political participation shown by the United States over other nations. American and German men have, overall, much the same levels of conventional political involvement.

One really deviant group stands out in Table 2.2: young British men. Only 2% of them regularly involve themselves in serious kinds of conventional political activity compared with 15% and 17% in The Netherlands and Austria and 26% and 32% in the United States and Germany. Older men in Britain show increased levels of activity but still well below the average elsewhere. In what is normally held to be a mature and reasonably participative political culture, these rates of recruitment to party activity are very low. Britain seems to be the one country where young people have taken a positive view of political protest, at least as positive as their German peers, but shun conventional political involvement. Their higher rates of trade union membership may account for this difference. This finding is particularly ironic because, compared with Germany, the British protest movements of the 1960s were muted. It was thought that in continental Europe the young would desert the existing system for new forms of political action while in Britain continuity would prevail. The data shows the opposite.

It is instructive carefully to compare Tables 2.1 and 2.2. The most compelling generalisation that strikes one is that among the whole Dutch sample, among most of the British and, of course, among young people everywhere, a commitment to direct action politics is substantially a more popular idea than involvement in conventional political activity. One cannot be entirely sure about this because the scales are different and corresponding scale scores have different real values. Yet most people familiar with data of these kinds would agree that this is a reasonable conclusion. Among the very youngest respondents one would expect this because they are emotionally attracted to protest behaviour while they have not yet established themselves as tax paying members of the community. It is when people become settled in one location in jobs and homes that they tend to be drawn into local community politics. They have a stake in local affairs and more readily see the point of supporting local political life. But a preference for protest is a pattern that persists among those in their 20s and 30s.

TABLE 2.2 Conventional Participation by Age, by Sex, by Country

	Conventional Participation	16-29		30-49		50 & over	
		Men	Women	Men	Women	Men	Women
The Netherlands	Low (0, 1)	40%	61%	36%	56%	43%	64%
	Medium (2, 3)	46	29	46	37	44	31
	High (4-7)	15	10	18	7	13	5
	(n=)	(202)	(222)	(187)	(191)	(200)	(179)
Britain	Low (0, 1)	55	60	41	58	43	63
	Medium (2, 3)	43	33	46	35	44	28
	High (4-7)	2	7	13	8	13	9
	(n=)	(142)	(166)	(220)	(220)	(303)	(391)
United States	Low (0, 1)	39	45	17	34	27	40
	Medium (2, 3)	35	38	37	35	39	34
	High (4-7)	26	17	46	31	34	26
	(n=)	(215)	(280)	(255)	(303)	(260)	(380)
Germany	Low (0, 1)	40	59	32	65	48	73
	Medium (2, 3)	28	26	34	25	26	20
	High (4-7)	32	15	34	10	26	7
	(n=)	(199)	(210)	(458)	(447)	(406)	(575)
Austria	Low (0, 1)	50	66	43	64	43	31
	Medium (2, 3)	33	27	36	25	34	58
	High (4-7)	17	8	21	11	23	11
	(n=)	(139)	(166)	(279)	(371)	(227)	(394)

Less easily explained is the position of women. In every country, young women seem attracted to political protest quite as much as are young men but they record very low levels of conventional political activity. The youngest women tend to be no less available for political mobilisation than are the youngest men. It may well be that their distinct bias toward protest and away from the conventional political arena has more to do with choice than tradition. This question will be taken up again soon. If choices are being made, and of course they are, then mental skills are being used. At this point it is time to introduce the third element of the baseline model: the impact of education.

Previous studies of this kind have shown that the more education a person has received and the better the quality of that education, the more likely it is that sooner or later they will engage in party political activities. Education provides people with what psychologists call cognitive skills, the ability to fit new information into an established mental map. This is as true for politics as it is for any other aspect of life. Political information is especially difficult to learn and interpret. Political problems are often vexing and intractable. Clear and unbiased information is hard to come by. Without some rudimentary map of the political landscape most people become quickly lost. Education can provide such a map. This is not to say that such guidance is always provided to schoolchildren and students alongside maths and language teaching. In some countries, notably in Germany, it is provided, but usually the process is indirect. The emphasis is upon learning-how-to-learn. To pursue this line of reasoning now would anticipate too much of the following chapter where these cognitive skills in politics are examined directly. For the moment we will examine only the extent of the relationship between education and political action.

Age was earlier found to be strongly associated with protest potential but less so with conventional political participation. Sex was earlier found to be strongly associated with conventional political participation but less so with protest potential. We now find that education is associated equally strongly with both conventional and unconventional forms of political action. This is true when education is measured in forms of the number of years of schooling a respondent has had and is equally true when education is measured in terms of the kind of school a respondent last attended: primary, secondary, or higher education. In terms of quantity and quality, therefore, the more and better education one has received the more likely it is that one will be in the habit of conventional forms of political involvement *and* the higher one's protest potential is likely to be. This is true in each of the five nations in the study though the relationship is expressed in differing aggregate terms from country to country.

Using only the type-of-school measure, Tables 2.3 and 2.4 show respectively how levels of conventional and unconventional political action rise under the impact of education. With respect to protest potential, for example, the relationship is most marked in the United States. Among the least well educated Americans, one half will go no further than signing a petition and only a quarter will go further than demonstrations. Among Americans with even secondary level education these figures reverse: only a quarter will go no further than petitions and a half will go beyond demonstrations. Among Americans with at least some college education (and there are many such people in the United States) the preference is overwhelmingly in favour of the more committed forms of protest: only 15% will go no further than signing a petition and two thirds will go further than demonstrations. The proportion who will go even further and use unlawful means of protest increases almost four-fold from 8% among primary educated Americans, to 21% among the secondary educated to 31% among the college educated. These are large differences and something of the kind is observable in each national sample.

Leaving aside The Netherlands, this division of each national sample into three educational strata, crudely done though this may be, does show that some of the cross-national differences examined earlier are accounted for by differing educational structures. The least well-educated in Britain, Germany, the United States and Austria all have similarly low levels of protest potential. The higher levels of protest potential associated with secondary and college education that occur evenly in Britain, Germany and the United States are strongly echoed, if not quite matched, by similar increases in protest potential among better-educated people even in Austria.

In The Netherlands the relationship between better education and a higher protest potential is blunted somewhat by the sheer weight of potential protesters crowding the ranks of even the least well educated Dutch. Among Dutch people having only primary education 42% will go further than demonstrations on the protest potential scale and two thirds of these (28% of the total) will go further even than boycotts and use unlawful means of protest. These figures are respectively twice and three times higher than the average among primary-educated people elsewhere and are similar to the figures for

TABLE 2.3 *Conventional Political Participation by Type of Schooling Received*

Conventional Political Participation			Primary only	Secondary High School	University College	(tau-b)
			%	%	%	
The Netherlands	Low	0	35	14	7	
		1	23	17	13	
		2	28	34	43	
		3	8	11	14	
	High	4–7	7	24	24	(.26)
Britain	Low	0	32	20	9	
		1	27	25	15	
		2	28	34	46	
		3	6	9	12	
	High	4–7	7	13	18	(.17)
United States	Low	0	26	16	2	
		1	23	17	11	
		2	23	25	20	
		3	11	12	15	
	High	4–7	16	29	51	(.27)
Germany	Low	0	28	15	4	
		1	34	28	14	
		2	16	18	19	
		3	7	14	21	
	High	4–7	15	26	42	(.23)
Austria	Low	0	41	18	0	
		1	22	25	29	
		2	17	32	42	
		3	7	7	16	
	High	4–7	13	18	13	(.19)

college-educated people in the other four nations in the survey. Thus, a higher protest potential is very much a common property in The Netherlands in a way that it is not elsewhere. Among the Dutch intelligentsia, *none* of whom have a protest potential of zero, it is almost the norm.

With respect to conventional political participation (Table 2.3) increased rates of activity are strongly associated with a background of better education. This is especially true, once more, in the United States and quite strikingly so in Germany where the proportion who are most active rises from 15% among least well educated Germans to 26% among those with some secondary education and jumps to

TABLE 2.4 *Protest Potential by Type of Schooling Received*

	Protest Potential		Primary Only	Secondary, High School	University, College	(tau-b)
The Netherlands	Low	0	11%	4%	0%	
		1	22	13	17	
		2	26	24	24	
		3	14	22	18	
	High	4–7	28	37	42	(.14)
Britain	Low	0	29	13	5	
		1	24	21	5	
		2	23	29	30	
		3	12	18	34	
	High	4–7	12	20	26	(.22)
United States	Low	0	19	5	4	
		1	31	20	11	
		2	25	25	19	
		3	18	28	35	
	High	4–7	8	21	31	(.27)
Germany	Low	0	23	11	5	
		1	23	18	12	
		2	28	34	33	
		3	18	21	27	
	High	4–7	8	17	24	(.19)
Austria	Low	0	26	10	6	
		1	35	32	6	
		2	23	30	44	
		3	9	16	18	
	High	4–7	7	13	27	(.23)

42% among college-educated Germans. In fact, once the distortion introduced by the greater numbers of college-educated people in the United States is controlled for, as is the case in Table 2.3, Americans and Germans have very similar rates of conventional political participation. Elsewhere, the impact of education is more muted, especially so in Britain and Austria where its effects are confined to raising interest in politics and more passive forms of involvement like attendance at meetings rather than provoking high levels of campaigning activity among graduates.

Underlying quite a lot of this relationship between better education and higher rates of political activity of both kinds is the latent effect of youth and sex, mainly youth in the case of protest potential and mainly sex in the case of conventional political participation. The problem is that the young are better educated than the older age cohorts and men are better educated than women. So when we see that college-educated people have a higher protest potential than those with only primary education, is their higher potential associated with their education or their relative youth or both? The same problem arises with respect to the joint effects of sex and education upon conventional political participation. Are higher rates of conventional participation really associated so strongly with education or is it because men are better educated than women and, for many other reasons, men are more active in the conventional political sphere than are women?

These and similar questions were examined in two ways. The first involved combining the analyses shown earlier for age and sex with the tables for education. For each country, the relationships between levels of education and the two political action scales were examined separately within each of the six age-and-sex groups defined earlier (young, middle-aged and older men and women). Thirty tables are far too many to set out here. If they may be taken on trust, the results broadly confirmed that higher education is associated with higher levels of both conventional and unconventional political participation independently of the effects of age and sex. That is to say, even though young men, for example, have a higher protest potential than others, young well-educated men have a higher protest potential than young poorly-educated men. Exceptions to this are young men in The Netherlands, the majority of whom seem to favour political protest regardless of their educational background.

The results contained one or two surprises. Young and middle-aged women students and graduates tended to have a *higher* protest potential than their male student and graduate peers. This certainly reflects the radical and assertive mood that so characterised the young female intelligentsia in Europe in the 1970s. It is particularly intriguing to note that in Germany this higher protest potential among women graduates is accompanied by strikingly *lower* levels of involvement in conventional political activity. We shall return to this point later.

This is about as far as one can take this kind of analysis. Even three-way tables can stretch the modestly sized samples in the five national surveys too far. There are, for example, rather too few college-educated people in the European samples, especially in Britain and Austria, to examine closely in this way. One finds only handfuls of older college-educated women. This of itself is an important qualification to add to earlier discussions. One should not be oversold on the single idea of education as an explanation of higher rates of political action. To quote the original volume:

It is true that the majority of the best educated are prone to political action but by no means the majority of all those prone to political action received the best education.

A second means of testing the relative independence and relative impact of age, sex and education upon political action was the use of multiple regression analysis. The details of this analysis need not detain us here but some interesting conclusions can usefully be quoted.

In The Netherlands, Britain, and most especially in the United States, conventional political participation is most significantly associated with education. In Germany and Austria education is also important but is slightly outweighed by the importance of membership of the male sex. With respect to protest potential, the dominant influence remains youth, except in Austria where it is quite clearly higher education rather than youth. Elsewhere, being male and better educated does contribute significantly to higher levels of protest potential independently of age. The additional role of education is particularly significant in the United States.

It seems fair to conclude from these relatively simple findings that our dual concept of political action has passed its second test. The first test was to show that conventional and unconventional political participation are related, that they tend to go together. The previous chapter showed that they are related; not identically of course, but that each style of participation lies in the same quadrant. Each style suggests and expresses a positive and (usually) a democratic urge for political participation which may be élite-directed or élite-challenging but one that is not directed at the overthrow of existing regimes. The two scales are measuring a widening of people's political action repertoire. There are two styles but one repertoire. This analysis has strengthened this idea. The second test has shown that the two styles of political participation share common sources in the baseline model of political participation. The uniting factor is better education; not, it must be stressed again, solely degree-level education but simply better education. Conventional political participation is associated first with better education, second with membership of the male sex and (a little) with being middle-aged. Protest potential is associated first with youth, second with better education and (a little) with being male. This being so, the next step in this analysis is an obvious one. If the baseline model selects different kinds of people for recruitment to both kinds of political participation in a *similar* way, what is the social

The Social Background

composition of the five political action types defined in the previous chapter? How does the baseline model fit the political action repertory? Some of the answers are highly predictable from the results discussed so far in this chapter. Others are quite surprising.

A glance back to the previous chapter could be useful at this point, especially to Figure 1.5 which shows how the five political action types are created and to pages 30 to 31 which describe them in detail. Inactives, remember, will do little or nothing in politics; the conformists confine their involvement solely to conventional political participation; the reformists combine conventional participation with lawful forms of protest; the activists possess a complete political action repertory, combining high levels of conventional and unconventional actions; lastly the protesters favour only protest tactics but not conventional political involvement. We shall re-examine each in turn in the light of the baseline model:

2.1.1 The Inactives

Of the five political action types, the inactives most faithfully reflect the core elements of social status implied by the baseline model of political involvement. Typically inactives are poorly educated older women. Their lack of education is overwhelmingly the key factor in assigning the inactives to a life devoid of political activity of any sort. Age and sex are also important. Political passivity of this kind becomes more and more common among successively older age cohorts. Likewise, women are consistently more numerous among the inactives in every age group. These effects are exaggerated somewhat by the powerful underlying effect of poor education that supresses political activity. Older people generally and women in all age groups but especially older women had far fewer educational opportunities in their youth compared with those that were offered to men, especially now to young men. Even though the ratio of men to women among the inactives is more equitable among those (relatively few) better educated people among them, the bias towards political passivity among women remains strong among all ages and education levels. The consistency of this result across five nations is very striking. Even in these five advanced industrial countries in the 1970s, the social disadvantages visited upon women of all ages and conditions of life still imposed a bias against their involvement in political action of all kinds. Better education had weakened this bias considerably but had not eliminated it.

2.1.2 The Conformists

In contrast to the clear composition of the inactives, the conformists are a far more difficult group to summarise. Some historical forces have been at work that have recruited different people to this category at different times in different countries. The only point that is consistent across all nations is that conformists tend to be somewhat older than average. They may equally be men or women, except in Germany where the male dominance of party politics is so complete that even the conformists are predominantly male. In Germany and The Netherlands, education is quite unrelated to conformity while in Britain, Austria and most especially in the United States, a good education actually decreases the likelihood that a respondent will be a conformist. This seems odd. Conformity is a form of active participation and the baseline model insists that participation increases with better education. This paradox arises because conformity is typically the means to participation of the older respondents. It is a 'generational' or an 'historical' effect and has two origins. First, the kinds of political participation offered in their youth to those who are now older *but still politically active* were overwhelmingly of the conventional party political kind. It is the style of participation they learned when young and, since they still practice it, they learned it well and are unlikely to expand their personal action repertory now to include protest activities. Second, the educational opportunities offered to these older age cohorts were significantly poorer compared with the expanded and enriched educational systems that were developed in postwar Europe and the United States. They tend to be the poorer-educated older party faithful.

If this generalisation effect is true, then we ought to find that education has a very different effect upon the tendency to be a conformist among different age groups. Among older conformists, the classic baseline model should hold fast: better education encouraged them to take up party politics a long while ago and party politics is what they still do and they do no other kind. Among the (fewer) young conformists the reverse should be true. Young people who follow only the conventional political pathways are likely to be those whose lack of education has inhibited them from expanding their political action repertory to become, as others of their generation have become, fully-fledged reformists and activists. This broadly speaking, is what is found. Among the 16–29 year olds conformism is associated with poorer education, least so in Germany but strikingly so in Austria and Britain. Among those over 50, conformism is associated with better education, especially in The Netherlands. This last point does not hold in the United States where even among older respondents conformism is still associated with less education. Generational effects are different in American politics. A far greater range of political activities were freely available to ordinary Americans far earlier in this century than was the case in Europe. In the 1930s the baseline model was working in its now familiar way in America while European political life was being ploughed under by radical totalitarianism. This difference shows clearly in the data even 40 years later.

What is even more intriguing is that the generational effect has had a similar impact upon the relationship between sex and conformism *among the better educated*. Among the over-50s who experienced some higher education in their youth, women rather than men are likely to be conformists. Among the under-30s who are similarly (and more commonly) well educated, men are more likely to be conformists, women much less so. Thus, when those relatively few well-educated women among the older age cohorts became attracted to politics they were drawn easily into conventional pathways of political activity and, as always, they were given conventional tasks to do. They looked no further. Nowadays, when young well-educated women take an interest in politics they are not attracted to the sole service of a political party. In fact, they recoil from it. Let them stick their own envelopes. Young women, as we shall see in a moment, have other things to do.

2.1.3 The Reformists

Among the reformists, the baseline model is reasserted as clearly as it is among the inactives. The reformists' profile is almost a mirror-image of the inactives'. Whereas the inactives had among them disproportionate numbers of older poorly-educated women, the reformists are made up from large numbers of younger better-educated men. They are 'younger' rather than 'young' and in Britain, Germany and the United States they tend quite strongly to be 'young middle-aged' – between 30 and 49. But they are predominantly men. The reformists' choice of political style, combining higher levels of conventional political participation with lawful forms of protest, accords well with commonsense ideas about what kinds of political involvement are typical of Dahrendorf's 'natural group' – young well-educated men. Indeed, a closer analysis of the reformists testifies, as the original volume put it '. . to the enormous deficit less educated women have to overcome in political involvement; the gap between men and women is reduced from an average 19 percentage points among the least educated to an average 6 points among the most highly educated'. Put another way, the correlation between better education and entry into the reformist category is far stronger among women that it is among men. Men tend to need some education to enter this central position in political involvement; women need a lot.

2.1.4 The Activists

This group, the least numerous of the five political action types, extends the political repertory of the reformists to include the more forceful and often unlawful kinds of protest activities that define the higher reaches of the protest potential scale. They too, like the reformists, tend to be well educated but they are on average, somewhat younger. This one would expect, given their taste for unlawful forms of protest. This combination of youth and education means that activism is a style of participation typical of students even though students are not the majority of activists. Unlike the reformists, however, the balance of the sexes among activists is fairly even. This, however, is what is known as a 'compositional effect'. Being so much younger, female activists tend to be better educated. If one looks solely at those (relatively few) activists who had only elementary education, men outnumber women by about three to one. Only among the very best educated activists do women approach parity of numbers with the men. Thus, to quote again from the original, '. . . a poor education, while hampering political involvement both by men and women, still discourages and disadvantages women to a much greater extent'. It is about as hard for women to break into the vanguard of political activity as it is for them to gain entry into most other kinds of élite positions.

2.1.5 The Protesters

This group drew the Study Group's most eager attention. The creation of the political action repertory isolated the protesters as the group who have strong leanings toward the use of protest tactics, including often unlawful means of political coercion, yet who reject conventional political participation. They make this choice against a general trend among politically active people to combine conventional and unconventional methods (that is, to be reformists or activists). Are these people the majority who threatened the decisive break with the existing political system that seemed possible in the late 1960s and early 1970s? Are they the vanguard of a movement that might bring massive political change?

They certainly possess the first qualification for such a role: compared even with the activists, they are very young. This fact, it can be argued, means only that they have acquired their protest potential (the 'natural state' of the very young) *before* an involvement in conventional politics that tends, as we know, to follow a little later in life. Surely many protesters will transfer to the ranks of the reformists or the activists as they grow into their late 20s or 30s. Which of the two they become will depend on how much of their protest potential they retain as they grow older. Another fact argues against this: compared to reformists and activists they tend *not* to be well educated. Being very young, they tend less to have only elementary education (a lack characteristic of older people) but typically to have some secondary schooling rather than a college education. This does not advertise them as potential reformists and activists.

Another fact complicates the picture even further: in all countries except Austria, women are slightly *more* likely than men to be protesters. This is not a compositional effect; it holds true within each of the educational strata defined by primary, secondary and college education. This is especially true in Germany where women are over-represented among the (comparatively rare) college educated protesters by 23 percentage points. This implies that the protester category, while composed largely of young and not especially well-educated people, contains significant cells of highly-educated young women. They are not there by accident but by choice. They are there, to quote a phrase from the original that has achieved some wider currency, because they '. . . declare a willingness to be mobilized in political protest activity while shunning the grey-suited male dominated world of "politics"'. They, among all kinds of people active in politics, are the most élite-challenging and the least élite-directed. If you cannot join them, beat them.

2.2 THE POLITICAL ACTION REPERTORY AND THE BASELINE MODEL

2.2.1 A Summary

In Figure 2.2, the five political action types are represented as segments of a globe – rather as you might cut an orange. The baseline model is represented as three arrows – age, sex and education – each piercing the globe in the direction of its impact on the action repertory. Thus, as one moves from north to south, people get younger. As one moves from east to west, one encounters fewer women and more men. And as one moves from north-west to south-east, people get better educated. Note that the arrow representing education is not at right angles to those representing age and sex. It traverses the same two-dimensional plane across the diagonal. This is because poorer education is associated with older people and women (the north-west territory, as it were) and higher education is associated with youth and men.

To understand the value of this illustration choose any point on the globe. Now see which points on the arrows are closest to the point on the surface you have chosen. Among the inactives, for example, one is closest to the points of impact of the arrows representing women, older people and, especially, poor education. On the opposite side of the globe, therefore, one is closest to the points representing youth, men and, especially, better education and one has found, of course, the Reformists and the Activists. Over on the south-west area of the globe one encounters the protesters and one is closest to the impact of youth, women and medium (that is, secondary) levels of education, and so on. Like all summary devices, it does not illustrate the important exceptions discussed above and these should not be forgotten. The most important of these are the older well-educated women conformists and the young well-educated women protesters. But it does show very clearly how the baseline model of political participation is both supported and qualified by the political action repertory. The well-known impact upon increased political participation of higher social status (represented in our Western societies as being a well-educated man) is clearly present. But the strong association between protest potential and youth and a bias among women to move towards protest means that the impact of the baseline model is no longer unidirectional. It swings around into the two dimensions defined by the political action repertory. It means that conventional

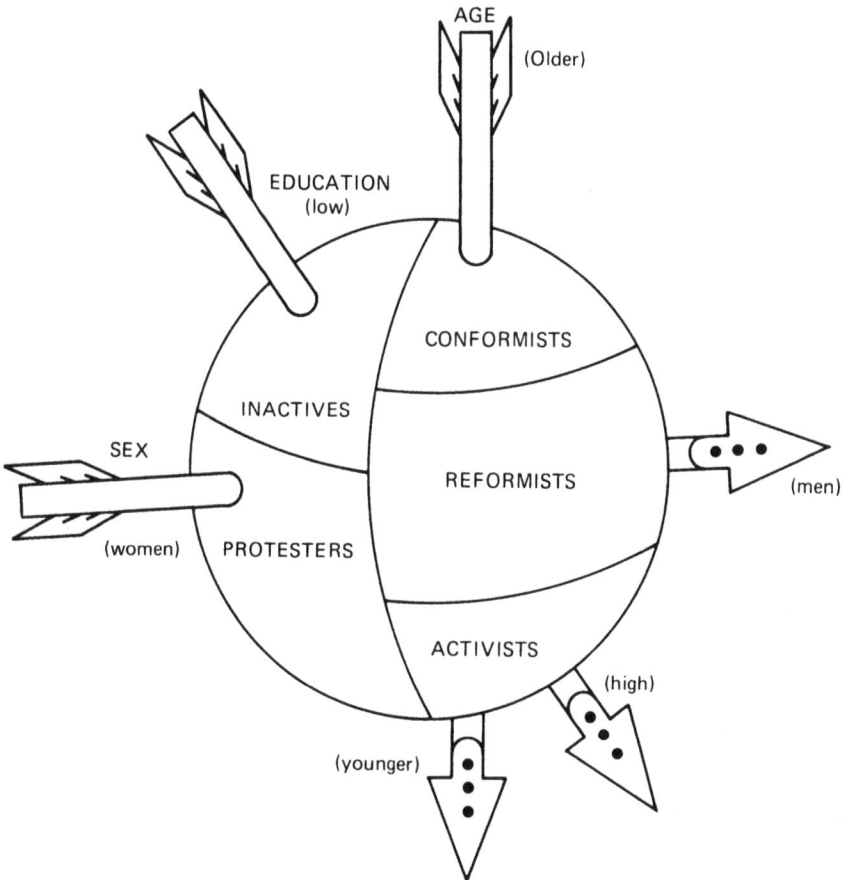

FIGURE 2.2 *The Impact of the Baseline Model upon the Political Action Repertory*

political participants must now be seen as three quite distinct groups of people – conformists, reformists and activists. Each group has different social characteristics that are not *individually* predictable from the traditional interpretation of the baseline model. There are also three quite distinct groups of potential (and actual) protesters – reformists, activists and protesters – and they too have different social characteristics that are not at all predictable from a unidirectional view of the baseline model. This is especially true of the protesters since they have none of the characteristics that traditional political theories of mass participation would allow for. Thus, the introduction of this dualistic idea of political participation has expanded our understanding of the social causes of political behaviour.

2.3 SOCIAL CLASS AND OTHER PROBLEMS

Pages 122 to 128 of the original volume dwell in detail on an analysis of the relationship between the two political action scales and 'social class'. This was a dauntingly difficult task. In any one country, social scientists fail to agree on the best way to measure social class. In a survey in five countries having differing class structures the problems are immense. Four measures were examined in the hope of bracketing the concept of a class heirarchy in a way that would reveal its influence on political action. These were:

(1) occupational prestige (a score derived from Treiman's scales of the level of relative prestige people assign to different occupations);
(2) subjective social class (whether people thought of themselves as 'working class', 'middle class' or 'upper middle class';
(3) Income; and
(4) trades union membership.

The results showed clearly that, as the baseline model would broadly predict, higher occupational prestige, identity with the 'middle class', and higher income were all associated both with higher levels of conventional political participation and greater protest potential. This was not, however, true of Trades Union membership which was unrelated to either scale. The problem with these results was that higher social class, however measured, is strongly associated with better education. Whenever the influence of education was held constant in the analysis, the effects of social class disappeared. This was true even when the five political action types were examined separately. Your present author had cherished the idea that social class would have special meaning in the case of the protesters. Whereas the reformists and the activists used their expanded political action repertory to increase their middle-class leverage on the political system, surely the political thrust of young workers would be best expressed by an exclusively protest orientation? This seemed especially likely since strikes and occupations feature strongly in the protest potential scale. So one looked hardest for such a result among the British data. After all, immediately following fieldwork the British Conservative administration of Edward Heath was defeated in an election brought about by a vigourously protracted strike by the National Union of Mineworkers with heavy support from their allies in the British Labour movement.

But it was not so. Being a protester is not an exclusive badge of working-class militancy. The analysis also controlled for the effects of larger numbers of women among the protesters. Was it at least a badge of militancy of young working-class men? It was not, not exclusively. It was true that more young workers were to be found among the protesters than among their well-educated peers among the activists. But so were large numbers of young non-manual workers who shared with young manual workers only moderate levels of education. Protesters are ordinary young people of all kinds, few of whom (except some of the women among them) made it to college.

It should not be forgotten at this point that social class is still an important influence upon the world of politics. This is especially true in Europe and truest of all in Britain. The division between manual and non-manual workers (the 'political cleavage' as it is called) still has a determining influence upon the direction of people's party choice at election time. If, as most political scientists do, one wishes to explain political partisanship, then the well-informed analyst turns first to occupational class background for enlightenment. Education will also help but its influence is secondary to class. For example, among the majority of moderately well-educated people, those following manual occupations will still tend to vote Left, those in non-manual occupations will tend towards parties of the Right. In this analysis, in contrast, we are trying to explain what people *do* in politics, not the cause in which they do it. In our case, the relative power of education and social class to explain the political style of our respondents is the opposite of their power to explain the direction of their vote. All that is accounted for by social class is accounted for equally by education but education accounts for more. We now need to know *how* education has this effect and what are the limits of its effects. This question provides the starting point for the next chapter as we examine the development and impact of ideological thought in politics.

3 Ideology and Political Action

The Political Action Repertory showed us new choices among political behaviours. Groups of people who differ sharply in their social composition are choosing to combine their political options from both conventional and unconventional actions, or to choose one kind or the other, or to reject both. The task for the remainder of this book is to show why they make these choices and what this development might mean for mass politics in Western democracies.

The answer that will occupy us in this chapter is that they choose differently because they think and feel about politics differently. By 'think' and 'feel' is meant the distinction that psychologists make between the cognitive aspects of mental life and the affective or evaluative aspects. That is to say, the distinction that is made between people's knowledge and understanding of political matters on the one hand and their political values, desires and feelings-for-and-against on the other. Both are important in determining the way people choose their preferred means of political action. A few paragraphs now will explain why this is likely to be so. The evidence for the way each area of influence functions will then be examined separately. Lastly, a combined analysis will show how, crucially, knowledge and values interact to direct people toward one style of political action rather than another.

3.1 IDEOLOGY, VALUES AND THE NEW POLITICS

Almond and Verba's famous study, *The Civic Culture*, proposed that successful democracies draw much of their vitality from a stratum of their citizens who demonstrate their 'subjective political competence'. These are people who feel able to influence political events and have the mental skills to interpret their meaning. They tend to be located, unsurprisingly, in the better educated, higher social classes and compared to others they have much higher rates of political participation. This activity is due partly to sheer social position; they are better placed to influence events, officials defer to them and they use their connections. Undeniably though, their better education and training also leave such people with the mental skills to process political information in ways that suggest, when necessary, action for change and they do not always act in their own material class interest. They are guided by an ideology. It is this combination of mental skills, this blend of political competence and its guiding system of values, that in this study is given the name of ideology. Such people have an ideological conception of politics.

Ideology has been given many other names, of course, and their recitation would detain us a long while. All that need be stressed at this point is that, as in any empirical study of mass politics, we are dealing with the impact of political ideas from the consumer's point of view. Political ideology is a cultural product. It reaches people through all the communication and organisational channels of society. It is learned by individuals, to a greater or lesser extent, and used by them in their comprehension of the political world. This stress upon learning and comprehension places the knowledge or cognitive aspects of ideology to the fore. It places this cultural definition of ideology firmly in the research tradition established by Campbell *et al.*, by Converse and by others. It is a way of defining specific groups who have specific skills. It is not, of itself, a statement about power relations in the political world.

It is reasonable to expect that the content of the ideological concepts people use will reflect the overarching principles of the political contest itself. Ideas like 'the common ownership of the means of production', 'the defence of liberty' or 'the preservation of social and political order' will have wide currency among those who, in the following pages, will be called ideologues. Much will be heard too of differences between Left and Right, of Socialists, Liberals and Conservatives, of progressives, reactionaries or revolutionaries. The most important point to grasp at the outset is that ideologies are learned but they are not learned by rote. What distinguishes an ideological way of thinking from simply having heard and remembered some of its vocabulary is the element of organising principles. Many may know what goes with which in the political world but fewer will know why. In this sense, the first function of ideology is to help an individual order, retain and understand political information. It provides a framework into which new information can be placed, coded and given wider meaning. Events are no longer seen as isolated in time but as typical of similar events and as representing one or other elements of the political contest. As Converse says: 'the more political information one already has, the lower the costs of acquiring and, perhaps more important, retaining new information'.

Although people's level of ideological thinking is seen here as the first and most important precondition for making and acting upon political judgements, it is not always a sufficient condition. It is when the holder of an organised body of political knowledge identifies with one set of ideological values, with the Left, the Right, or whatever, that strong political judgements are made. More than that, the possession of organised knowledge will help the holder to make *consistent* judgements. They are consistent in the sense that judgements on differing issues will be organised to serve a single set of preferred goals. These will often be quite long-term goals. It is the same for the choices of political action. These too will be guided by ideology. New forms of political action that do not enjoy majority support, typically those that define the higher levels of the Protest Potential Scale, will be rejected by knowledgeable people whose ideology is organised toward the defence of the status quo but will be embraced by those bent on radical social change.

This last argument leads us back to an important distinction made in chapter 1 between two fundamentally different forms of political participation, between 'élite-directed' and 'élite-challenging' kinds of action. Elite-directed participation is the older, more familiar form whereby national institutions like labour unions, the churches and mass political parties mobilise large numbers of people. It is the form of political participation that characterised the growth of mass politics in the nineteenth and early twentieth century. Newly enfranchised mass electorates, the first generations to have benefited from compulsory elementary education, were mobilised to mass rallies and to the polling booths. Only rarely did mass political action stray beyond these élite-directed paths, the most important exception being the six or seven years following the 1914–18 Great War in Europe. Then, large numbers of workers and freelancing ex-soldiers organised themselves politically, on the Left and the Right, outside the parties and the trade unions.

Lately though, and this point lies close to the whole *raison d'être* of the Political Action Study, new forms of élite-challenging political participation have emerged. Many have called this trend the rise of the New Politics. Skillful amateurs have moved out from the bureaucratic structures of the old institutions and formed ad hoc groups whose aims are often limited to a single issue. It is a much more precise form of political participation and aims at specific policy changes. It demands more of its practitioners, more energy, more resourcefulness and an ability to compete with the skills of existing élites. It demands education, certainly, but more than anything it demands a combination of organised knowledge and value-driven judgements that we call ideology. It may as well be said now that it is among the practitioners of élite-challenging kinds of participation – those who practice the New Politics – that one should expect to meet the Activists and many of the Reformists too. Much that follows will sift the evidence supporting the relationship that exists between ideology and styles of political action. Before that, however, one final introductory word is needed about the special role of value choices.

People do not challenge élites simply because they have the necessary political skills to do so. They do so because they have also made different choices. They see a difference between the goals served by existing élites and their organisations and those they themselves prefer and think better. To see such a gulf between what is and what ought to be is the basis for political motivation and always has been. However, the difference in choices that concerns us here is not one tied to specific issues, it is a fundamental difference in *value priorities*.

It was shown earlier that protest potential – the means by which élites may be challenged outside existing political structures – was not the sole property of the traditional constituency of the Left, namely, the organised workers and the dispossessed. To the contrary, those that would protest and especially those who are Activists, contain disproportionate numbers of young well-educated people who have enjoyed social and economic advantages and the patronage of the élite. While now in the 1980s we may have grown used to the most favoured youth in Western societies, especially the students, making political nuisances of themselves, it was a surprise when it happened in the 1960s and it is still not easy to explain. What has happened, and what among other things has caused the emergence of New Politics among the well-provided youth of the West, is a fundamental shift in value priorities between succeeding postwar generations.

Briefly, the key argument is that value priorities endure. The goals that one believes are ultimately the most important ones to attain and defend are chosen early in life and will change little in later years. The older generations of Europe and America had their value priorities set for them by the privations and insecurities they experienced, first in the Great Depression, later during the Second World War and its aftermath in Europe. They formed then, and who could blame them, an overwhelmingly materialist set of value priorities. Not that they placed no value on the higher things of life, on love, beauty or social justice, but especially when political or social goals were to be set, material priorities won out. The provision of food, work, money and security from violence were what they needed and what they wanted society first to guarantee. Even when social justice was sought, it was sought in material terms. The important point is that the relative affluence enjoyed subsequently by the pre-1945 generations had little impact on the value priorities they had formed in harder times. They did not forget and they continued to stress their desires for material and social security.

In contrast, those born into the rising affluence of the 1950s onward were freed, relatively speaking, to demote these basic needs in their value priorities and to place greater stress on higher-order values. First among these is a sense of belongingness, followed by powerful urges toward self-expression. These together attract their adherents toward greater access to decision-making in their communities. It is a process that the psychologist Abraham Maslow called the path to self-actualisation, and nowadays there is a lot of it about.

These higher-order or, as they will be called in what follows, postmaterialist value priorities were not taken up wholesale by the postwar generations, nor even by the majority of them. Poverty and privation were not abolished and have lately returned in the form of mass unemployment. There remain many who have good reason still to cleave to materialist values. Nor does the conspicuous consumption of many young people encourage the view that an essentially nobler and *non*-materialist generation will supplant the old. There has, however, grown up a larger and larger minority of postmaterialists to whom these 'self-actualising' values are important, especially when they are asked to make *political* rather than personal choices. If they do so in addition to and not at the expense of their continued material affluence, this is not important. The political issues they raised in the 1970s, especially racial justice, sexual equality, environmental protection, an end to the nuclear arms race, and, more than anything perhaps, the establishment of more democratic and open systems of political decision-making, were all apparently quite beyond the competence of existing political élites. This gulf between their new values and the continuing materialist preoccupations of the existing élites left the postmaterialist minority with an acute need to press for social and political change, and to do so outside the conventional pathways of political redress. It is through this intergenerational shift in value priorities that many of the Reformists, most of

the Activists and some of the Protesters were recruited.
This value-change thesis will occupy the latter part of this chapter and all of the next. For the moment we return to the task of understanding the basis for political judgements of these kinds, namely the distribution of ideological thinking in the political communities of Western Europe and America.

3.2 MEASURING IDEOLOGICAL THOUGHT

The survey obtained from respondents three measures of ideological thought whose development was the special contribution to the study from Hans Dieter Klingemann:

(1) *The Active Use of Ideological Thought* which is the extent to which respondents were able spontaneously to use ideological ways of thinking to evaluate, in this case, political parties.
(2) *The Recognition and Understanding of Ideological Thought*, which is the extent to which respondents could recognise and describe political ideas in ideological terms, in this case, the ideas of Left and Right.
(3) *Levels of Ideological Thinking in Politics* which is a measure combining elements from both the above.

3.2.1 The Active Use of Ideological Thought

It would be nice to believe that one could equip survey interviewers with a neatly precoded scale that asked respondents to indicate precisely their personal levels of ideological thinking; nice, but hardly likely. Instead, more indirect methods are necessary. In this case, respondents were asked to say, *in their own words*, what they liked and then what they disliked about the major party of the Right appropriate in each country (see Figure 3.1) and then to say what they liked and what they disliked about the major party of the Left. In this way a large amount of open-ended material was collected in each national survey representing ordinary people's spontaneous views on the virtues and shortcomings of their major political parties. Such views are interesting and not all were politely expressed, but their explicit content was of only passing interest to the study. What was important was the *way* respondents expressed themselves. The question, innocuous enough in itself, threw respondents back on their own resources to provide an answer. They had to select their own frames of reference in making a reply and it is these frames of reference that the coding scheme was designed to capture. The measure is therefore one of the saliency or centrality of ideological kinds of thinking to the way each respondent makes a commonplace political judgement. Briefly, this is the coding scheme that was used:

Ideological concepts: Overwhelmingly these were expressed in terms of the Left-Right dimension in politics and consistently so in all five nations. Descriptions of the Left parties diverged between radical ideas concerning the class struggle and reformist ideas about social equality. Likewise, descriptions of the Right parties diverged between the consensus politics of liberal conservatism and radical or reactionary Right ideas. Remember it was the *use* of the idea that was coded, not the respondents' approval or disapproval of it. Often ideological terms denoting the radical Right or Left were used perjoratively to describe the party that the user did not support.

Social groups: These respondents judged parties as representatives of social groups – 'workers', 'big business', 'middle class' and so on.

Party organisation and competence: These ideas focused upon party unity, professionalism and their competence to form governments and conduct affairs of state.

Domestic policy issues and *Foreign policy issues*: Descriptions in terms of where parties are believed to stand on specific issues.

Politicians and party leaders: Usually these were simply named in association with their parties.

Intrinsic values: This last group merely identified with the party, or not, in a purely personal way unaccompanied by any political terms or reasons.

The use of ideological concepts was confined to about a fifth of the British, Austrian and American samples and about a third of the Dutch and German (see Table 3.1). Considerably more preferred to cast their judgements in terms of the parties' identification with social groups, their organisational competence or the domestic policies they were thought to support. Far fewer mentioned foreign policies, except in Germany, where 'Ostpolitik' (Brandt's overtures to the Eastern Bloc) was a live issue at the time of the survey. Also in Germany and in the United States, politicians and leaders were mentioned more often than elsewhere. In Britain, intrinsic values – sheer emotional attachment to a party – was a more frequent basis for judgement than elsewhere. Sixty-five percent of the British used such ideas, accounting for 34% of all the ideas used by all the British

Ideology and Political Action

Countries	Non-extremist "left" system party	Non-extremist "right" system party
The Netherlands	Partij van de Arbeid	Volkspartij voor Vrijheid en Democratie
Britain	Labour Party	Conservative Party
United States	Democratic Party	Republican Party
Germany	Sozialdemokratische Partei	Christlich Demokratische Union/Christlich Soziale Union
Austria	Sozialdemokratische Partei	Österreichische Volkspartei

In Germany the Christlich Soziale Union has been used as the stimulus object in Bavaria only.

Question wording:
Now, I'd be interested in knowing your opinions of what you feel are the good and bad aspects of the political parties in the (United States).
Let's start with the (Democratic Party).
What do you like about the (Democratic Party)? (Probe fully)

What do you dislike about the (Democratic Party)? (Probe fully)
And what about the (Republican Party)? What do you like about the (Republican Party)? (Probe fully)
What do you dislike about the (Republican Party)? (Probe fully)

FIGURE 3.1 *The Political Parties Judged by Respondents in each Country*

sample compared, for example, to only 13% of the total number of ideas deployed by the German sample.

Among those who make ideological judgements, some used them of one party, some of the other but only a few of both. These last, who see clearly the two main parties as occupying places in a continuum of Left and Right, will be called 'ideologues'. They are rare: 4% in Britain and Austria, 7% in Germany and the United States, 9% in The Netherlands. The remainder, who see one or other party in ideological terms, will be called 'near-ideologues'. They are commoner: less so in Britain (17%), Austria (15%) and the United States (only 13%); more so in Germany (26%) and The Netherlands (27%).

TABLE 3.1 The Use of Different Kinds of Ideas in Judging Political Parties

	The Netherlands %	Britain %	United States %	Germany %	Austria %
Ideological	36	21	21	34	20
Social Groups	40	41	40	45	39
Party Organisation and competence	31	35	49	66	49
Domestic policies	32	38	34	53	51
Foreign policies	6	8	11	42	2
Politicians and leaders	15	18	40	38	16
Intrinsic values	32	65	46	49	42
No reply	28	18	13	6	17
(Base for percentages)	(1201)	(1483)	(1719)	(2307)	(1584)

Columns total more than 100% because many respondents gave more than one kind of reply and so appear in more than one category.

Thus, the remaining proportion of the population who are 'non-ideologues', of one kind or another, are a majority in each country. It is a small majority in The Netherlands (64%) and Germany (66%); larger in Britain (79%), the United States (80%) and Austria (81%). Among the minority of ideologues and near-ideologues, the character of the ideas they used were predominately focused, as might be expected, on ideas describing the reformist rather than the radical Left and the liberal, status quo rather than the reactionary Right. The ratio of 'moderate' to 'extreme' judgements was at least three to one on each side, Left and Right, except in Germany where radical Left ideas were freely deployed, comprising half the Left ideas used. This is not because the Germans identified freely with the radical Left; the ideas were expressed most often in hostile terms, reflecting the strong anti-Communist sentiment that endures in the German polity.

3.2.2 The Recognition and Understanding of Ideological Thought

The requirement that people should actively and spontaneously use ideological ideas in judging parties to earn the name of ideologues was a strict one. It may well be that there are others among those who judged parties in terms of groups or policies who, while they do not spontaneously reach for an ideological frame of reference, can nevertheless recognise one when asked to do so. This is the distinction made earlier between knowing why different things in the political world are linked together and simply knowing that they are.

Consequently, a measure was included in the survey that in some senses reverses the procedure described for the 'active use' measure. The terms 'Left' and 'Right' were put before respondents, quite literally, in the form of a scale (see Figure 3.2). They were handed a pencil and asked to indicate their own position in one of ten boxes making up the 'Left-Right Scale'. Most European respondents obliged, ranging from 75% in Austria to 92% in Germany but somewhat fewer in the United States (62%) where a 'liberal-conservative' dimension is a more familiar idea. They tended to mark the scale accurately too: supporters of Left parties appeared in the left-hand boxes, supporters of Right parties on the right, and supporters of Centre parties, where they existed, in the centre.

A moment's work with a pencil, however, is not an adequate measure of ideological recognition even if the results do encourage the belief that most people can find a place to put themselves. Their task complete, respondents were then asked (a little meanly, per-

> Question wording:
>
> "Many people think of political attitudes as being on the "left" or the "right".'
> This is a scale stretching from the "left" to the "right".
> When you think of your own political attitudes, where would you put yourself?
> Please mark the scale in the box ☒ ."
>
> LEFT   RIGHT
>
> "What do you mean by "left" in politics?" (Probe fully)
> "What do you mean by "right" in politics?" (Probe fully)

FIGURE 3.2 *The Left-Right Self-Placement Scale*

haps) to say in their own words what they meant by 'Left' and what they meant by 'Right' in politics. Here again they were thrown back on their own resources and had to select a frame of reference to respond. A minority, ranging from 13% in Austria to 20% in The Netherlands, failed to respond at all or, happily in fewest numbers, managed to reverse the terms (see Table 3.2). The remainder, who were able to offer an explanation of Left and Right, fell clearly into three groups:

(1) *Ideological understanding*: These respondents associated Left and/or Right with broad social movements, social change, the class struggle, and with all the ideological symbols of the classic political contest between Left and Right.
(2) *Political parties*: These respondents simply labelled, correctly, the Left and the Right by the parties located in their country on the Left and the Right. Whereas the 'active use' measure coded those who judged parties in terms of Left and Right as ideological, this 'recognition' measure does not code the association of parties with Left and Right as ideological. This is not a contradiction. Those who earlier actively used the language of Left and Right (and all its associated symbols) to evaluate parties were spontaneously showing that they knew *why* the political world lines up the way it does. Those who now say they merely know what is associated with what are not, as the ideologues do, saying why but are saying simply that it is so.
(3) *Idiosyncratic or affective understanding*: These respondents did

TABLE 3.2 *The Use of Different Kinds of Ideas to Recognise the 'Left' and the 'Right'*

	The Netherlands %		Britain %		United States %		Germany %		Austria %	
Higher ideological recognition :	27	⎤ 48%	11	⎤ 23%	24	⎤ 34%	30	⎤ 56%	21	⎤ 39%
Lower ideological recognition :	21	⎦	12	⎦	10	⎦	26	⎦	18	⎦
Political parties or groups :	19	⎤ 52%	30	⎤ 77%	2	⎤ 66%	24	⎤ 44%	18	⎤ 61%
Idiosyncratic or affective :	3		10		16		3		5	
Wrong or no understanding :	20		19		15		9		13	
No recognition :	10	⎦	18	⎦	33	⎦	8	⎦	25	⎦
(Base for percentages) :	(1201)		(1483)		(1719)		(2307)		(1584)	

not describe Left and Right; they expressed a general moral opinion. Thus, the 'Left' might be 'bad' or 'untrustworthy' and the 'Right' might be 'good' 'moral' or, just as often, the other way round.

Table 3.2 shows how these different ways of recognising Left and Right, or not, are distributed in the five national samples. Those showing some ideological understanding are divided into those recognising *both* Left and Right in ideological terms ('higher') and those recognising only one or the other ('lower'). Ideological recognition is least common in Britain (23%), more common in the United States (34%), Austria (39%) and The Netherlands (48%) and is actually the dominant category in Germany (56%). Higher or lower levels of ideological recognition occur in equal balance, except in the United States, where both Left and Right tend to be recognised, if they are, in ideological terms. Among the non-ideological terms used, the British tend to prefer to recognise Left and Right, if they do at all, as a contest between the Labour and Conservative parties. In contrast, Americans rarely define Left and Right in terms of Democrats and Republicans, preferring, more than other nations, to use the moralist terms of affection or abuse or they fail to recognise Left and Right at all.

In summary, then, and taking the two measures together, less than one-in-ten people spontaneously use fully-elaborated ideological terms to make political judgements. About a fifth more come close to doing so. Up to a half, however, are able both to recognise an ideological dimension when they see one and understand it in ideological terms.

3.2.3 Levels of Ideological Thinking in Politics

What is the relationship between the active use of ideological thought and its more passive recognition and understanding? There should be some connection, otherwise one would doubt their meaning. In Britain, only a narrow majority (63%) of the 'active use' ideologues go on to discuss Left and Right in ideological terms. The remainder prefer an interpretation based on political parties and social groups. This reflects the clearly-defined political contest in Britain, typical of a country so sharply divided by social class. Elsewhere, about four fifths of ideologues recognise with ease the Left-Right dimension in ideological terms. Those that actively use ideological thought in politics tend to know whereof they speak.

Since there are more who are capable of recognising ideological concepts than there are who actively use them, it follows that recognition and understanding are necessary preconditions of active use. Between a third and a half of those who discuss both Left and Right in ideological terms are also ideologues or near-ideologues according to the active use measure. Among those that discuss only Left *or* Right in ideological terms, still between 24% in the United States and 43% in The Netherlands are found actively using ideological concepts in their judgements of political parties. Among those having a non-ideological understanding of Left and Right, near-ideologues are rare and ideologues almost completely absent. This is less true in Germany where still about a quarter of those having a non-ideological understanding of Left and Right appear for the most part as near-ideologues. This is due again to their use of anti-Communist ideological terms to abuse the Social Democrats.

Taken together, these two measures of ideological thought represent a progression from blank incomprehension of politics, through a variety of specific but non-ideological frames of reference, then through a passive recognition of political ideology, up to a point where ideological concepts are actively deployed by people, to a greater or lesser extent, in making political judgements. This progression can be expressed in a single scale and the way this is done is illustrated in Figure 3.3 and the resulting index is called the Level of Ideological Thought in Politics. Five levels are specified, as follows:

1 HIGH These are ideologues who also recognise and understand *both* 'Left' and 'Right' in ideological terms.

2 MEDIUM These are ideologues who recognise *either* 'Left' *or* 'Right' and near-ideologues who recognise both in ideological terms.

3 LOW These are ideologues unable to recognise 'Left' or 'Right' in ideological terms or near-ideologues with only lower understanding or non-ideologues with a higher ideological understanding. They are a mixed group of the rarer 'either/or' type.

4 VERY LOW These are a lower level, 'either/or' group. They either have some active use and little or no understanding or some understanding and no active use of ideological thought. Additionally, a very few actively use ideological concepts but cannot recognise one at all when asked to do so.

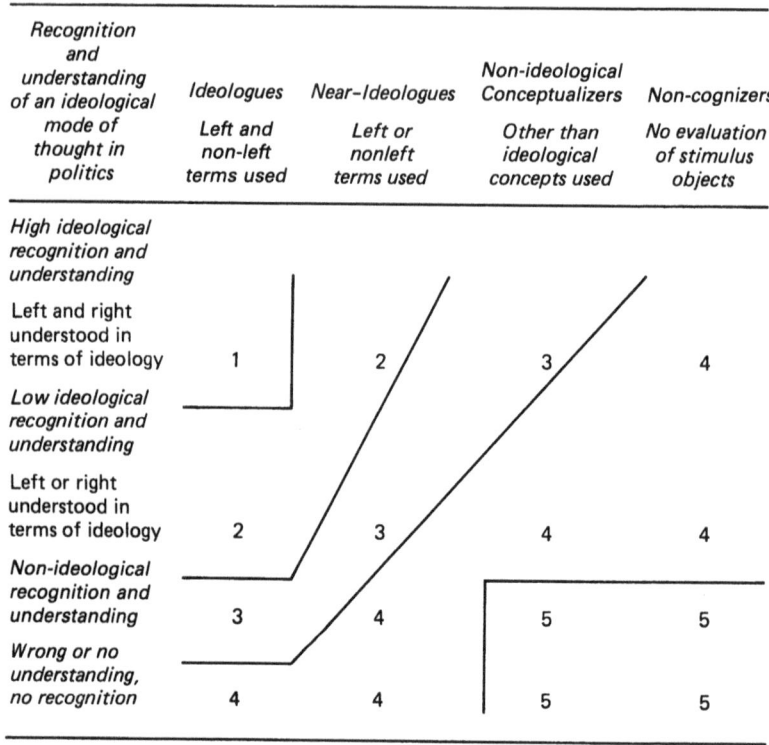

FIGURE 3.3 *Levels of Ideological Thought in Politics: Definition of Types*

5 NONE This group have no penetration at all into the world of political ideology. They neither understand ideological notions nor do they use them.

The distribution of these Levels of Ideological Thought in Politics is illustrated for each country in Figure 3.4.

Looking first at the two ends of the scale, it is clear that the lowest category is the largest in each national sample. Two thirds of the British have no access to ideological thought, nor have more than half the Americans and Austrians, 41% of the Dutch and a third of the Germans. At the other end of the scale, a high level of ideological thought is rare, not exceeding 5% in any country and is present in only tiny minorities in Austria and Britain. This latter finding is hardly surprising since those who qualify have, in the space of two

Ideology and Political Action 71

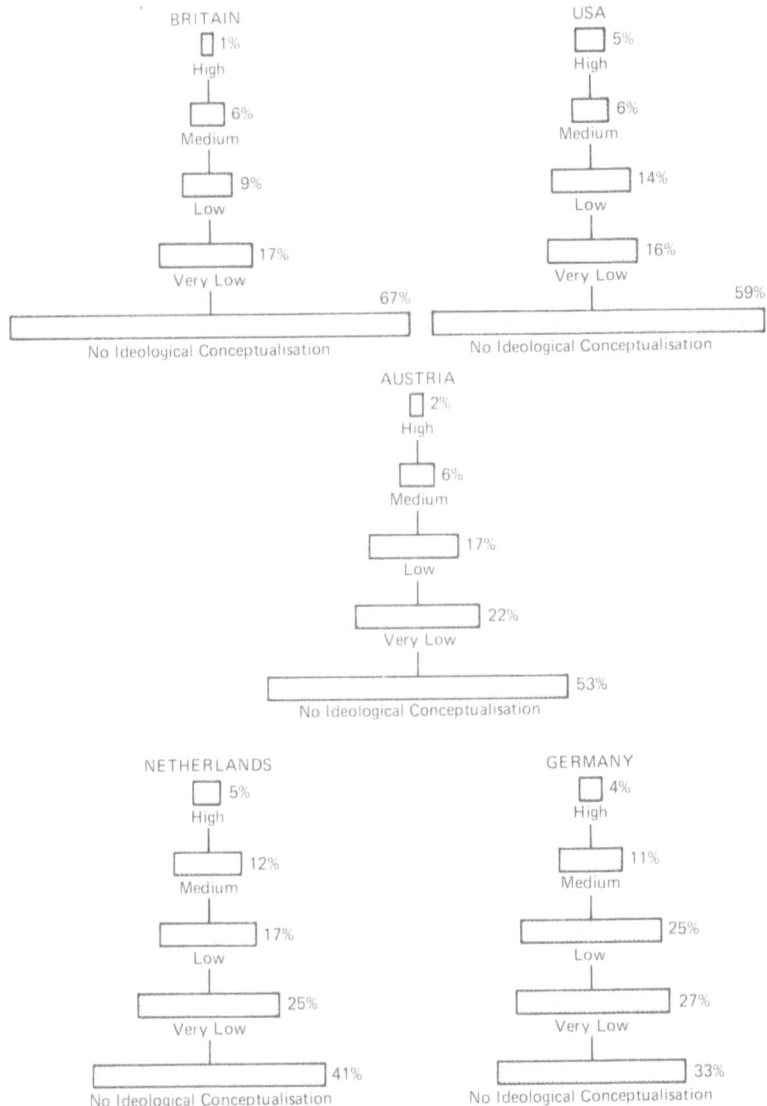

FIGURE 3.4 *Levels of Ideological Thought in Politics*

questions, demonstrated a fully active use and a complete understanding of ideological thought. On bad days your present author might not qualify. Even so, a good deal of the literature on this subject tends to treat the history of mass politics as a contrast between the unequal size of these two groups: between a tiny élite and the ill-informed masses. Such discussions favour what is called the 'élite-mass interaction' model of politics. Thus Converse and Pierce:

> The broad contours of elite decisions over time can depend in a vital way upon currents that are loosely called the history of ideas. But, of any direct participation in the history of ideas and the behavior it shapes, the mass is remarkably innocent.

To follow this reasoning uncritically would be a serious blow to the argument of this book: that there is a large stratum of society capable of being mobilised into élite-challenging forms of political action in an informed and self-motivated way. The data in Figure 3.4, however, point to some modifications of the 'élite-mass' model that fit our theory very well. The wider net that the survey cast has found many who, if they are not fully-paid up political sophisticates, certainly have considerable potential for understanding and using ideological thought in politics. Taking the widest possible view, only in Britain is there real shortage of ideologues, while in Germany they are a majority. They are a group too large to be called an élite. Probably the old social psychological term of 'opinion leaders' fits them better. They read the serious pages of the newspapers, watch current affairs programmes and understand at least some of this information even when political ideology is invoked. Many of them will discuss these things with others and will retain an ideological vocabulary when they do. If all this means what we think it means, that there is a wide constituency for political action among the politically informed, then two further things must be shown: first, that levels of ideological thought are related both to a background in rising levels of education and to political motivation; second, that ideology is related in a politically consistent way to political action itself. The evidence supporting these ideas is examined now.

3.3 IDEOLOGY, EDUCATION AND POLITICAL INTEREST

In a cross-national study such as this, the relationship between levels of education and the distribution of ideological thinking are more difficult to show than one might think. This is because these levels, especially that of education, differ widely from one country to another. The greatest contrast is between the United States, where 19% of the population can claim university education (far more among the young), and the European countries (only about 5%). In Europe, about two thirds have only basic education compared to 28% in the United States.

The diagrams in Figure 3.5 show that, as expected, people with higher levels of ideological thinking are far more commonly found among those who have experienced higher education. Ideological thought is detectable in the great majority of those who attended university or some similar institution of learning: about 80% in British and American graduates, even more elsewhere. It is worth pointing out though, that still only a minority of the best educated display *higher* levels of ideological thought. Among those with some intermediate form of secondary education, these higher levels of ideological thought are even rarer. In Britain and the United States, the majority who have secondary levels of education show no understanding of ideological thought at all while in the remaining European countries, a lower level of ideological thought is typical. Among the least educated, higher levels of ideological thought are all but absent. In Britain, the United States and Austria, large majorities of those having only basic education are unable to recognise political ideology at all, though some traces of ideological recognition remain in narrow majorities among the least educated in Germany and The Netherlands. This again is probably due, at least in the German case, to the intrusion of anti-Communist sentiments.

Though it may appear so, it would be wrong to conclude from this evidence that education has a greater impact upon the formation of ideological thought in Britain and the United States than it has elsewhere. The difference between the Anglo-Saxon and European countries is due, paradoxically, to the much higher levels of education in the United States and lower levels of ideological thought in Britain. Within each category of education, levels of ideological thought are simply higher in The Netherlands and Germany than they are in Britain and the United States. Using statistical techniques that need not detain us here, it was quite easy to show that the *core association* between higher levels of education and higher levels of ideological thought was much the same in each country.

It follows, of course, that since education is an important antecedent of ideological thinking, this measure of levels of ideological thought is also associated with higher social and economic status,

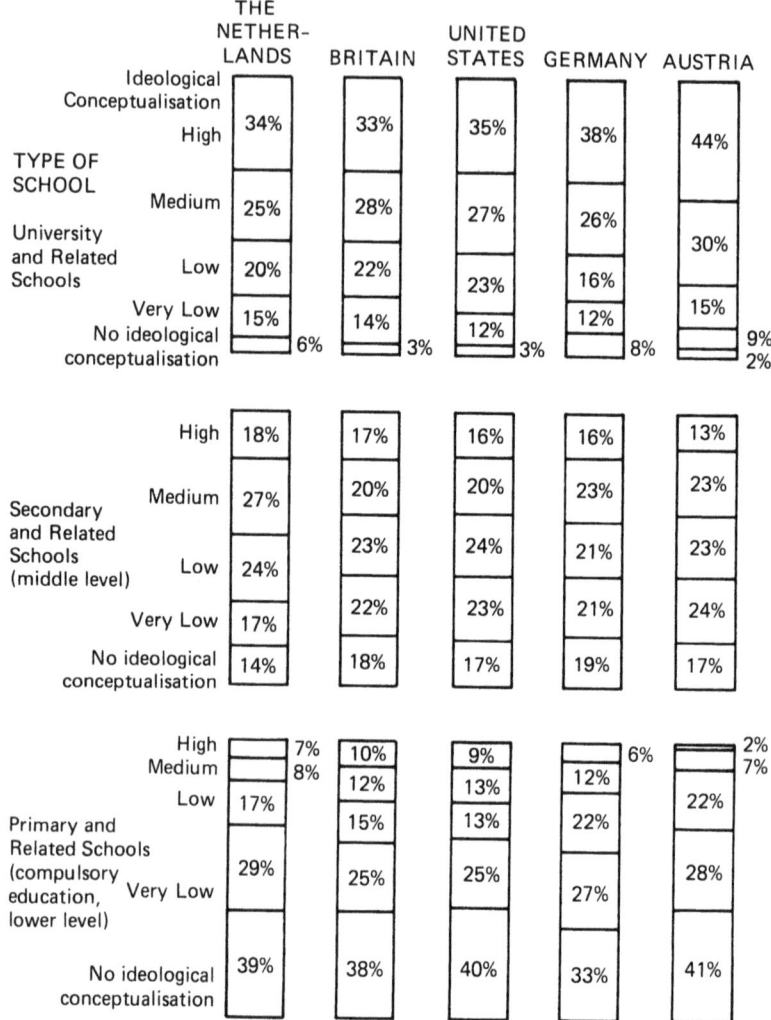

FIGURE 3.5 *Levels of Ideological Conceptualisation in Politics and Education (controlling for country-specific effects)*

social background and income. Our earlier argument was that the mental skills bestowed by education and training are a more important determinant of ideological thinking, judgement and of political action than is sheer social position. The data showed that it was education itself and the skills it provides which was the most important factor, not the social advantages acquired by the educated.

It seems fair to conclude, then, that the greater availability of secondary and higher education and, perhaps more importantly, improvements in the quality and diversity of secondary education, have admitted a much larger stratum of the population of Western Europe and America than before to the 'issue public'. There are now quite large numbers of people who do not necessarily occupy élite positions but who are capable of processing political information in ideological terms and do so.

Lest we too appear to succumb too much to an élitist drift in this argument, it is well to point out again that still quite substantial numbers of less well-educated people understand and use ideological thought. As the previous chapter showed, many participate in politics too. The political field is not left solely to the well-educated flowers of the middle class.

A second and independent source of the development of ideology may well be sheer political interest and motivation.

The simplest and in many ways the most effective measure of political motivation is to ask people how interested they are in politics. The proportions who said they were 'very', 'somewhat', 'not much' or 'not at all interested' in politics are shown for each country in Table 3.3. Political interest, in this most general sense, appears highest in the United States and Germany where large majorities declared themselves at least 'somewhat interested' while in Britain only a minority do so. Only 9% of the British sample say they are 'very interested' in politics compared to 22% of the Germans and 24% of Americans.

The relationship between higher levels of political interest and higher levels of ideological thought follows much the same pattern as that observed for the effect of education. Those with the highest levels of ideological thought are most commonly found among those expressing the highest levels of political interest. Among those expressing only moderate levels of interest, lower (but not the lowest) levels of ideological thought are more typical except, again, in Britain and the United States where a complete lack of ideological thought characterises a narrow majority. Among those who are 'not much' or 'not at all interested' in politics, higher levels of ideological thought are mostly absent and, again typically in Britain, the United States and Austria, such lack of political interest is accompanied overwhelmingly by a corresponding lack of ideological thought.

Once more, the apparently greater effect of political interest upon

TABLE 3.3 *Distribution of Political Interest by Country*

Political Interest	The Netherlands	Britain	United States	Germany	Austria
Very interested	14%	9%	24%	22%	14%
Somewhat interested	43	35	45	41	39
Not much interested	23	32	22	21	27
Not at all interested	20	24	9	16	20
N	1193	1471	1708	2302	1582

ideology in Britain and the United States is a result of the lower levels of both interest and ideological thinking in Britain and higher than average figures for the United States. When these differences are accounted for in the analysis, the core association between higher political interest and higher levels of ideological thought is again much the same in each country.

This similarity of effect would lead one to suppose that education and interest in politics overlap to such an extent that their impact on ideology is indistinguishable – that they are really different measures of the same thing. They are indeed quite strongly associated, though less so in Britain; the better educated are more interested in politics. Nevertheless, there is good evidence from previous research to suggest that political interest does have an independent effect on the formation of ideology, even if the effects of education tend to dominate. This is because mental skills are held to be more important than motivation; thus Campbell *et al.* in *The American Voter*:

> Whatever the depth of a person's involvement, there are rather basic limitations on cognitive capacities which are likely to make certain of the most sophisticated types of content remain inaccessible to the poorly endowed observer.

The importance of the 'cognitive limitation' idea is examined in Table 3.4. Clearly, the American data fit the above American hypothesis best. Among the better educated Americans, political interest does increase ideological thinking but the dominant contrast is between levels of education. The least educated Americans do not, as they might put it, get off first base where ideology is concerned even

TABLE 3.4 *The Proportion Having High or Medium Levels of Ideological Thinking Among Those with Differing Levels of both Education and Political Interest*

Education Level	Higher Education			Medium Education			Only Basic Education		
Interest in Politics	High	Medium	Low	High	Medium	Low	High	Medium	Low
The Netherlands	67%	44%	(15%)	47%	40%	16%	21%	15%	4%
Britain	(16%)	40%	(30%)	31%	15%	4%	15%	8%	1%
United States	37%	27%	15%	15%	10%	1%	3%	5%	1%
Germany	47%	39%	(30%)	33%	18%	19%	13%	12%	9%
Austria	(61%)	(50%)	(25%)	31%	17%	4%	10%	4%	1%

Figures in brackets indicate the base for percentages was less than 20 respondents.

if they say they are interested in politics. The British follow a similar pattern, though there are so few who are interested in politics and are also ideologically aware, even among the best educated, that it is hard to tell for certain. The same is broadly true for the Austrians. But among the two countries where ideological thinking is a more widely distributed habit, Germany and The Netherlands, political interest and ideology have a more balanced influence. Overall though, the verdict should go to education as the main source of higher ideological development: better educated people with only a passing interest in politics are still better able to use and understand ideological concepts than are those who express an enthusiasm for politics but are hampered by a poor educational background.

Finally in this chapter it remains to examine the impact of ideology on political judgement and political action. With respect to conventional political participation, we are on familiar ground. All research in this area leads one to expect a clear pathway: higher education leads to higher levels of ideological thinking, greater political interest and greater participation in the everyday business of party political and civic affairs. It matters little whether participants bring with them a 'pro-change' or a 'pro-status quo' view of politics. They may enter the political arena from different sides but it is the same arena and they do the same things.

The pathway toward unconventional political participation – protest potential – is likely to be different. Not all those with a developed ideology will favour protest as a means of political redress. Those who have a pro-status quo view are likely to reject such techniques because they tend to lie outside the pathways of political redress that the existing structures favour. Some of the actions defining the protest potential scale may be legitimate in a narrow legal sense, but few are likely to be acceptable to those whose values commit them to the defence of the political status quo. In contrast, those whose political values compel them to seek social change will naturally be drawn to protest actions. This division of values among the ideologically aware will reduce the direct association between ideological thinking and protest potential. However, those choosing to protest in pursuit of social change carry an additional burden. They have to improvise ad hoc political structures as they go along and they have to make some original political judgements. This means that the coincidence of high levels of ideological thinking and a committed set of values is more important in triggering protest actions than it is in promoting conventional participation. The higher the level of ideological thinking, therefore, the greater will be the impact of value choices on levels of protest potential. What support can the data offer for these ideas?

First we find, as others before us, that the impact of higher levels of ideological thinking upon people's rates of conventional political participation is clear. In Europe, about half of those who show no ideological thinking in their political judgements also refrain from all forms of conventional political participation. Among those with low levels of ideological thinking, this figure falls to 19%. Among those having the most developed ideology, only 6% are non-participants; the remaining ideologues are all busy discussing politics, contacting officials, going to meetings, and so on. In the United States there are fewer non-participants among the ideologically unaware, a quarter compared to a half in Europe. As anyone who has lived in the United States will tell you, political activity, especially at the local level, is actually quite hard to avoid.

This relationship between ideological thinking and conventional political activity can be summarised by the use of correlation coefficients. (These are gamma coefficients which may range from +1 to −1 and indicate the magnitude of association between two measures in the data. Large positive coefficients indicate that higher levels of one measure are strongly associated with higher levels of the second, large negative coefficients indicate that the opposite is true, that higher levels of one measure are strongly associated with correspondingly lower levels of the second). The strongest associations are found in Britain (.48) and The Netherlands (.47), followed by Austria (.42) and the United States (.39) but are lower in Germany (.27) (see Figure 3.6). The impact of political interest is even greater, being correlated with conventional political activity at higher values ranging from .59 in the United States to .72 in The Netherlands. Even so, it is interesting to note that when the effects of political interest are taken account of in the analysis, the impact of ideological thinking remains strong and positive. This is because people with higher levels of ideological thinking tend to participate in conventional political activity in an habitual sort of way even though they may have relatively low levels of political interest. The mental skills involved in acquiring an ideological way of thinking can lead to behaviour guided as much by a sense of habit or duty as it is by inspiring political motives.

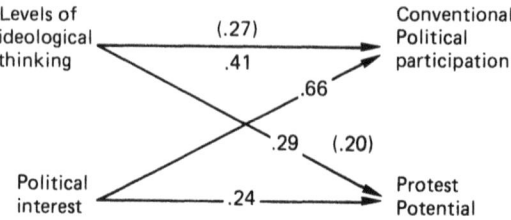

NOTE The figures in brackets are first order gamma correlations for controlling political interest.
FIGURE 3.6 *Relationship Between Ideological Thinking, Political Interest and Political Action*

The corresponding relationships between levels of ideological thinking and protest potential are, as expected, weaker. The correlation coefficients range from .23 in Germany up to .36 in the United States. So too are the parallel relationships between political interest and protest potential, ranging from .13 in the United States and .36 in Austria. Again though, it is interesting to note that the impact of ideological thinking upon protest potential remains unclouded by the effects of political interest. Even so, the modest value of the relationships at this general level of analysis supports the view that other factors must also be important. We turn now to the influence of political values.

These measures of political values will be considered:

(1) A Left-Right self-anchoring scale;
(2) An index of materialism *versus* postmaterialism;
(3) An index to measure the political importance of social equality.

The first was encountered briefly earlier in this chapter: it is the position people assign themselves to when presented with a simple ten-box scale stretching from the Left to the Right (see Figure 3.2). The second is an index describing the extent to which people hold either materialist or postmaterialist values. This is a complex measure and will be dealt with in detail in the next chapter, as its importance to our story requires. If it may for the moment be taken on trust, it measures, on a single dimension, the extent to which people cleave to a set of values that stress, on the materialist side, basic social and economic security or, on the postmaterialist side, opportunities for self-expression, self-realisation and greater political participation of a democratic nature. The third measure, the political importance of social equality, asked respondents to consider three issues: (1) guaranteeing equal rights for men and women; (2) providing equal rights for racial or ethnic minorities; and (3) trying to even out differences in wealth between people. They were asked to say how important was each of these issues to them personally and to what extent they felt the government had a responsibility to do something about achieving these goals. Thus, people who found equality of these kinds important and felt the government should act in this direction scored high on the scale; those that did not, scored low. Figure 3.7 summarises the relationship between these three measures and the two measures of political participation.

Clearly, political values do not determine levels of conventional participation except in Germany where, to a small extent, postmaterialists have higher rates of activity. Equally clear, Leftism, postmaterialism and a concern for social equality are all associated with higher levels of protest potential. This is particularly true in The Netherlands where such values tend to abound but less so in Austria, where they do not. The values of these correlations are modest. Levels of protest potential in these populations are not accounted for alone by political values. The thesis of this chapter, however, is that higher levels of ideological thinking imply higher levels of value consciousness. More than that, only when ideological thinking is developed beyond a basic level will political values act as a guide in the choice of styles of political action. We have now assembled all the measures we need for a test of these ideas.

The first test is to see whether higher levels of ideological thinking cause people to make more *consistent* political judgements. It is reasonable to expect that Leftism, postmaterialism and a concern for social equality are positively associated, one with another. This is called the 'level of constraint' or the extent to which holding one idea implies that, to be consistent, one holds another idea in a similar, related way. This can be measured simply by the value of the correlation coefficients between each of the three measures in each country. For the total sample in each country the average of these three correlations is quite low. It is the highest in The Netherlands (.29), lower in Germany (.20), Britain (.18) and the United States (.14) and lowest in Austria (.08). Overall, then, the level of constraint in political values is not high. Many respondents guess some of their answers, others fail to relate one answer with another. The important question now is: are these people also those who lack the

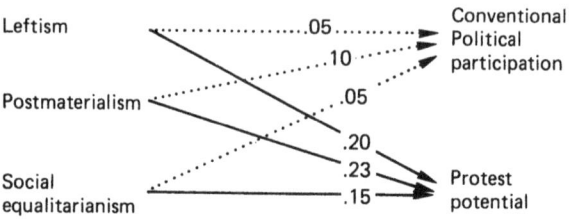

FIGURE 3.7 *Political Values and Political Action*

skills associated with ideological thinking? In contrast, are those who show higher levels of ideological thought much more likely to relate one answer to another – to be consistent in their choice of political values?

The evidence is that, in both cases, they are. Among those who show no ideological thinking, the relationships between holding one political value and another are hardly more than random. Those having only low levels of ideological thinking show more consistency. Those showing the higher levels of ideological thinking are very consistent indeed. For example, the most obvious relationship to expect is that Leftism is associated with a concern for social equality. Across the five countries, the correlation between these two measures averages only .02 among those who showed no ideological thinking. Among those at the intermediate levels of ideological development it averages .21. Among those showing the higher levels of ideological thinking this average correlation rises to .40. The improvement in this indicator of value consistency is most striking in Britain, rising from .12 to .31 to .60 and is least noticeable in Austria.

The next test brings in behaviour. Is the relationship between political values and political behaviour different at different levels of ideological thinking? With respect to conventional political acitivity this ought *not* to be so. At each level of ideological consciousness and at each level of participation, Left and Right give battle in similar numbers. In contrast, the gates to the *un*conventional arena where boycotts, demonstrations, strikes and occupations are the means of contest, should be opened by political values that favour radical social change. In this case, the gates to protest should be thrown open by Leftism, postmaterialism and a concern for social equality. The test of the argument is that this happens only at more developed levels of ideological consciousness.

The evidence clearly supports these ideas. Overall, the impact of political values on levels of conventional activity remains low at all levels of ideological consciousness. Britain provides one exception to the uniformity that prevails elsewhere. Conventional political activity is higher among those who place themselves on the Left and who show greater concern for social equality. Interestingly for our argument though, this is true only among those who show the highest levels of ideological thinking. In Britain, those active in conventional politics on the Left tend to be Left-wing ideologues. Those active on the Right – at least this was true in 1974 – tend far more to reflect consensus, almost an apolitical view that challenges or annuls the class-based politics of the Left.

In contrast, levels of ideological thinking intervene decisively to allow political values to determine a preference for protest methods. Among those showing no ideological thinking, Leftism, postmaterialism and concern for social equality (unconnected as they tend to be among this group) neither impel nor impede the choice of protest as a means of political expression. Among those showing only low levels of ideological thought, there is a clear positive relationship between holding these values that imply social change and choosing protest methods. Among those showing higher levels of ideological thought, this relationship is generally very strong. It is highest in The Netherlands where the correlation between the political desire for Leftist social change and protest potential averages .51. It is almost as high elsewhere except in Austria where the corresponding figure is .15. It is as well to bear in mind that, at the time of the survey, Austria was governed by a successful and popular Socialist administration whose record must have muted the demand for social change from the Left and discouraged protest.

The third test involves the use of the Political Action Repertory. From what we know now, it is a routine matter to predict that those with higher levels of ideological thinking will congregate among the activists and reformists. They do, though they are not of course a majority, averaging 27% of activists and 20% of reformists. Although those active in the conventional political arena were found earlier to have higher levels of ideological thinking, only 10% of the conformists do so. This is because many ideologues desert them to the ranks of the reformists and activists by adding protest methods to their political armoury. The protesters, their choice of élite-challenging methods notwithstanding, muster only 8% of ideologues among them. This again casts doubt on the consistency, the direction and the real political thrust that may be attached to their willingness to engage in political protest. More predictably, the inactives contain only a handful of ideologues.

Finally, Figure 3.8 represents a simple summary of the main story of this chapter. It shows, in a summary measure, the proportion who, more than average, tend to favour a set of political values that implies social change compared to the proportion whose values favour the defence of the status quo. This contrast is illustrated separately for the five political action types averaged for the five countries in the survey. The top chart shows this comparison for those with the higher levels of political thinking, the bottom chart for those with none.

Among the ideologues, the contrast in political values between those choosing very different combinations of political activity is extreme. Activists are overwhelmingly in favour of Leftism, postmaterialism and social equality. The reformists also, if narrowly, incline toward such social change. The conformists were not so named for nothing: large majorities of them are keen to defend the status quo and the most politically active among them no doubt do just that. Since we are speaking now only of those with higher levels of ideological thinking, it is difficult to be certain about the value position of the inactives and the protesters because they are so few among the ideologues. The inactives appear to give their informed consent to the status quo. The protesters are less sure. They contain substantial numbers who favour Leftist social change but many also who favour the status quo. The idea of street protest in this latter political direction among political ideologues who also reject conventional means of protest still has uncomfortable echoes in European politics. It is as well to restate that they are a small minority of the whole.

Standing in mute proof of the crucial role of the ideological development just described is the same analysis in Figure 3.8 conducted among those who showed no ideological thinking. Taking a cross-national average once more, the balance of values between the desire for social change and defence of the status quo is more or less equal within each political action type. Their very different preferences for contrasting styles of political action are not informed by their value choices. They lack the binding threads of ideological thought that would inform them that different political stances imply different styles of political action.

Ideology and Political Action

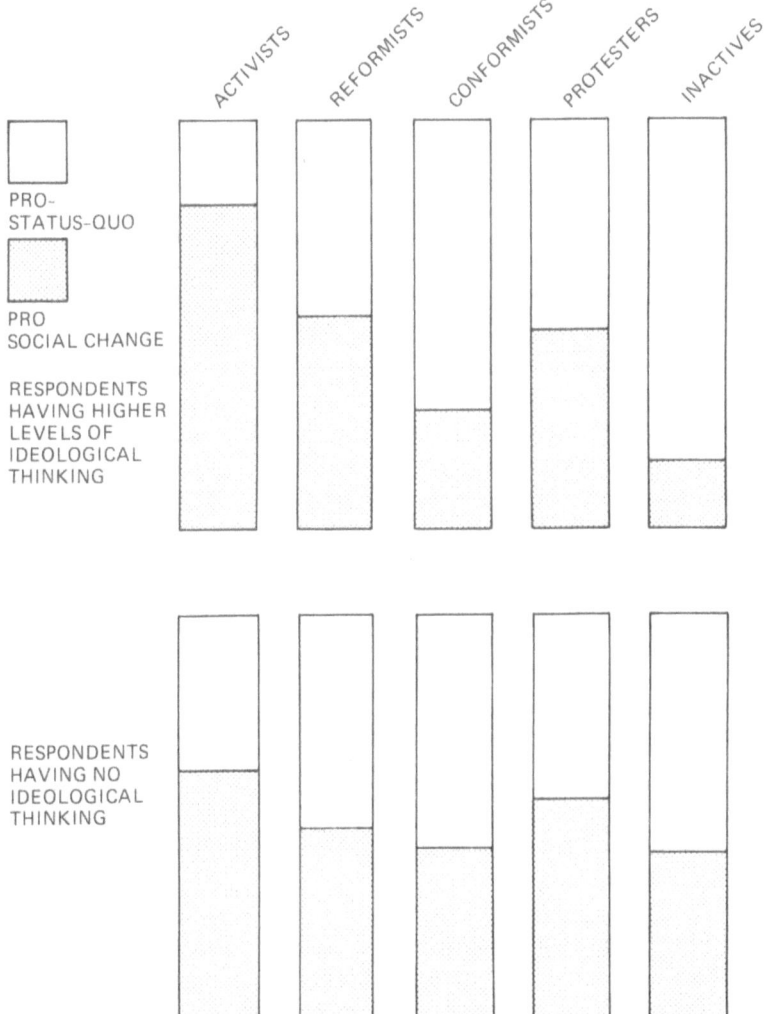

FIGURE 3.8 *The Balance of Political Values Among the Five Action Types, Averaged over Five Countries, by Levels of Ideological Thinking*

4 Values and Political Action

The previous chapter showed that as people's capacity for ideological reasoning increases, so their political values begin to take on an instrumental as well as an expressive meaning for them. That is to say, they no longer express only basic feelings in favour of or against one political view or another, issue by issue. Patterns begin to form, political objects and events become linked together in their minds, and one thing seems to follow from another. These connections emerge in a special way. First, under the influence of growing ideological awareness, a commitment to a *set* of political values is formed. Second, this set of values will suggest action. Most important, one set of values will direct the holder towards an appropriate style of political action, other sets of values towards others. The data that showed this process best were the familiar political values of Left and Right and their allied feelings for and against the need for social equality.

This may seem obvious, but it leaves a puzzle to be solved. Why is protest potential among the young associated with both Leftist views *and* higher education and social status? Those who have most to gain from social equality are often the least likely to protest: the poor, the ill-educated and the socially disadvantaged. This is not a new puzzle. As Dahl points out:

> To the dismay and astonishment of activists who struggle to organise a disadvantaged group to oppose its lot, the human psyche does not invariably impel those who are deprived of equality to seek it, or sometimes even to want it.

All the data discussed so far show this and show to the contrary that it is the better educated and often the most advantaged youth who have placed themselves in the vanguard of the New Politics with its demonstrations, boycotts, occupations and so on. While it must also seem obvious that such people have the time, energy and resources to engage in this sort of behaviour, their impulse to use them in Leftist causes is new. In 1926 in Britain, for example, students poured out of the universities and, just as energetically, helped break the General Strike. In the 1950s all that interested them was material self-advancement. What now have these people to gain by challenging political élites in new ways to achieve Leftist goals of social equity and economic redistribution? There are far too many of them to write them off as a Bolshevik clique seeking to excite the masses to revolution. Nor is that really their style. Their concern for democratic participation, freedom of expression, new political demands for racial and sexual emancipation and their constant excursions into all forms of community politics would be the despair of the average Bolshevik. Where is the class struggle in all that?

Indeed, one can point to a moment in modern political history when it all went wrong for the unity of class struggle. It was in May 1968 when the French Communist Party and the Communist Trade Unions pulled the rug out from under the Student Revolution. They settled for short-term material gains, leaving the students exhausted and bewildered. This was not at all what the students had in mind. Their demands were for a new society where creativity and free expression would lead everyone to a far more satisfying way of life. The problem was that the students had developed new values. They were of the Left, to be sure, but what that meant to them was not at all the steely materialism that guided every move of their comrades up the road at Communist Party Headquarters. On top of their basic Socialist values that favoured social justice they had heaped a whole new set of value priorities. They wanted a new political agenda entirely. It is the emergence of this new political agenda and the fundamental shift in value priorities it reflects, that will be examined now.

The basic idea was introduced in the previous chapter. Sustained economic growth and widespread social insurance programmes introduced since 1945 have freed the postwar generations of Europe and the United States to set aside many of the material preoccupations that had beset their parents. For the majority, food, shelter, protection from violence and the chance to earn a decent living were no longer in short supply. The young, encouraged by an expanded and liberalised education system, could set their eyes on new goals. As they neared adulthood what *they* found in short supply were social opportunities for self-expression and the chance to participate fully in the decision-making of their communities. Many of them began to cleave to a set of social and political priorities that emphasised postmaterialist values.

The means to measure this new dimension of political values – materialism vs. postmaterialism – owes everything to the work of Ronald Inglehart. It was his singular contribution to the Political Action Study. In previous work, using a measure of engaging simplicity, he was able to show that postmaterialist values had emerged among the younger age cohorts of postwar Europe and the United States. In successive national surveys in many countries he asked respondents to choose between just four basic political goals; like this:

> In politics it is not always possible to obtain everything one might wish. On this card several different goals are listed. If you had to choose among them, which would be your *first* choice? Which would be your second choice? Which would be your third choice?
> A. Maintain order in the nation.
> B. Give people more say in the decisions of the government.
> C. Fight rising prices.
> D. Protect freedom of speech.

This is not an easy choice to make. Many people would regard all these things as important. However, those who chose *both* maintaining order and fighting rising prices as their first and second priorities (in either order) were labelled materialists. Those who, in contrast, chose both the protection of freedom of speech and giving people more say in the decisions of the government were labelled postmaterialists. Those who chose some other combination were assigned to an intermediate category.

The data from these surveys did *not* show that a postmaterialist revolution had swept Europe and the Western world. Postmaterialists remained a minority and were always heavily outnumbered by the materialists in every country surveyed. What they did show, however, was of great importance. First, the ratio of materialists to postmaterialists in each age group changed dramatically from the oldest to the youngest. Among the older age cohorts, whose values were formed in the difficult and dangerous world of the Depression and the war, there was an overwhelming preference for materialist values. Among the younger age cohorts there remained, on balance, a preference for materialist values but among successively younger age groups, the proportion choosing postmaterialist values grew larger and among the youngest the balance of choices between materialist and postmaterialist values in some countries approached parity.

Second, and most importantly, the *rate* at which this balance of choices changed from the oldest down to the youngest was strongly related to the rate of economic growth each country had experienced. Britain, having experienced relatively more prosperity in the first part of the twentieth century than the rest of Europe and having been spared at home the worst horrors of defeat and occupation during the Second World War, had a larger proportion of postmaterialists and fewer materialists among its older age cohorts than elsewhere. Having also experienced a slower rate of economic growth during the 1940s and 1950s, Britain showed correspondingly fewer postmaterialists among its youngest age cohorts than is the case elsewhere in Europe. Germany, on the other hand, had suffered the economic collapse of the 1920s, the depression of the 1930s and the national disaster of the war. As a result, one can search all day among samples of older Germans before one finds a postmaterialist. The younger Germans were brought up in a very different country. By 1960, German standards of living were ahead of those in Britain. By 1974 the average German income was almost double that of the British. Consequently, the proportion of postmaterialists to materialists among young Germans was by then noticeably higher than in Britain.

Inglehart's work showed clearly that the ratio of materialists to postmaterialists in the 1970s was closely related to the rate of economic growth in each country according to a law of diminishing returns. That is to say, postmaterialist values appear quickly among the young as soon as the economy meets the basic economic needs of the majority. Their spread then slows down as affluence increases far beyond basic levels.

Findings such as these linked the idea of newly emerging postmaterialist values to basic changes in the structure of Western societies. They were the first clue that change from a predominantly industrial society towards a postindustrial society would result in new political values and new divisions of social interests. New class groups would emerge in the vastly expanded professional, public administration and service sectors of the economy. The political divisions that so plainly represented the dual class interests typical of industrial societies would start to give way to a far more diverse scattering of interests. The first clear split of this kind was the parting of the material values of the Old Left and the postmaterial values of the New Left during the 1960s and 1970s. This was the point of greatest interest to the Political Action Study. The first task was to seek an improvement in the measurement of the materialist-postmaterialist dimension.

The original four-item measure ('hold down prices + maintain order' versus 'freedom of speech + more participation') was open to many rival interpretations. If it were not for its power to show the differences between age cohorts and to predict postmaterialists' interests in New Left causes, it would be hard to believe that so simple a device could really tap so complex a dimension of political attitude. For the sake of continuity, the original four-item version, which had become known affectionately to the study group as the 'Model-T' version, was retained. It was followed up with a more developed scale of eight items, like this:

On these cards are some goals and objectives people say our country as a whole should concentrate on. Of course, all of these are important to all of us in one way or another, but which *three* are *most* important to you personally?
And from these three goals, which one, for you, is most important?
next most important?
third most important?
Please look at the rest of the cards and tell me which are the *three least* important?
Now which of these three is least important?
next-to-least important?
third least important?
The goals offered in this second group were:
A. MAINTAIN A HIGH RATE OF ECONOMIC GROWTH
B. MAKE SURE THAT THIS COUNTRY HAS STRONG DEFENCE FORCES
C. GIVE PEOPLE MORE SAY IN HOW THINGS ARE DECIDED AT WORK AND IN THEIR COMMUNITY
D. TRY TO MAKE OUR CITIES AND COUNTRYSIDE MORE BEAUTIFUL
E. MAINTAIN A STABLE ECONOMY
F. FIGHT AGAINST CRIME
G. MOVE TOWARD A FRIENDLIER, LESS IMPERSONAL SOCIETY
H. MOVE TOWARD A SOCIETY WHERE IDEAS ARE MORE IMPORTANT THAN MONEY

The choices that respondents made using both the four-item and the eight-item measures were pooled in a single factor analysis. In each country it was clear that the original materialist choice – maintaining order and fighting inflation – was closely associated with the tendency to go on to give higher priority to a stable economy, economic growth, strong defence forces and a firm hand with crime. Likewise, the original postmaterialist choice – freedom of speech and more say in government decisions – was closely associated with the tendency to go on to give higher priority to achieving a less impersonal and more humane society where ideas counted more than money and one that gave people more say in how decisions are taken at work and in their communities. Thus a clear single dimension exists in public attitudes that juxtaposes the basic materialist needs for a productive, secure and firmly controlled social order with a postmaterialist ambition that will satisfy 'higher order' needs of self-expression, belongingness and free participation in a less regulated society. This dimension is illustrated in Figure 4.1.

There is one anomaly. The 'more beautiful cities and countryside' item was intended to reflect the higher order aesthetic needs that might attract postmaterialist favour. It did, but in equal numbers it attracted support from materialists who would wish their cities to be a lot safer than they are. As the present author has written elsewhere, (Marsh, 1980) environmental concern finds its political expression in a strange alliance between the postmaterialist Left and the *pre*materialist Right. It is an alliance more often seen outside cities. Postmaterialist young people are often found shoulder to shoulder with older people from the agricultural classes, bucolic ex-officers and landed minor gentry demonstrating together against a new road or power installation.

Combining the pattern of respondents' choices, a simple four-category index was constructed. The first group made consistently materialist choices, the second a mixed but predominantly materialist set of choices, the third a mixed but predominantly postmaterialist set of choices and the fourth made consistently postmaterialist choices. Table 4.1 shows how these four 'value types' are distributed in each country.

Two countries remain haunted by the past. In Germany, the pure materialist group are a majority and less than one in five Germans make any postmaterialist choices. In The Netherlands, which inherited from the war a set of public attitudes unswervingly hostile to any unreasonable authority that would constrain public freedom, half the population make postmaterialist choices and 21% make purely

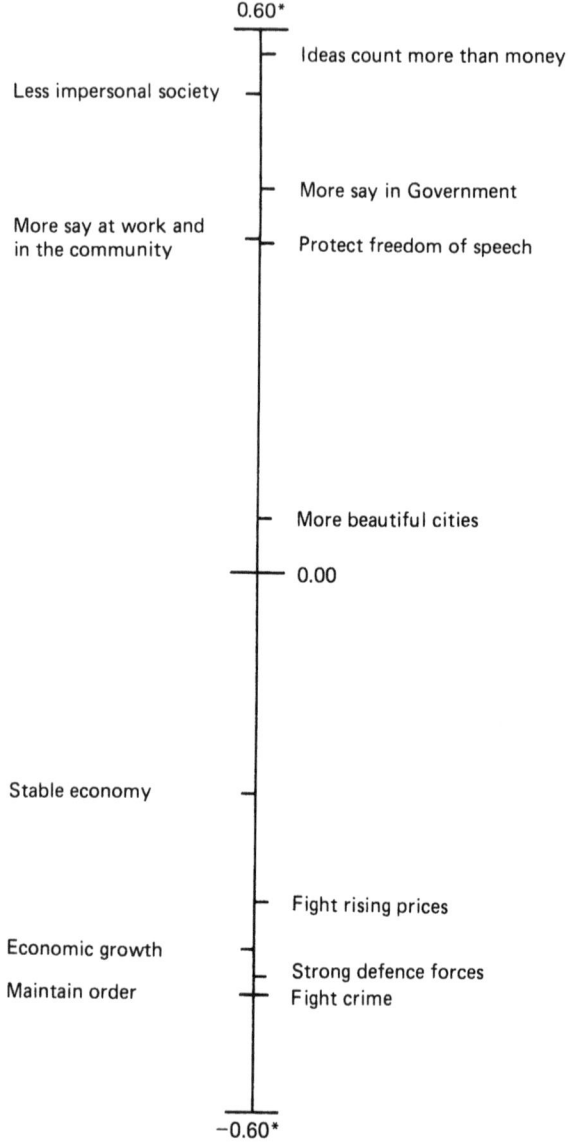

FIGURE 4.1 *The Materialist-Postmaterialist Dimension*

TABLE 4.1 *Distribution of Value Types*

Index Scores:	The Netherlands	Britain	United States	Germany	Austria
1–3 Materialist	19%	30%	39%	56%	41%
4–5 Mixed (Materialist)	31	38	31	28	37
6–7 Mixed (Postmaterialist)	29	25	20	11	18
8–10 Postmaterialist	21	8	10	6	5
	100%	101	100	101	101

postmaterialist choices, more than three times the proportion in Germany (6%). Austria veers close to the German position overall with a heavy predominance of materialist choices. Britain and the United States take up a middle position sharing a similar balance of opinion with materialists outnumbering postmaterialists at about two to one.

These comparisons are of only marginal concern; the main issue is one of intergenerational change. This is examined in Table 4.2 which shows the proportion making purely materialist or postmaterialist choices (leaving out the two intermediate categories) separately for each of six age groups. In each country, the ratio of materialists to postmaterialists changes dramatically among successively younger age groups. In The Netherlands, for example, materialists outnumber postmaterialists by three to one among those over 70 while among those under 30 it is the postmaterialists who outnumber the materialists by almost the same margin. It is fair to add that in all countries pure postmaterialism remains a minority interest even among the young. Many are still found in the intermediate categories. But, especially in Germany, the decline of *pure* materialism among the young compared to the old and the sudden appearance among them of significant minorities of *pure* postmaterialists is very striking. Something of importance has clearly been going on, but what?

One doubt that may have crept into some readers' minds already is that what we are looking at in Table 4.2 is not intergenerational change at all but a 'life cycle effect'. Surely people become more

TABLE 4.2 *Value Priorities by Age Cohort, 1974: Percentage Falling into Materialist or Postmaterialist Category*

Ages	The Netherlands		Britain		United States		Germany		Austria	
	Mat.	Pmat.	Mat.	Pmat.	Mat.	Pmat.	Mat.	Pmat.	Mat.	Pmat.
16–29	11	28	21	13	28	17	32	15	25	9
30–39	18	27	27	8	38	11	50	8	41	6
40–49	21	13	25	9	49	4	56	5	44	3
50–59	26	17	29	10	45	8	64	2	40	1
60–69	23	11	40	6	51	3	65	1	52	3
70+	38	11	46	2	42	4	74	2	–	–

conservative as they grow older and this is all the figures really show. This is a problem that will not go away. There must be some truth in it. It is a matter of common observation that some of the most radical students of the 1960s, for example, are now to be found in comfortable circumstances explaining at dinner parties how they have been obliged to move to the Right for tax purposes. Likewise, many of those of the older generations may well have been idealists in the 1930s. There were quite a few about then, enough to send whole divisions to fight on the Republican side of the Spanish Civil War. Even so, if the differences shown between age groups in Table 4.2 are to remain constant in the future, then the young are going to have to change their minds about some very basic value priorities in enormous numbers as they grow older. This is too strong a challenge to the imagination and it offends commonsense. People do change as they get older but not that much, nor in those numbers. Commonsense aside, can the data help sort out this problem?

First we observe that postmaterialist values are *not* strikingly prevalent among those whose head of household is employed in non-manual occupations compared to those in manual working-class families. So it is not only the middle class we are dealing with. There is, however, a stronger tendency for the minority in each country who have some higher education to make postmaterialist choices compared to those with less education. In Germany, for example, only 10% of those with basic education are even predominantly postmaterialist compared to 32% of those with higher education. Austria and The Netherlands contain similar differences, Britain and the United States rather less so. Even so, the overall effect of education on the choice of postmaterialist value priorities seems less than one might have supposed it to be. It gives a clue, however, to an important point that would weigh heavily in favour of the intergenerational change interpretation and against the life-cycle interpretation. Postmaterialism is related far more strongly to *'formative affluence'* – to one's family's circumstances when one was growing up – than it is to *present* affluence.

Table 4.3 pursues this last point in this way: a scale is created which combines respondents' education and present employment status (manual or non-manual) into a single, three-category measure of 'socio-economic status': lower, medium and upper. The proportion who made predominantly postmaterialist choices is entered against each group. Alongside each of these figures is the same calculation but this time according to the socio-economic status of respondents' fathers which is coded according to the respondents' accounts of the jobs their fathers were doing *during the time the respondents themselves were growing up*.

In the case of The Netherlands, a respondent's own status is a better predictor of the choice of postmaterialist values than is her or his father's. Higher status people are somewhat more likely to choose postmaterialist values. This is what one would expect – one's own personal characteristics really ought to determine one's values more certainly than someone else's, even if it is one's father. The difference in the Dutch case is marginal. Fathers' education and occupation come very close to describing their offspring's value priorities as well as their offspring's own.

The Dutch case is the exception but one that is not at all in the expected direction. In the United States, Austria and Germany, fathers' socio-economic status is a *better* predictor of their offspring's value choices than is their offspring's own. The differences are not great but it does mean that people's family circumstances during their youth contribute heavily to their choice of political values as they mature. Their subsequent fortunes are likely to have only a marginal effect on their values as they grow older. This speaks strongly in favour of enduring values and suggests that the relative differences in value priorities chosen by different age cohorts reflect real change over time. While postmaterialist values may be a youthful whimsey for some, the more likely outcome is that, if we are all spared, their new values will endure as they advance into middle age. Other things being equal, more postmaterialists will follow them and the balance of public opinion will continue to accommodate this new and growing dimension of political attitudes.

TABLE 4.3 Value Priorities by Respondent's Socio-Economic Status (by Respondent's Father's Socio-Economic Status)
Percentage predominantly Postmaterialist: that is, scoring 6 to 10 on values index.

Socio-economic Status	The Netherlands		United States		Germany		Austria	
	Status of Respondent	Status of Respondent's Father	Status of Respondent	Status of Respondent's Father	Status of Respondent	Status of Respondent's Father	Status of Respondent	Status of Respondent's Father
Lower	45	47	25	25	12	13	18	20
Medium	47	53	30	30	18	22	25	28
Upper	65	60	31	38	45	36	34	42
Gamma:	.19	.16	.03	.16	.28	.30	.20	.24

NOTE: Question on father's socio-economic status not asked in Britain.

As we know already, this new dimension of political attitudes has not departed completely from older established dimensions of Left and Right and so on. The data show this. For example, the postmaterialist minority are substantially more likely to award their vote in elections to the major party of the Left, particularly so in Germany and The Netherlands. Correspondingly, they are far more prepared than others to say that fair treatment for ethnic minorities, equality between men and women and trying to even out differences in wealth between people are important political goals for the government to achieve. Their latter view is particularly interesting since pure postmaterialists contain somewhat larger numbers of better-off people among their ranks. Objectively, they have scant interest in a redistribution of wealth since it may well be *their* wealth that is redistributed. Those who speak against their own class interests always intrigue political scientists.

The materialists, for their part, show a good deal of ideological consistency. Unlike the postmaterialists, they urge their governments to 'make neighbourhoods safe from crime' and tend to reject notions of greater social or sexual equality. They tend more to be religious too, though this might be put down to the greater numbers of older people among them.

The extent of the correspondence between the 'old' Left-Right dimension (represented by respondents' self-placement on the now-familiar Left-Right scale) and the 'new' Materialist-Postmaterialist dimension is illustrated in Figure 4.2. The slope is steep in each country: materialists congregate on the right. The two mixed value types – predominantly materialist or postmaterialist – are found either side of the centre of the scale. The postmaterialists alone take an unequivocal lurch to the left. These positions are reflected in the partisan choices shown by each value group at election time. In addition, there is a particularly intriguing element in the political family background of the different value types. People brought up in families whose fathers voted for Left parties tend themselves to continue this family tradition and vote Left. This is true almost regardless of their present value choices except that, particularly in the United States, those that have since developed pure materialist value preferences tend in the privacy of the polling booth to desert to the Right. People whose fathers voted for Right parties tend also to follow their family voting tradition and award their vote to present-day parties of the Right. Not so the postmaterialists among them. They desert wholesale to the Left. In Germany, for example, only

16% of materialists whose fathers voted for Right-wing parties (yes, some were understandably coy about *which* Right-wing party) now give their own vote to parties of the Left and 84% remain on the Right, voting for the present Christian Democrats or their allies. In contrast, 58% of those whose fathers also voted for Right-wing parties but who have themselves become postmaterialists desert the family tradition and vote for the Left, usually for the Social Democrats. In The Netherlands, the corresponding figures for left-voting among the offspring of Right-wing fathers show the same value-directed differences: 16% among materialists, 55% among postmaterialists. In Britain, the figures are 11% and 37%, in Austria 26% and 56%, in the United States 14% and 46%. It is a clear statement of the power of new values to rupture the main lines of old political socialisation.

It was said at the outset of this chapter that, for those who come to hold them, postmaterialist values create a new definition of what it means to be 'Left'. For postmaterialists to be 'Left' is but one facet of an elaborated set of political attitudes. It appeals to needs far beyond the traditional aims of the materialist Left of raising the standards of living of the working class by a more equitable distribution of the fruits of their labour. While the manifest content of the scale itself ('a less impersonal society', 'ideas count more than money' and so on) tells of new aims and ambitions beyond economic equity, it is time to offer better evidence of this.

It is said that men, and presumably women also, may be judged by the company they keep. The survey used this idea in a political sense by inviting respondents to indicate how close or distant they felt themselves to be with respect to 12 groups. These were: the major party of the Left and Right, Labour Unions, Big Business, Clergy, Police, Civil Servants, Minority Groups, Women's Liberation Movement, Student Protesters, Revolutionary Groups and Small Businessmen. Each group, whose precise nomenclature differed from country to country in more ways than language alone, had an obvious political resonance in the early to mid 1970s. Respondents were asked to say how sympathetic or unsympathetic they felt toward each group using a 'thermometer scale' rising from '0' to '100'. A score of 50 would indicate an entirely neutral feeling.

These kinds of data can be difficult to handle because some people who prefer to think well of everyone use the top range, others with a jaundiced view of the world use the bottom of the scale. It is better then to treat such scores as relative judgements. This is done by

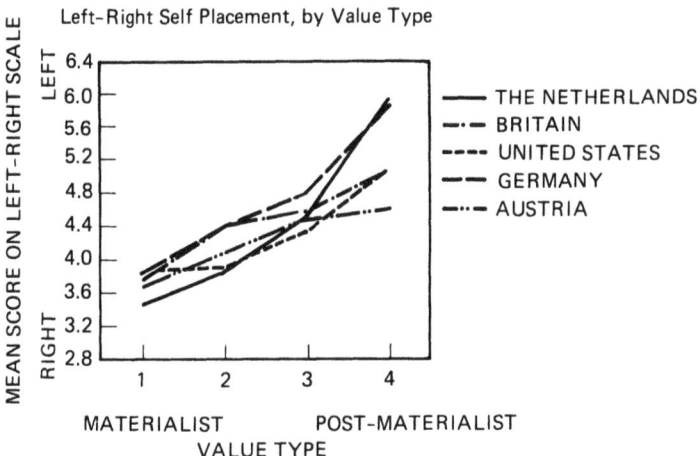

FIGURE 4.2 *Left-Right Self-Placement, by Value Type*

calculating the average of the 12 scores awarded by each respondent and recalculating each score as a departure from that individual's average in a positive or negative direction.

By the use of factor analysis these data can provide a mapping of people's broader political sympathies on the basis of a 'what goes with which' principle. In each of the five countries, in a very similar way, two distinct dimensions of political affiliations emerged. The first reflected the traditional Left-Right dimension, juxtaposing the major party of the Left together with Labour Unions on one side and the major party of the Right and Big Business on the other. In The Netherlands, Germany and Austria a religious dimension is still incorporated into the industrial class dimension of politics. European Socialism contains an enduring anti-clerical sentiment and the parties of the Right are still careful to announce their Christian affiliations even in their titles. Consequently, feelings towards the Clergy in these countries are closely related to feelings towards the Right-wing parties and to big business.

The second dimension, largely unrelated to the first, reflected attitudes for or against the Establishment. Sympathies towards the police, civil servants, small business and, in Britain and the United States, the clergy are juxtaposed with sympathy towards minority groups, women's liberation, student protesters and revolutionary groups. If it seems odd to some that anti-establishment sentiments are largely unrelated to the traditional Left one should remember

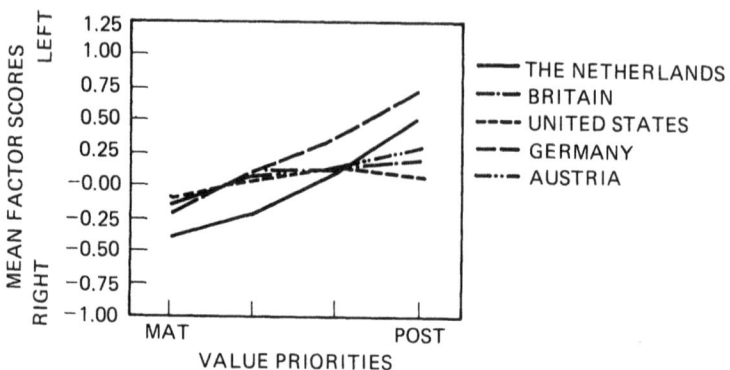

FIGURE 4.3 *Value Priorities and Partisan Attitudes*

that there are many who support Left parties and labour unions who also respect and like the police, for example. Admittedly, it is harder to see reasons why supporters of Right parties should have a good word to say about revolutionary groups but equally there are many among them who have little time for civil servants.

The feelings reflected by this Establishment and Anti-establishment dimension align closely with the New Politics; the Left-Right dimension, almost by definition, aligns with the Old Politics. If what has been said about the emergence of postmaterialist values as the guiding impulse toward the New Politics is at all true, value choices should be much more closely associated with the Anti-establishment dimension than they are with the traditional Left. Comparing the two graphs in Figures 4.3 and 4.4 shows this to be so. The four value types differ relatively little in their average scores on the Traditional Left-Right dimension. Only the pure postmaterialists show any significant deviation to the Left. This graph may appear to conflict with the much stronger relationship shown between value choices and the Left-Right self-placement scale shown in Figure 4.2. There it was much clearer that materialists congregated on the Right, postmaterialists on the Left. In Figure 4.3, however, the Left is much more objectively defined by the extent of people's relative sympathy toward the major party of the Left and the labour unions. Many postmaterialists, while happy to define themselves as Leftists, are distinctly lukewarm about the major party of the Left even if they vote for them. This is particularly so in the United States and Germany. Often they are dismayed by the relentless materialism of the party's programme. For the same reasons, they are often out of

Values and Political Action

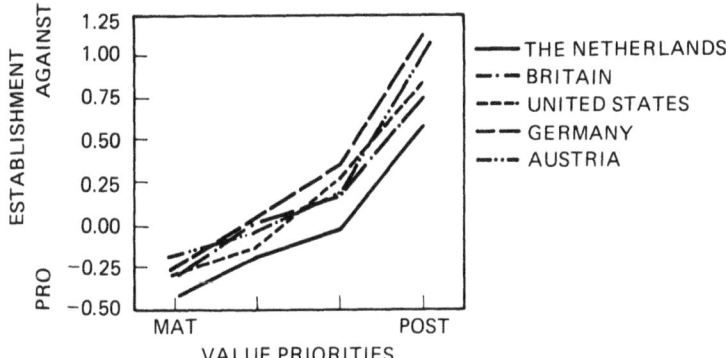

FIGURE 4.4 *Value Priorities and Attitudes Toward the Establishment (factor scores)*

sympathy with the labour unions. It is clear evidence that they have a different definition in their minds of what it means to be Left.

Much more of what they have in mind is shown in Figure 4.4. The four value types differ very widely in their views for or against the Establishment. Materialists deprecate the radical movements, minorities and so on while giving strong allegiance to the police, civil servants and other Establishment bodies. The postmaterialists are almost alone in identifying strongly with radical movements and ethnic minorities and they take a less than generous view of the police. Other studies have shown this too. Miller and Levitin found that materialists and postmaterialists in the United States differed relatively little in their support for the Democratic Party (38% against 46%) but differed hugely in their support for what they called 'New Liberalism'. Only 16% of materialists favoured a package of new liberal aims including civil rights, student protest and the use of marijuana, compared with 60% of the postmaterialists.

In the societies in which they live, postmaterialists have clearly set their faces against what they see as the materialist hegemony of the existing political order. If they want to pursue their revised programme for an enlightened and consultative community they can expect to make only limited headway using the existing conventional party political structure. They need more leverage. The adoption by them of protest tactics has provided this leverage. The evidence for this is shown in Table 4.4. In Britain, only 21% of materialists will engage in protest tactics beyond the use of boycotts compared to 55% of postmaterialists. And Britain provides the *weakest* example. In

TABLE 4.4 *Protest Potential by Value Type**

	The Netherlands	Britain	United States	Germany	Austria
Materialist	27%	21	38	23	17
Mixed (Materialist)	38	30	46	30	19
Mixed (Postmaterialist)	47	33	50	43	24
Postmaterialist	74	55	72	74	48

*Percentage scoring "3" or higher on protest potential scale.

other countries these differences are huge. In Germany and The Netherlands, for example, only a quarter of materialists stray into the higher reaches of the Protest Potential Scale compared to three quarters of the postmaterialists. One is not accustomed in survey analysis to observing differences of this magnitude between a fairly abstract measure of political attitude and a measure having such strongly behavioural implications. Postmaterialists say they will do as they feel. They are sufficiently out of favour with the existing system of political values to use radical means to do something about it. If they lived in a postmaterialist society, they would not have to act in this way; probably they would be running it. They live, instead in a materialist system and as a result their new value choices impel them strongly in the direction of political protest.

None of this means that the majority of postmaterialists exclude themselves from the conventional political scene even if they are sometimes uncomfortable participants. As Table 4.5 also shows, the postmaterialists are a little *more* likely than other value types to engage in conventional political activity, especially in Germany. This confirms in detail the summary provided in the previous chapter. If one is searching for an activist – someone willing to employ the widest range of tactics to achieve political goals – then one should look first among the ranks of postmaterialists.

We are now in a position to update the argument outlined in the previous chapter and to take a much closer look at the crucial intervening role played by levels of ideological thinking in allowing people's value priorities to direct them into alternative paths of political action.

The impression given in the previous chapter was that *only* under conditions of higher levels of ideological thinking do value-choices imply corresponding choices of styles of political action. In the case of the traditional distinction between Left and Right, this is almost certainly so. Supporters of the Left, for example, who show no

TABLE 4.5 *Conventional Political Participation by Value Type**

	The Netherlands	Britain	United States	Germany	Austria
Materialist	50	40	68	43	38
Mixed (Materialist)	33	44	65	55	43
Mixed (Postmaterialist)	48	48	63	64	57
Postmaterialist	67	64	76	83	59

*Percentage scoring "2" or higher on conventional political participation scale.

understanding of what either Left or Right means in ideological terms, are very unlikely to choose protest methods even though their values might be supposed to point them in that direction. The case of postmaterialism is likely to be different.

Just as the earlier analysis would lead us to expect, among the ideologues protest potential rises sharply across the four value types. It does so almost as sharply among the near-ideologues. Among those showing no ideological thinking the materialists differ very little from the two intermediate categories in the levels of protest potential; none of them are very interested in it. Among those few postmaterialists to be found in the non-ideological stratum, however, protest potential rises substantially, particularly in The Netherlands and Germany. Here, 'non-ideological postmaterialists' have a much higher protest potential than ideologues and near-ideologues among the intermediate value types. It is a little hard to imagine what their views really are; 'non-ideological postmaterialist' sounds like a contradiction in terms and there are relatively few of them. A possible explanation is that respondents were placed in the non-ideological category if they twice answered 'nothing' and 'everything' when asked what they liked and disliked about the two major political parties. Most of these were genuine non-ideologues but it would be an appropriate response for radical postmaterialists who, as we know they can be, were well out of sympathy with both the major system parties. Their choice of protest methods is therefore no longer a surprise. This aside though, the overall message is plain – materialist and postmaterialist value choices respectively suppress or encourage the choice of protest methods equally at any level of ideological consciousness beyond the most basic level. Postmaterialists with only a low level of ideological thinking are far more likely to choose protest methods than are materialist ideologues.

Finally in this chapter we must come back to the vexing problem of competing explanations for these findings in terms of life-cycle or intergenerational causes. For example, is the strong relationship between values and protest potential due solely to the fact that postmaterialists are young and better educated? If the influences of age and education are held constant in the analysis, does the association between values and protest potential disappear? If it does, then the puzzle that started this enquiry will have returned unsolved. Why do the better educated young now choose protest methods? They are not fools; they know they are well-placed. The rewards that await them in the future give them every reason to keep quiet and go along with the system just as their predecessors did in the past.

The technique used to sort out this problem was path analysis. This uses multiple correlation and regression analysis to predict causal paths between 'predictor' measures like age, education, values and so on and 'dependent' measures like protest potential, while taking simultaneously into account the degree of association between the predictor measures. Before things get too complicated, however, it is worth mentioning one finding that appeared to establish the power of postmaterialist value choices to raise protest potential independently of age and education.

The British study interviewed an additional sample of 286 students from 12 universities and 12 polytechnics. As a group, they had, unsurprisingly, a very high protest potential. Half of them scored at the highest point on the scale. Their average score was twice that even of young people in the main British sample and many times higher than the rest. One could wish for no clearer demonstration of the independent effect of age and education in increasing protest potential. Yet within this student sample the relatively small number of materialists among them had a *low* protest potential and the mixed value group not much higher. The large number of postmaterialists among them, however, were protesters almost to a man and, equally, to a woman, too. Thus, even when the impact of youth and education is at its greatest, postmaterialist value priorities still have the power to impel their holders toward political protest and materialist values to deter.

What then of the general populations of the five countries surveyed? The path models established for each country were very similar and these are illustrated in Figure 4.5. In each case, the effects of age and education on protest potential are mediated by value choices and levels of ideological thinking. Let us take this finding point by point. Age is directly related to protest potential. Other factors aside, youth alone can account for a portion of the

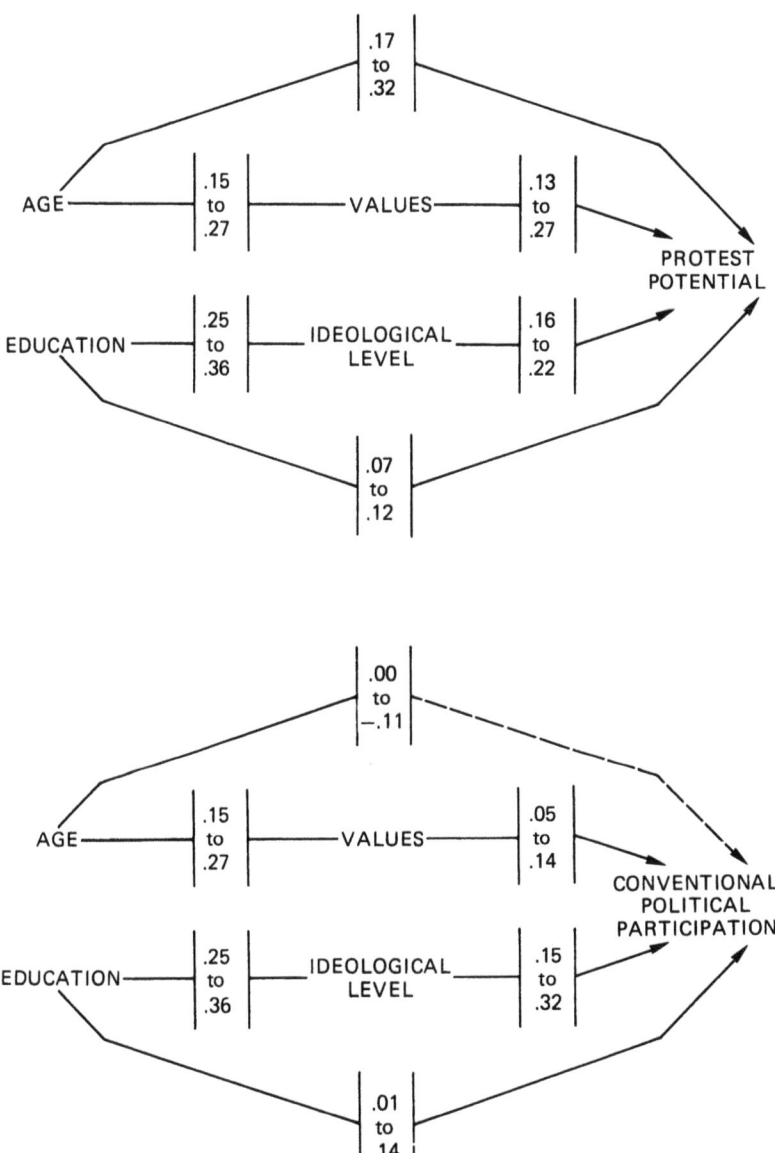

FIGURE 4.5 *The Combined Influence of Age, Education, Value Priorities and Levels of Ideological Thinking upon Political Action*

protest potential measured in each country. Thus, some support is found for the life-cycle interpretation. As people get older, their protest potential will fall simply because they are getting older. But it may not fall all that much. This is because age and values also combine in a joint impact on protest potential. Put at its simplest, postmaterialists are more likely to choose protest methods almost regardless of their age. This means that equal support is found for the generational change interpretation: the young protest because they are young *and* because they are choosing value priorities that are different from those of older generations. In Britain and the United States, the life cycle explanation tends to be the stronger. In Germany and The Netherlands, generational change – new values among the young – tends to dominate.

Unlike the effects of age, the direct relationship between education and protest potential is weaker. The effects of education are largely mediated by levels of ideological thinking. If one manages to graduate from higher education having acquired no glimmer of ideological thinking, and some do, one's education alone will rarely be sufficient to impel one toward political protest.

These four factors, age, education, ideological thinking and values, taken together explain a good deal of the amounts of protest potential found by the five national surveys. In statistical terms, they explain between 16 and 25% of the variance in protest potential; most in Germany, least in Austria. This may not sound all that much but a large portion of the remaining variance will be attributable to measurement error. Find someone, man or woman, who is young and better educated, who has a high level of ideological thinking and has a chosen set of purely postmaterialist values and it is a fair bet that he or she will score noticeably higher than average on the Protest Potential Scale.

The same analysis was carried out to estimate the causal paths between these four measures and levels of conventional political participation. As the earlier discussion would lead one to expect, the model is somewhat different. The direct association between better education and increased conventional political activity is still modest but is definitely stronger. Some better educated people participate in civic affairs and party politics solely because they are educated and not because they are ideologues. Overwhelmingly though, it is the mediating effects of higher levels of ideological thinking that promote conventional political participation. Age has a slight *negative* effect; younger people, many of whom will not yet have established a secure place in their communities, are not yet drawn into the community-based activities that are reflected by the Conventional Participation Scale. Partly because of the absence of the young, values matter little, except in Germany where postmaterialists are taking more interest in the conventional political arena. Elsewhere, the Right and the Left, materialists and postmaterialists compete in party politics to a more or less equal extent.

The implications of all this might now be more obvious. Since the younger age cohorts in Western Europe and the United States are so much better educated than those older, the proportion of better educated people in the polity will rise in the future. This is true even if the scale of higher education does not expand further: a better educated generation will replace those who are now old and be succeeded in turn by equally or better educated sons and daughters. Correspondingly, the average level of ideological thinking in each country will also rise. It may also be fostered by other factors, perhaps by better communications and more skilled explanations from political leaders. This means that the *potential* for mass participation in mainstream political life will continue to rise under the impact of a greater spread of cognitive skills and ideological understanding in the population. If such rates of participation appear to some actually to be falling, the evidence of the surveys is that this is not the people's fault. The ability of the political élites to mobilise mass support will always depend on other things too. Mostly it will depend on their ability to demonstrate that getting involved in politics and actively supporting a party brings tangible rewards both to the participants and to the community as a whole. It is called leadership but is of a kind that inspires confidence and optimism and *involvement* in a democratic process, not a narrow appeal for electoral support.

The surveys also show that, should this process of political involvement continue to falter or even to fail, then people have an alternative. Levels of protest potential are also being driven upwards by the spread of education and the cognitive skills it bestows but they are being driven up even more strongly by the spread of postmaterialist values among the young. Since these new values are very much the property of the young and if they endure as we think they must, the proportion of postmaterialists in the population will increase even faster than the increase in the proportion of well educated people.

Notwithstanding their appeal to a more humane society concerned more with ideas than money, a key element of postmaterialism is the demand for more political participation in decision-making at work, in the community and in government. This has led some authors, the present included, to take a more sober view of the postmaterialists than they themselves might welcome. They may have 'higher-order' political goals but they are interested in power too. Given their education and social expectations this is not surprising. They seek it in the conventional political arena no less than others. Their tendency to *add* protest methods to their political repertory will be a direct function of the amount of new political consultation and influence they can achieve and whether or not they can get their issues onto the national political agenda. That is what political protest is really about: getting new demands onto the political agenda. That is why political skills and new values combine so powerfully to predict protest potential. The next chapter will examine more closely the contest for possession of the political agenda: who is dissatisfied with what?

5 Dissatisfaction and Political Action

It is difficult to escape the impression that the explanations of political action discussed so far are somehow 'middle-class' explanations. Education, mental skills, new values and so on, they all point to an expansion of the political action repertory among new non-manual class groups thrown up by the growth of the post-industrial economy. This may of course be no more than simple truth. The choice of protest methods, in particular, has spread well beyond the student communities who road-tested them in the 1960s. The data show this. Yet we have been continually driven back on explanations of people's behaviour that take for granted the presence of some trained intellectual skills. To be educated is to understand, to understand is to choose and to choose is to act. While it may yet be true that, as Moorehouse and Chamberlain say, '. . . it is not necessary for men to encompass the world intellectually before they set out to change it', the data keep insisting that such skills are extremely important.

What such explanations lack is an explicit motivational basis. However reasonable it may be to infer, for example, that new values imply a desire for social change and that the denial of such desires will impel their holders toward protest, it remains no more than a reasonable inference. The aim of the Political Action Survey was to cut deeper into this process and try to establish what mass social psychological processes may underlie the growth of New Politics. What goes on in people's minds when they are impelled toward unconventional forms of political redress? What kind of impulse do they subjectively experience? Why really do men and, saving Moorehouse's and Chamberlain's blushes, do women protest?

The Study Group was confronted with a wealth of literature on this subject. Most of it pointed to one conclusion: people protest because they are fed up, or, since we are political scientists, because they experience a subjectively-held sense of dissatisfaction. How could it be otherwise? Protest on the streets is invariably an expression of some grievance and grievances are expressed by the aggrieved. One of the leaders of the student revolution in France, Daniel Cohn-Bendit, was clear on this point: 'Yes', he agreed, 'we are in revolt. We are fed up with everything.' The implied tautology can be avoided simply by accepting that dissatisfaction, not to say anger, is a necessary antecedent of political protest. That surely is how it always happens. As soon as people realise in sufficient numbers that they are not getting the things they want and feel they ought to have, they become frustrated. Frustration leads to dissatisfaction which leads to demands which, if unmet, will lead to anger and aggression and thence to protest actions.

This process has been easy enough to demonstrate in the laboratory. Frustrate and provoke people enough in controlled experiments and they will behave more aggressively than those not so provoked, especially if some aggression-provoking cues like weapons are left lying around. Another research tradition entirely, aggregate data analysis, has shown that societies that foster increasing relative deprivation have much higher rates of political violence and insurrection than those which, while some of them may be poor, are more equitably organised.

Though suggestive, neither of these bodies of literature were of direct use to the Study Group since the first assumes that people behave on the street as they do in the laboratory and the second assumes that aggregate measures imply subjective psychological states. A third area was more helpful since it embraced the study of protesters and social movements. Most intensively studied were the Civil Rights Movements and the Black Revolt in the United States between 1959 and 1969. No-one doubted that feelings of frustration and deprivation underlay the enduring force of the Movement but research results were uneven. Some studies showed participants in the struggle recording high levels of frustration and deprivation, other not. Much was learned about protesters, less about the role of protest behaviour in Western societies. It was rather a special case.

So much depends upon what one means by deprivation and frustration. The key concept in this field of enquiry is 'relative deprivation'. This can be conceived of as deprivation relative to others or relative to some personally-defined standard of need or entitlement. The first idea, deprivation relative to others, has been found useful in explaining political stability in unequal societies. In Britain, for example, Runciman was able to show that manual workers do not waste much time comparing their lot with the rewards enjoyed by the upper classes. Instead they watch carefully the rewards and conditions obtained by occupational groups like themselves. The second idea is called by Muller and Grofman the 'just deserts' measure. It is deprivation seen relative to some personally-defined standards and has been found more useful in explaining people's propensity to seek political remedies for the shortcomings they see.

In seeking an appropriate means of measurement for the Political Action Study, the Group opted for this second strategy. It was particularly appropriate because the first would rely on the use of different reference groups in different countries. The second uses very simple measures that are easy to administer cross-nationally and have been found effective in similar studies. The measure that was adopted was derived from the work of Cantril. In fact it is called the 'Cantril Self-Anchoring Scale' and consists of a ten-rung vertical ladder printed on a card and labelled '0' at the bottom and '1', '2', '3' up to '10' at the top – an *eleven* point scale. This was shown to respondents who were then asked:

> First I'd like to ask you how you feel you and your family are doing these days. Number ten here at the top of the ladder represents the very best possible situation that you could imagine for yourself. And zero down here at the bottom represents the worst possible situation for you. Now, let's think first about the material side of your life today – the things you can buy and do – all the things that make up your material standard of living.
> (Interviewer: hand card to respondent)
> All things considered, how satisfied or dissatisfied are you overall with the material side of your life today?

Respondents replied simply by giving the interviewer a number from '0' to '10' representing their present material standard of living. They were then asked for three more numbers, in this way:

> Where would you have put yourself five years ago? And where do you expect you might put yourself in five years' time? And – still thinking just about your material standards – what do you think is the right point on the scale for people like yourself? I mean, what level of material satisfaction do you feel that people like yourself are entitled to?

This done, the same sequence of four questions was repeated but this time respondents were invited to consider their lives as a whole, like this:

TABLE 5.1 *National Dissatisfaction Levels**

	The Netherlands	Britain	United States	Germany	Austria
Material Satisfaction	7.6	6.6	6.9	6.7	6.6
Material Entitlement	7.8	8.4	8.3	8.0	7.9
Material Deprivation**	−0.2	−1.8	−1.4	−1.3	−1.3
Life as a Whole Satisfaction	7.6	7.3	7.4	7.1	7.1
Life Entitlement	7.9	8.4	8.6	8.3	8.2
Life Deprivation**	−0.3	−1.1	−1.2	−1.2	−1.0

*Figures are mean scores on 0–10 scale: 0 = low satisfaction and no deprivation.
**Deprivation scores are difference between actual and entitlement levels.

Now, let's think about your life as a whole. All things considered, how satisfied or dissatisfied are you overall with your life these days? Where do you put yourself on the scale?

Note carefully that the 'just deserts' measure lies not in the first ranking given – how things are in relation to some 'best possible' ambition. It lies in a comparison between the 'best possible' and the 'entitled' measure. Table 5.1 shows how each national sample rated their material and overall satisfaction and their entitlement and, the second subtracted from the first, the amount of shortfall they saw between achievement and entitlement.

The poorest of the five nations, Britain, records the lowest level of material satisfaction and the highest level of entitlement, leaving an average shortfall of nearly two scale points. Given that the majority of the sample locate themselves in only half of the ten-point scale (in the '5' to '9' range) that is a large discrepancy. Three much wealthier countries, the United States, Germany and Austria, are not that much less discontent, having discrepancies ranging from −1.4 to −1.3 scale points. Overall life satisfaction is very similar in all four of these countries with lower discrepancies of between −1.2 and −1.0

scale points. These four, however, contrast dramatically with The Netherlands. On both measures, the Dutch sample are the most satisfied and claim the lowest levels of entitlement, leaving them more or less at parity: they have, *on average*, what they feel entitled to. Small wonder then, that we earlier found postmaterialism so rife among them. If nothing else, the survey did serious violence to the Dutch stereotype of a nation of materially obsessed trading folk. Whatever its causes, it means that by far and away our most protest-prone nation is also outstandingly the most content. This does not bode well for the dissatisfaction theory of political protest. We had better go straight to the evidence.

Neither material nor overall levels of satisfaction, nor even the relative deprivation measure relate systematically to protest potential or to conventional political participation. In the samples taken as a whole, the signs of the correlation coefficients are in the right direction – that greater deprivation is associated with higher protest potential, for example, but attain statistically significant values (and then only just) among randomly distributed subgroups like older people in The Netherlands or younger people in the United States. Looked at more closely, there is some significant tendency for those occupying the extremes of the satisfaction scales to differ: the least satisfied scoring higher on the Protest Potential Scale, the most satisfied scoring lower. The deprivation measure too shows those most deprived scoring higher compared to others, especially compared to those who feel privileged but this is really true only of the youngest, the under 21-year-olds. In Germany though it is both the deprived and the privileged who have the higher protest potentials. Many of these under 21s will be in fulltime higher education and many readers will not need survey data to tell them that students are often poor and feel they ought not to be.

The use of the Political Action Repertory provides somewhat more interpretable results. Table 5.2 shows that the most protest-prone group – the Activists – record the largest discrepancies between what they have and what they feel entitled to while the Inactives and Conformists tend to record less deprivation. This finding fits a little uncomfortably with earlier discussion because the Activist category is full of young postmaterialist middle-class men who might be expected to acknowledge, at least in material terms, the rewards they receive. Probably the scale is picking up as much aspiration as it is judgement of the present. On the other hand, the protesters, who tend to be

TABLE 5.2 *Satisfaction and Action Typology (Figure is Mean Satisfaction)*

	The Netherlands	Britain	United States	Germany	Austria
Material Satisfaction					
Inactives	7.7	6.8	6.9	6.6	6.5
Conformists	7.7	6.9	7.1	6.9	6.9
Reformists	7.8	6.8	7.0	6.9	6.5
Activists	7.5	6.2	6.6	6.2	6.7
Protesters	7.4	6.4	6.7	6.6	6.9
Life as a Whole Satisfaction					
Inactives	7.8	7.4	7.6	6.9	7.1
Conformists	8.0	7.7	7.5	7.2	7.3
Reformists	7.8	7.4	7.5	7.3	7.2
Activists	7.4	6.8	7.1	6.9	7.3
Protesters	7.6	7.2	7.3	7.1	7.4
Material Deprivation					
Inactives	−.1	−1.6	−1.3	−1.2	−1.2
Conformists	−.3	−1.5	−1.2	−1.3	−1.0
Reformists	.0	−1.7	−1.2	−1.1	−1.3
Activists	−.4	−2.1	−1.8	−1.6	−1.5
Protesters	−.5	−2.1	−1.6	−1.3	−1.1
Life as a Whole Deprivation					
Inactives	−.2	−1.3	−1.0	−1.2	−.9
Conformists	.0	−1.2	−1.1	−1.1	−1.0
Reformists	−.2	−1.2	−1.1	−1.0	−1.1
Activists	−.4	−1.8	−1.8	−1.5	−1.2
Protesters	−.3	−1.5	−1.3	−1.2	−1.0

young but not middle class, do show some of the highest levels of *material* deprivation. This is more encouraging from a theoretical point of view. If value-change explains much of middle-class protest, does material deprivation provide more motivation for militant young workers? It is particularly interesting to see that this relationship is most striking (perhaps literally) among the protesters in Britain. One point that detracts from this promise is that young people generally tend to be less satisfied than older people. One of the more engaging findings from this field of research was provided by Campbell *et al.*, who showed that as people get older they become more 'satisfied' but less 'happy'.

Perhaps we should not be too disillusioned by the uncertainty of these relationships between deprivation and political action. Such measures ask, fundamentally, 'how are you feeling at the moment?' and people's basis for judgement will be drawn from a wide range of contributory factors, many of which will have little to do with politics. Other research has shown that the state of one's personal relationships can be a major source of variance in life satisfaction and only a few will manage to blame those on the political system or the Government. More interesting from a theoretical point of view are not these static measures of well-being alone but a comparison between these and what one feels is likely to happen in the future and what has been the case in the past. This is so because political action, and especially political protest, is about the future – people urging a different future through social change. Political theorists have argued this strongly.

Davies, for example, was puzzled, as others before him, as to why Marx attributed impending revolution to the increasing misery of the masses while de Tocqueville came to the opposite conclusion, that revolution occurs when the expectations of the masses start to rise, but do not rise fast enough. Davies proposed his famous J-curve explanation, that revolt is most likely when expectations rise only to be dashed once more by economic or political reversals. Grofman and Muller found some interesting confirmation of this idea in ways that align closely with our interests. They showed that people whose domestic and work satisfactions had recently increased but were expected by them to decline in future did score high on a measure very similar to the Protest Potential Scale which they called Potential for Political Violence. Strangely though, people who had had the opposite experience, that is, falling satisfactions that were later expected to rise, were also those with higher Potential for Political Violence. Those lacking in such potential were those whose life satisfactions had remained and were expected to remain stable, whether these be high or low. They proposed a 'V-curve' explanation, that political action is typical of those with changing fortunes in either direction and less likely among those leading stable, unchanging lives.

The Political Action Study replicated all these complicated pathways of satisfaction over time by comparing life satisfaction scores now with those that people recalled as the case five years ago and with those they expected to achieve five years hence. Like Grofman and Muller, the highest protest potential was found among the 'drop-and-rise' group in each country. Those who had had a poor time in the past but expected to do better in the future were the most

TABLE 5.3 *Changes in Expectation and Protest Potential (Mean Protest Potential 0–7)*

	The Netherlands	Britain	United States	Germany	Austria
		Material Expectations			
Decreasing	2.79	1.77	2.18	1.80	1.47
No Change	2.60	1.61	1.96	1.87	1.48
Increasing	3.02	2.22	2.83	2.30	1.87
		Life as a Whole Expectations			
Decreasing	2.74	1.78	2.00	1.76	1.45
No Change	2.63	1.74	2.11	2.02	1.46
Increasing	3.10	2.23	2.88	2.33	2.02

inclined toward protest. Contrary to the J-curve idea, and unlike the similar Grofman and Muller study, those suffering the more painful experience of an expected reversal in recently rising fortunes, were *least* inclined toward protest. Generally speaking, people who felt their fortunes were rising, who were optimists, were higher on the Protest Potential Scale than those who were pessimistic. There was some tendency too for optimists to engage more heavily in conventional political activity. These two findings are shown most clearly in Table 5.3 where the comparisons between people's view of their past, present and future material satisfactions are summarised by three groups: those whose fortunes are declining, remaining unchanged or improving.

These three groups shown in Table 5.3 were examined separately as they occur among the five types of the Political Action Repertory. First one notices quite strong national differences. Especially among the more numerous Reformist, Conformist, and Inactive groups, Germans and Austrians tend far more toward a pessimistic view than do the British and, especially, the Americans. This is odd. If the economic record of Germany and Austria did not, in 1974, give reasonable grounds for optimism, what could? Certainly not the British, yet in the British sample as a whole optimists outnumber the pessimists by nearly two to one and in the United States by three to one, while in Germany and Austria the two groups are of equal size. Perhaps the Germans felt they had more to lose.

Across the five political action groups, however, comparisons are similar within each nation. The activists are strikingly the most optimistic and, more strangely, in Britain, the United States and

Austria the protesters almost match their optimism. This is not at all what the literature led one to expect. Political action and especially political protest does not, in these five Western nations, feed upon discontent and fear for the future but upon hope and optimism. (The next time someone asks you why social scientists do surveys only to show what everyone knew already you may like to quote this finding.)

Cynics may point out that anyone who engages in mass political action, especially if they seek social change, simply has to be an optimist by nature. This may be so, but there is a simpler explanation for what we have found. Optimism is overwhelmingly associated with youth. In the most optimistic nation, the United States, 81% of the under 30s have increasing expectations of material satisfaction compared to only 38% of those over 50. In the most pessimistic nation, Germany, the corresponding figures are 64% and 28%. When the analysis shown in Table 5.3 is carried out separately within age groups, the relationship between optimism and activism tends to break down. There remains a tendency for inactives in each age group to be more pessimistic than others. One can be too preoccupied with financial problems to be bothered with politics. But otherwise optimism no longer varies systematically with a choice of styles of political action. Activists and protesters are more optimistic simply because they are younger.

This discrepancy between the widespread assumption that political action derives from people's dissatisfaction with their material and other expectations and clear evidence that it is associated instead with youthful optimism is instructive. The world view that insists that there is an obvious link between life dissatisfaction and protest encompasses many places and events where the dissatisfied suffer objectively miserable conditions rarely encountered in the five nations examined here. To become dissatisfied with a life of poverty in a South American country, for example, is to become angry indeed and with good reason. Also, it reminds us forcibly that we are dealing for the most part with protest *potential*. While we have good reason to believe that such potential is associated with real protest, it is usually of a kind that seeks sophisticated remedies for grievances that grow out of mature and comparatively well-provided political systems. Probably the one thing that detracts most from the impact of life satisfaction upon political dissent is that, despite recent setbacks, these societies still offer the chance of considerably upward social mobility to their younger members or, failing that, the chance of steady improvement in material and social well-being throughout the life cycle. Thus, the first remedy for deprivation seems to most people to lie more in the personal than the political domain. It is the core problem with which all Socialist parties in Western Europe have to struggle. If deprivation does play a role in promoting political action we must look for it in a politicised form.

The place to look first for this meeting between deprivation and political remedy is in the national 'issue agenda'. What issues are really important to people? Do they feel that these also are things that the Government should do something about? If so, how well or how badly do they judge the Government's performance to be in these key areas? These questions are the very stuff of politics and are heard loudly in the few weeks before general elections.

The Study Group chose ten key issues to place before respondents; these were:

Looking after old people
Guaranteeing equal rights for men and women
Seeing to it that everyone who wants a job can have one
Providing a good education
Providing good medical care
Providing adequate housing
Fighting pollution
Guaranteeing neighbourhoods safe from crime
Providing equal rights for ethnic or racial minorities
Trying to even out differences in wealth between people.

Respondents were asked to consider each one and say how important it was '. . . to you personally', then to say how much responsibility, if any, they felt the Government bore for each policy area and finally to say how well or how poorly they thought the Government was presently handling each area. The list of issues was not intended to be exhaustive – foreign and defence policies are absent, for example. It is, however, a fairly comprehensive list of policy areas embracing issues that were least likely to attract cross-national distortions of meaning. Note also that the judgements respondents were asked to make were ideologically neutral. No reasons were sought in the sense of why an issue may be important, nor the nature of the Government's responsibility, nor the direction of the Government's success or failure.

Respondents agreed that the issues they were asked to consider were important to them personally. The ten items attracted an overall average importance score of 3.4 in the United States and 3.5 in each of the European countries on the four-point scale. Thus the majority of items were felt to be 'important' or, more usually, 'very important' to individual respondents. With respect to the extent of Government responsibility they were less emphatic. On a similar four-point scale (where 1 = no responsibility up to 4 = an essential responsibility) average scores across all items were 3.3 in Germany and Austria, 3.2 in Britain and The Netherlands and down to 3.0 in the United States. The latter score indicates an enduring doubt in the minds of many Americans about just how 'big' Government ought to be. They are more likely than are Europeans to assign responsibility for such issues to actors other than governments.

The priorities assigned to these issue agendas in each country are summarised in Table 5.4. By priorities is meant a combination of people's views on the importance of each item and the extent of the Government's responsibility. A single score was calculated ranging from '1' to '5', where '1' indicated that respondents rated an issue as unimportant *and* felt the Government should leave well alone and '5' indicated the opposite, that this was a very important issue that the Government had an essential responsibility to do something about.

The rank-ordering of the five national issues agendas are very similar in each country. The 'bread and butter' issues of housing, job security, medical care and education dominate the upper half of the rankings in all five countries. This is hardly surprising. These issues are central to the welfare policies of Western democracies and define that area of government where personal need and benign intervention intersect. At least this was so in the 1970s and people recognised it. Equally clearly, the three issues dealing with material, sexual and racial equality tend to be relegated in each country to the bottom of the list. These remain controversial aspects of government policy. It may also be that many people otherwise sympathetic toward social equality gave lower importance rankings because they felt that only members of the nominated group – particularly minorities – had any business saying it was important to them '. . . personally'. On the other hand, a measure of special pleading was part of what the issue agenda is designed to capture: who wants what?

If majority social welfare issues define the Old Politics agenda and minority social equality defines the New, there are other issues floating between them that reflect a mixture of both. Crime control is ranked first in Germany, Austria and (more expectedly) second in the United States but receives a middle ranking in Britain and The

TABLE 5.4 Mean Score Rankings of Issue Agendas

The Netherlands	Britain	United States	Germany	Austria
Education (4.5)	Medical care (4.6)	Education (4.1)	Crime control (4.6)	Crime control (4.5)
Medical care (4.3)	Education (4.4)	Crime control (4.1)	Medical care (4.4)	Medical care (4.4)
Housing (4.2)	Old age (4.3)	Old age (3.9)	Job security (4.3)	Job security (4.3)
Job security (4.1)	Housing (4.3)	Medical care (3.9)	Pollution (4.3)	Education (4.1)
Pollution (4.1)	Job security (4.2)	Pollution (3.7)	Education (4.2)	Pollution (4.1)
Crime control (4.1)	Crime control (4.1)	Job security (3.6)	Old age (4.1)	Old age (4.0)
Old age (4.0)	Pollution (4.0)	Minority equality (3.4)	Housing (3.7)	Housing (3.7)
Wealth equality (3.4)	Minority equality (2.8)	Housing (3.3)	Sex equality (3.2)	Wealth equality (3.1)
Sex equality (3.3)	Wealth equality (2.7)	Sex equality (3.0)	Wealth equality (3.1)	Sex equality (2.9)
Minority equality (2.9)	Sex equality (2.6)	Wealth equality (2.0)	Minority equality (2.7)	Minority equality (2.4)

Netherlands. The care of the elderly and pollution control, objectively a 'New' issue, also received middle rankings in each country.

This division among priorities was clearly mirrored in a much more detailed analysis using multi-dimensional scaling techniques. People who assigned priority to one of the four social welfare issues tended strongly to promote the other three in their personal ranking and vice versa. The social equality issues behaved in the same way. Concern for one kind of social equality was associated with concern for the other two. On the other hand, we know already that these equality issues tend to attract the special favour of postmaterialists. We know also that such people favour the environmental movement strongly, so it is odd that neither pollution control nor concern for the elderly bonded to the social equality items in the same way.

Comparing the joint scores assigned to social welfare with those assigned to social equality, Britain clearly showed greatest concern for the former and least for the latter issues. In the United States the average rankings of social welfare and social equality were closest. This is due possibly to a greater concern for sexual equality among an increasingly equality-conscious female population and having quite large numbers of Blacks in the American sample who would naturally give priority to their advancement in Government concerns. These greater demands for equality in the United States are matched by noticeably less concern for government agencies to take full responsibility for social welfare which, in contrast, is something about which the British were adamant.

These issue priorities are given again in Table 5.5, with the social welfare and social equality issues picked out respectively in bold and italic type. Beneath these are given the *performance* rankings for each item in each country. These are determined by the extent respondents judged their respective Government's handling of each issues as 'very good', 'good', 'bad', or 'very bad'. Overall, there tended to be only a little more 'good' than 'bad'. The Austrians were the most satisfied, bestowing an average ranking of 2.8 on the 1–4 scale. It has been pointed out before that the late 1960s and early 1970s were something of a golden age for social democracy in Austria. The Germans were again the least satisfied (2.5). German authorities must wonder sometimes what they have to do to secure popularity.

Two of the social welfare items were the most favourably regarded – medical care (less so in the United States) and education. Job security, as well it might have at the time, was also thought good in

TABLE 5.5 Ranking of Issue Agendas

The Netherlands	Britain	United States	Germany	Austria
EDUCATION	MEDICAL CARE	EDUCATION[a]	Crime control	Crime control
MEDICAL CARE	EDUCATION	Crime control[a]	MEDICAL CARE	MEDICAL CARE
HOUSING	Old age[a]	MEDICAL CARE[b]	Pollution[a]	JOB SECURITY
Pollution[a]	HOUSING[a]	Old age[b]	JOB SECURITY[a]	EDUCATION[a]
Crime control[a]	JOB SECURITY[b]	Pollution	EDUCATION	Pollution
JOB SECURITY[a]	Crime control[b]	JOB SECURITY	Old age	Old age
Old age	Pollution	Minorities equality	HOUSING	HOUSING
Wealth equality	Wealth equality	HOUSING	Sex equality	Wealth equality
Sex equality	Minorities equality	Sex equality	Wealth equality	Sex equality
Minorities equality	Sex equality	Wealth equality	Minorities equality	Minorities equality

RANKINGS ON GOVERNMENT PERFORMANCE

The Netherlands	Britain	United States	Germany	Austria
MEDICAL CARE	MEDICAL CARE	EDUCATION	MEDICAL CARE	JOB SECURITY
EDUCATION	EDUCATION	Sex equality	JOB SECURITY	EDUCATION
Old age	Old age	Minorities equality	EDUCATION	MEDICAL CARE
Sex equality	Minorities equality	MEDICAL CARE	Sex equality	Old age
JOB SECURITY	Crime control	HOUSING	Old age	Sex equality
HOUSING	JOB SECURITY	Pollution	Minorities equality	Minorities equality
Wealth equality	Sex equality	Old age	HOUSING	Crime control
Minorities equality	Pollution	JOB SECURITY	Crime control	HOUSING
Crime control	HOUSING	Crime control	Wealth equality	Wealth equality
Pollution	Wealth equality	Wealth equality	Pollution	Pollution

NOTE: a and b represent tied rankings
All capital letters and words are individual well-being items.
Entries in italics are social equality items.

Germany and Austria, less so in The Netherlands and Britain, and was thought fairly calamitous in the United States. It is well then that Americans also rated job security the lowest in their issue agenda compared to other countries. The most painful discrepancies appear over crime control which most nations rated high and thought the Government's performance in providing it was poor. In Britain, housing shows a similar gap between priority and peformance and so does pollution control in Germany and The Netherlands. It is no coincidence that these latter countries are the natural home of the Green Movement.

One can see, then, that the performance rankings – the key measure of political satisfaction – are pulled this way and that by the mix of issues that were current at the time. Britain was tumbling into recession and living through the traumas of the Miners' Strike, the oil embargo, the three-day week and the coming dramatic demise of Edward Heath's Conservative Government. Austria was calm, Germany secure but anxious; the United States was also anxious about oil but obsessed by Watergate, and so on. Multidimensional analysis confirmed what is evident: the structure of public policy satisfaction, unlike the clear consensus that underpins the priority rankings, depends very much on what was going on at the time. It is this distinction, of course, that the survey design was intended to capture: an enduring issue agenda that provides a rank-ordered frame of reference within which ad hoc judgements of the performance of the incumbent authorities are made. Accordingly, a single measure of Policy Dissatisfaction was constructed by combining the importance and responsibility rankings with the 'good'-'bad' performance rankings. Those scoring high on this index felt that the Government was failing to provide those things that they felt were important to them personally and that the Government had a high responsibility to provide.

Before we do the obvious and confront this Policy Dissatisfaction Index with its relation to political action, there is more work to be done. The final task of integrating our understanding of political dissatisfaction with the role of ideology and voting to form a general model of political action will be undertaken in the next chapter. Since we have come this far and found already that the other factors are important in the explanation of political action, it is also important to know what are the antecedents of policy dissatisfaction. How is this bridge formed between private grievance and political dissent?

The diagram in Figure 5.1 suggests that there are three main sources of policy dissatisfaction: social stratification, value discrepancy, and electoral partisanship. An excursion into political theory will be necessary to explain the reasoning behind each of these.

5.1 SOCIAL STRATIFICATION OR THE OLD POLITICS MODEL

This derives from the classic Marxist theory of political mobilisation in societies divided by industrial-occupational class membership. In the way it is realised in Figure 5.1, the social stratification model puts forward three arguments. First, simply being placed in the lower and hence disadvantaged part of a hierarchically stratified society will lead to policy dissatisfaction because the authorities are bound to defend and favour the interests of the élites. Second, policy dissatisfaction will increase as those who are objectively deprived realise what is happening to them and *feel* subjectively deprived too. Third, dissatisfaction will increase still further when those who are and feel deprived identify the inequalities of society as the source of their deprivation. This realisation, called of course 'class consciousness', leads people to identify the need for a new redistributive regime as their best chance of remedy. Conceivably, too, others who are not deprived will nevertheless find objectionable Government policies designed to perpetuate social stratification and class cleavages. Marx himself laid considerable stress upon subjective processes in the way deprivation was to be translated into ideology and then into action. He wrote, for example,

> Although the enjoyments of the workers have risen, the social satisfaction that they give has fallen in comparison with the state of development of society in general. Our desires and pleasures spring from society. . . . Because they are of a social nature they are of a relative nature. (See James Davies, 1962)

Thus relative deprivation must be both subjectively experienced *and* politicised before it can become a realistic source of threat to a bourgeois regime that perpetuates inequality and minority class domination. This process is represented in the model in Figure 5.1 by four measures:

(1) The source measure, objective deprivation, is the Treiman

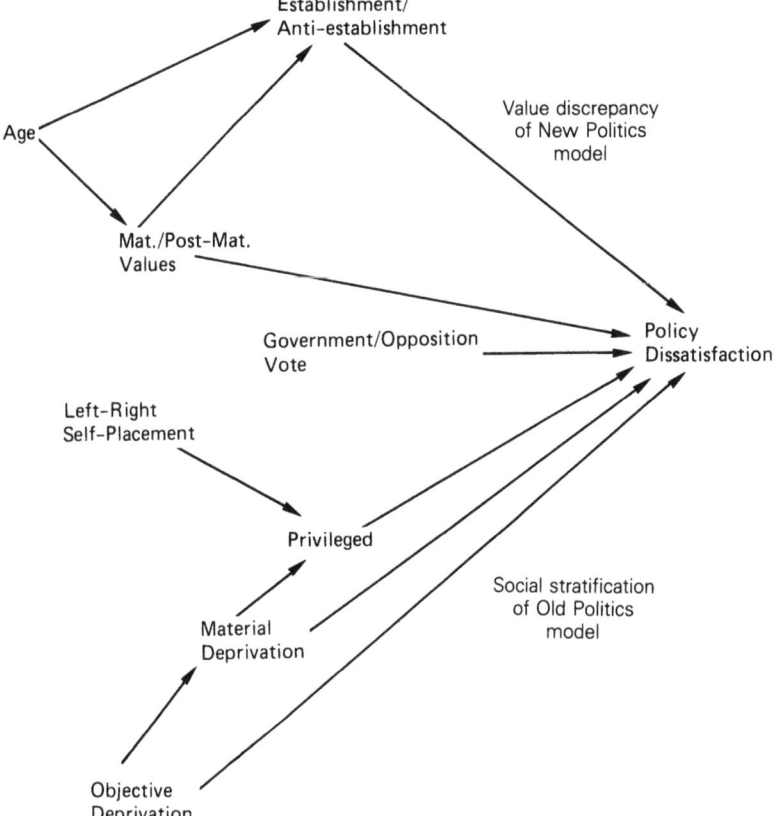

FIGURE 5.1 *Model of Policy Dissatisfaction*

Occupational Prestige Score introduced in chapter 2. It is difficult to guess what Marx might have thought of this measure since it describes a continuum of occupational prestige and not discrete class groups. But to be at the bottom is certainly to be poor and the lower scores usually denote manual occupations and the higher scores non-manual and professional occupations.

(2) Subjective deprivation is represented by the measure introduced earlier in this chapter, the difference between people's present material satisfaction and what level they feel entitled to have.

(3) The recognition of inequity in the social stratification of society is represented by a measure not previously discussed. Respondents were asked to say whether or not they felt there were groups in

society who were 'over-privileged', who were getting more rewards than they should, and also whether there were groups who were 'under-privileged', who were receiving less rewards than they should. Those who agreed that such groups existed were scored as those 'recognising inequality'. Those who denied their existence were scored as '*not* recognising inequality'.

(4) Finally, the identification of a political means of economic redistribution was represented by the Left-Right Self-placement Scale introduced in chapter 3.

5.2 VALUE DISCREPANCY OR THE NEW POLITICS MODEL

Here we reintroduce the postmaterialist critique of traditional politics. The emergence of new values among the young has caused them to embrace an expanded issue agenda. To the extent that their New Politics issues, in particular their championing of the causes of racial and sexual equality, remain low in official priorities, they will be politically dissatisfied. Since their political affiliations do not fit easily into existing industrial class-based cleavages, their political identity with groups in the polity will reflect shared values rather than stratified class interests. Thus, this portion of the model identified age (that is, youth) as its source measure leading of course to postmaterialism. In addition, it proposes that identification with anti-establishment élite-challenging groups (women's movement, minorities, revolutionary groups, and so forth) and opposition to establishment bodies (the police, clergy, civil servants, and the like) will be the agent that politicises value change into a view critical of the existing materialist regimes. It is represented by the Establishment/anti-Establishment dimension of the combined sympathy scores introduced in the previous chapter.

5.3 ELECTORAL PARTISANSHIP

In Britain, when the first Thatcher administration plunged into an early period of unpopularity in 1981, car-stickers appeared saying 'Don't blame me. I voted Labour'. These mimicked similar stickers absolving Conservative supporters of blame for the troubles of the Labour Government in the 1960s. The point is that present policy dissatisfaction always contains a strong partisan element – who did you vote for last time? Thus, the importance of the competing Old and New Politics Models described above cannot be fairly assessed unless this simple cause of dissatisfaction is also taken into account.

The complete three-part model was tested using regression analysis of a kind that allows the analyst to assess simultaneously the causal structures formed by the measures in each national sample. Students who have a special interest in these numbers are referred to pages 423 to 444 in the original *Political Action* volume. There they will find a satisfying array of standardised and unstandardised regression and slope coefficients combined in a series of linear models and equations. In a volume intended as a general student text, these intimidating numbers tend to get in the way and so in the narrative that follows, most of these may be taken on trust.

Let us start, then, with the social stratification component of the model of policy dissatisfaction. Objective deprivation, the Treiman Prestige scores, are directly related to policy dissatisfaction *but in the wrong direction*. Policy dissatisfaction is somewhat more characteristic of those *higher* on the social scale; lower social status is associated with *less* dissatisfaction. The relationship is weak, but it is negative. The same is true of the path between objective deprivation and subjective deprivation. People higher on the social scale are a little *more* likely to feel materially deprived and to connect this feeling with policy dissatisfaction. One reason for this is that the better-off occupational grades find their material fortunes more directly affected by day-to-day Government policies than do the low-paid. The better-off are at the whim of tax changes, insurance surcharges and interest rates. The low-paid are at the whim only of their employer, though one might have thought too that the inadequacy of welfare payments might have been a source of policy dissatisfaction. The real reason probably lies in the spread of issues the Policy Dissatisfaction Index embraces. If the social welfare items alone had been included then the above result might well have been quite different.

This anomaly apart, the remainder of the social stratification component makes a strong and independent contribution to policy satisfaction. Subjective deprivation and an affiliation with the political Left as its likely remedy, combine to create a politicised view of a stratified and unequal society that contains over- and under-privileged groups. The resulting sense of unfairness strongly increases policy dissatisfaction in each national sample. Its source, however, lies not in poverty itself but in a political view of a society unfairly divided by class.

Value discrepancy also provides a strong source of overall policy dissatisfaction. The source measure is youth, though the mediating effects of postmaterialist values and anti-Establishment sympathies are the stronger effects. Interestingly, the path from postmaterialist values *through* anti-Establishment sympathies is the strongest of all. This means that value change too has to be submitted to a politicisation process before it has its heaviest impact on a critique of Government policy. Not only does one have to develop new value priorities but one must also identify with new élite-challenging groups and oppose the present guardians of the materialist system. This process has gone furthest in The Netherlands, where the effect of a value-driven identification with New Politics groups upon policy dissatisfaction is twice as great as elsewhere. This fits very well with the special character of politics in The Netherlands. It has been called a 'consociational democracy' wherein different 'zuilen' or pillars represent different parts of a fragmented social structure divided by both class and religion. According to Lijphart:

> Dutch national consensus is weak and narrow, but it does contain the crucial component of a widely shared attitude that the existing system ought to be maintained and not allowed to disintegrate. (p. 102)

This means that the Dutch Establishment is strong and occupies the centre of the political arena. Groups on the outside will therefore experience far more policy dissatisfaction since they find themselves opposed not merely to the policies of an incumbent party but to the entire social order.

As expected, simply having voted for what became the opposition party in the last election is also a source of policy dissatisfaction. This is true, remember, independently of the effects of both the social stratification and value discrepancy paths. The Dutch case is again interesting. Since value change and its associated opposition to the establishment and identification with political outgroups is so strong a source of policy dissatisfaction in The Netherlands, it follows that voting behaviour will be a weak source. This is so. Dutch governments are broad coalitions of Catholic, Protestant and Socialist parties. If, for example, one voted Socialist (and there are five of these to choose among) and one's party finds a niche in a Centre-Left coalition government, there is little guarantee that one will identify strongly with all the policy outcomes of the coalition. One's quarrel remains substantially with the Establishment, whose values the coalition will defend.

Among these five nations, the Dutch party system contrasts most completely with the British. As it was in 1974, at least, the distinction between Government and Opposition is unambiguous in Britain and the two main parties which contest power reflect most clearly a single class cleavage in society. Consequently, having voted for the Opposition – the Labour Party at the time – was a far greater source of policy dissatisfaction than it was in the other four countries. In fact the five countries line up on this dimension precisely in an order corresponding to the degree of singular responsibility possessed by Government and Opposition parties, like this: The Netherlands, Germany, Austria, the United States, and Britain. That is to say, the greater the likelihood that one party takes sole responsibility for power and confronts a single Opposition party, the greater is the contribution to policy dissatisfaction of having voted for the Opposition. This is true even when strong alternative sources of dissatisfaction are held constant.

The main outcome of this analysis was to modify the original three-part model of political dissatisfaction into a four-part model: perceived stratification, objective stratification, values and incumbency. The most important facets of each source were then packaged up, so to speak, in the linear model represented in Figure 5.2. This form of analysis weights each contributing factor by a coefficient whose value is determined by its independent relationship with dissatisfaction. In this way the analyst can determine the relative contribution each makes to the level of political dissatisfaction in each country.

This analysis showed that the three major components of dissatisfaction were values, perceived stratification and incumbency (that is, having voted for the present Opposition party). Each makes a more or less equal contribution in each country except, for reasons discussed earlier, in The Netherlands where the values component (namely, postmaterialism *plus* opposition to the Establishment) tends to dominate. Objective stratification (that is, having *higher* social status) makes less independent contribution in each country and in Britain it makes none at all. Britain is the country which has by far the largest number of poorer people who depend in whole or in part upon the State for their material well-being. Thus, policy dissat-

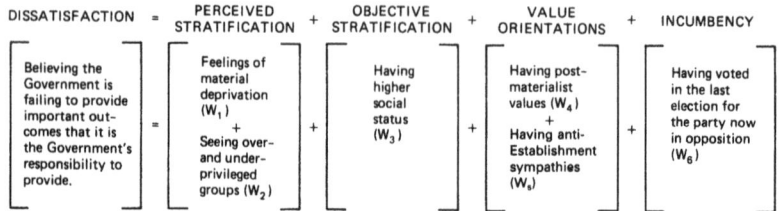

FIGURE 5.2 *A Linear Model of Political Policy Dissatisfaction*

isfaction among the better-off, when it arises, tends to be matched by dissatisfaction among the poor whose fortunes, more than in other countries, vary according to the welfare package delivered to them by the British Government.

5.4 SUMMARY

This chapter has shown that some seductively simple ideas concerning the role of dissatisfaction in political life give rise to dismaying complexity when confronted with data. Protest potential, for example, ought according to theory to be associated with a threat to gains so far achieved. It is not. It is associated with dissatisfied optimism which, in turn, is simply associated with being young and prone to protest. We have also seen, on the other hand, that political dissatisfaction is a reality. People do care about political outcomes and they assign clear priorities for government responsibility. They judge these outcomes, sometimes severely. The degree of political dissatisfaction that results has complex origins. People do not simply glance at the news and grumble. Dissatisfaction arises from abiding feelings about the way the political community should be organised. Some of these are traditional divisions of Left and Right, others are new and involve what we have called the contest for possession of the issue agenda.

Political dissatisfaction is the bridge between social structural and social psychological processes on the one hand and real political outcomes, including political behaviour, on the other. The next chapter will examine how this whole process works.

6 The General Model of Political Action

If this work has a single theme it is that political action arises from the way people evaluate their political system. These evaluations, conceived in the previous chapter as political satisfaction and dissatisfaction, have their origins in social structure. Here, age and education were found to be of primary importance. Political evaluations also have origins in social psychological processes. Here ideology and values were found to exercise a profound influence on the way people form their political judgements. All these factors also have a direct influence upon political behaviour. The task now is to bring together these five key factors – age, education, ideology, values and political judgement – into a general model of political action. By so doing, we will learn how this chain of social circumstances and social attitudes may be translated into a more complete understanding of political behaviour than has so far been achieved.

The most basic form of the general model is illustrated in Figure 6.1. The model ignores, for the moment, many of the important qualifications shown in earlier analysis. There is a strong need at this point to have the basic ideas very straight indeed. Building on what we know already, the model says that there are two parallel paths to political action. First, higher education and higher levels of ideological thinking lead to the formation of political judgement. Such judgement, especially when it involves strong views on what the present authorities are doing, will lead, primarily, to higher rates of conventional political participation. Second, youth and the growth of new political values among younger people will also lead to the formation of political judgements. The kinds of critique these judgments imply will lead toward the use of protest methods. This, as we said, is the simplest statement that can be made on the basis of the evidence sifted thus far. Readers can spend a diverting five minutes drawing in qualifying arrows on Figure 6.1. The interaction across the two main paths between ideology and postmaterialism is an obvious one.

What the model makes clear, however, is that we still do not know enough about the relationship between political judgement and pol-

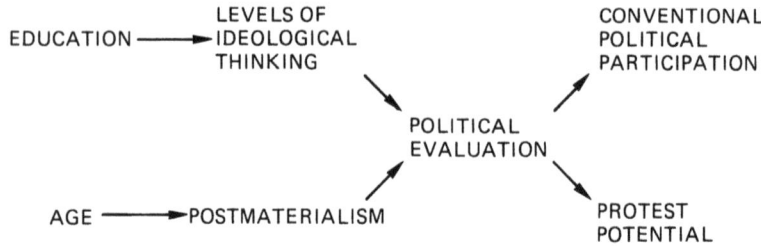

FIGURE 6.1 *A General Model of Political Action*

itical behaviour. Judgement, that is to say satisfaction and dissatisfaction, can be of so many kinds. How does this linkage work? Moreover, how does it work independently of the relationships we know already to exist between the source measures (age, education, ideology and values) and political behaviour? After all, if all these complex measures of political dissatisfaction add nothing to the explanation of behaviour beyond those shown before, then to some extent we have wasted our time. The data must now be organised in such a way as to show this final linkage clearly. In social science, to be organised is to have a theory.

The theory used by Political Action Study to develop these final linkages in the model owes much to the work of Easton and others. It is a 'systems theory' of politics. The theory concerns the nature of the *support* for political systems. This support is of two kinds: *diffuse* support and *specific* support. Diffuse support is an enduring assessment of whether or not the whole political system is generally good or generally bad. Is it the *kind* of system that *can* deliver preferred political outcomes? Specific support is the more short-term judgement of the kinds that obsess politicians as they scan the opinion polls. Is the system, and more especially, is the Government presently providing or failing to provide these preferred outcomes? Are election promises being kept? Are the things people need from governments being delivered as they should be?

The theory also makes a distinction between two different objects of support: between the political *authorities* and the political *regime*. The authorities are an obvious target, they are the party presently in power and, to a lesser extent, those who serve them. The support that most nourishes the authorities, and which they are known sometimes cravenly to seek, is specific support – an endorsement of their policies and approval of their record. Things have to get very bad before authorities are forced back on an appeal for diffuse support. A good example of this is President de Gaulle, who from time to time confronted the French electorate with a choice between his continued incumbency and the end of civilisation as they knew it: 'Après moi, le déluge!' The regime, on the other hand, is different. It is a term often used carelessly by modern commentators to refer to governing parties but it is really a much wider term. It refers to the whole political order, the great Institutions of State (the Law, the Civil Service, and so on, together with the party *system*) and also to the rules of procedure that govern the whole system. When things become difficult for the regime, during periods of rapid social change or some external threat to national security, for example, the extent of diffuse support becomes important. At such times, appeals for the preservation of 'our way of life' are intoned and party political differences (specific supports) are said to be transcended. For these reasons, authorities change faster than regimes.

To this well accepted theory, the Political Action Study proposed a qualification. The regime is seen by people in two quite distinct ways. One aspect concerns their respect for political institutions. It is, almost literally, a concrete view. The second concerns national purpose, a public philosophy of what the overriding priorities of the nation ought to be. It is this second aspect that is of greater interest here since it embodies a view of exactly what kinds of responsibilities and functions Government should assume for the well-being of its citizens. It is the key aspect of the political regime in which change most readily occurs. This kind of change is an obvious source of political mobilisation.

The intersection of these two kinds of support (diffuse and specific) and these two objects of support (authorities and the regime) define four areas of political evaluation or judgement. These are four areas where negative evaluation or 'political dissatisfaction' of different kinds can arise. These are shown in Figure 6.2.

Of the four cells defined in Figure 6.2, we are concerned with only three: A, B and C. The fourth, cell 'D', defines a rarer kind of political dissatisfaction when diffuse support is withdrawn from authorities, that is when the people in power at the present are seen to be at odds with the rules of the whole system. Such dissatisfaction has an unreal quality (though perhaps both Charles de Gaulle and Richard Nixon might disagree) because it will always be masked by dissatisfaction

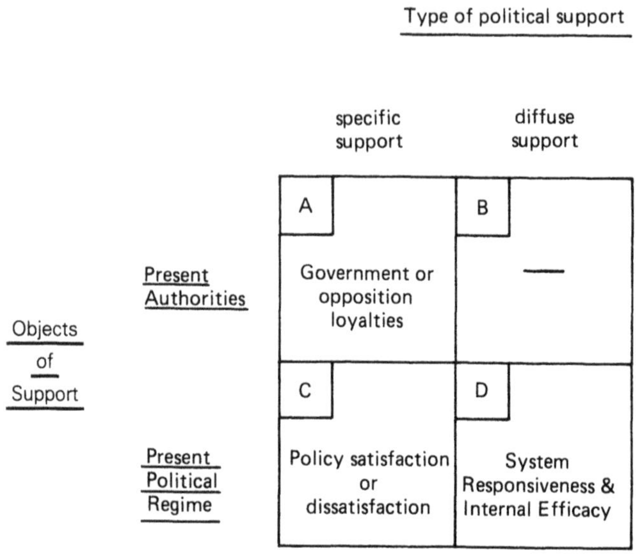

	Type of political support	
	specific support	diffuse support
Present Authorities	A Government or opposition loyalties	B —
Present Political Regime	C Policy satisfaction or dissatisfaction	D System Responsiveness & Internal Efficacy

(Objects of Support)

FIGURE 6.2 *How Political Judgement is Formed*

of the more specific kinds. Consequently, no measures of this kind were included in the survey. If you try to think up some questions that will measure people's diffuse support for the present authorities you will soon see why.

For the remaining three kinds of political dissatisfaction, measures are available, as follows:

(1) *Specific support for authorities (cell 'A')*:
This is defined simply by whether or not the respondent *currently supported* the party in power at the time of asking. Note that this is not the same measure used in the previous chapter, which determined whether or not respondents *voted* for the party now in power at the last election.

(2) *Specific support for the regime (cell 'B')*:
This focuses, as suggested earlier, on both the definition and the fulfillment of a public philosophy of what the national political priorities ought to be. Accordingly, the Policy Dissatisfaction Index described in the previous chapter fills this requirement. It is political dissatisfaction in relation to people's priorities for government responsibility.

(3) *Diffuse support for the regime (cell 'C')*:

The General Model of Political Action

This kind of political dissatisfaction focuses on the *responsiveness* of the whole political system to the demands its citizens make upon it. It is not, remember, a judgement about particular issues but about whether one has the kind of political system that can and will respond to people's political and social needs. Accordingly, respondents were asked to say how much they agreed or disagreed with the following three statements:
(a) I don't think public officials care much about what people like me think.
(b) Generally speaking, those we elect to (Parliament) lose touch with the people pretty quickly.
(c) Parties are only interested in people's votes, but not in their opinions.

Those *dis*agreeing with these three statements score high on a combined System Responsiveness Index, those agreeing scored low.

To these three kinds of political dissatisfaction, the survey added a fourth. It differs from the three defined above because the object of satisfaction or dissatisfaction is not the authorities or the regime but oneself. More particularly, it is oneself as a political actor. Respondents were asked to say how much they agreed or disagreed with two statements:

(a) Voting is the only way that people like me can have any say in how the government runs things.
(b) Sometimes politics and government seem so complicated that a person like me cannot really understand what is going on.

People who *dis*agreed with these two statements are held to have a high sense of Internal Efficacy, as the measure is called. Those who agreed were awarded a low efficacy score. A reduction in levels of personal, internal efficacy in the population will contribute to a reduction in the level of diffuse support for a regime.

Let us now take these four measures of political judgement – two kinds of specific support (authority and regime) and two kinds of diffuse support (both regime) – and see how they relate to the two measures of political action. This must be done in each case so as to show the influence of each measure on each kind of action (conventional participation and protest potential) independently of each other measure. More than that, this set of relationships must be shown independently of the direct relationships we know to exist already between behaviour and the four main antecedent measures of political action: age, education, ideology and values.

This exceedingly complex analysis was carried out in the Political Action Study using the same regression techniques described in the last chapter to assess the components of policy dissatisfaction. The results of this analysis are shown in Figure 6.3 in a diagrammatic form, omitting the controlling factors of age and so on for the sake of clarity. These will be reintroduced later. The numbers, in this case unstandardised regression coefficients, are available in pages 435 to 439 in the original volume for those who feel, rightly of course, that they need to see them.

6.1 CONVENTIONAL POLITICAL PARTICIPATION

What does the theory of system support lead us to expect? First, it leads us to expect that diffuse rather than specific supports are the mainstay of regular participation in the conventional political arena. There is something habitual about party politics, particularly at the grass roots level. It arises from an enduring belief that the party system and its institutions of State, for all their faults, offer the best chance for ordinary people to participate in the decision-making processes of their communities and of the nation as a whole. Specific forms of support will also play a role. Suspicion that the system is headed in the wrong direction, that it has the wrong goals and priorities also invites participation. It motivates people to intervene and make known their alternative vision. So too when the suspicion arises that the present authorities are making a mess of things. Opposition to incumbent authorities is always a better springboard than support. But it will be opposition within the context of a wider diffuse belief that campaigning within the system against the cause of those in power who are doing the wrong things will be effective – or at least that is the right way to go about securing their political demise. Thus, *positive* diffuse support makes conventional political participation a regular, approved option while *negative specific* support motivates it as the need is seen to arise.

The evidence summarised in Figure 6.3 supports these ideas. Diffuse support for the regime, especially the responsiveness measure, is strongly and independently related to higher levels of conventional political participation. Feeling that public officials do care, that

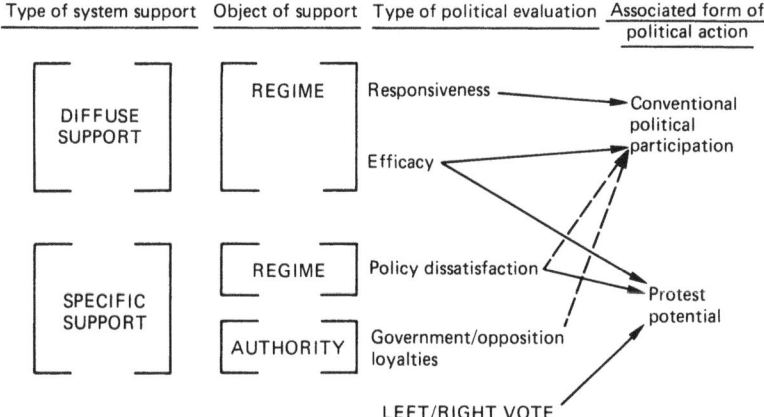

FIGURE 6.3 *System Support, Political Evaluation and Political Action*

elected office-holders do not lose touch and that the parties they represent are interested in people's opinions as well as their votes is associated with grass roots party activity in each country. The relationship is strongest in the United States, Germany and Austria, weaker in Britain and The Netherlands.

The role of internal efficacy is less certain, except in Germany where those who feel that they can do more than merely vote to influence government and who are not easily discouraged by political complexity are, all other things being equal, far more likely to participate in conventional politics. This accords well with what is known of the dramatic change in the political climate of Germany since the Second World War. The lingering political passivity of the German population, still detectable even in Almond's and Verba's 1959 survey, has been deliberately engineered out of the system. Germans are educated to believe in their individual civil rights and are sternly enjoined to use them to good effect: almost, as Henry Ford said of money, to use them or lose them. As a result, the impact of internal efficacy upon behaviour in Germany is twice as great as the impact of system responsiveness. In Germany, it is thought to be of little use simply waiting for the system to respond; it is up to the individual citizen to make it respond too. Germans know this and they do it.

In Britain and The Netherlands the impact of internal efficacy is about equal to that of responsiveness, while in the United States and Austria efficacy has no independent effect at all on conventional participation once all other factors have been accounted for. In the United States, even the inefficacious tend to get swept into the very high level of local political activity one encounters in that country. In Austria, it must be said, relatively few people become involved in political activity, whether they are efficacious or not.

As expected, specific evaluations play a lesser rôle in promoting conventional political participation than does diffuse support for the regime but their impact is in the predicted direction. In The Netherlands and the United States, but not elsewhere, policy dissatisfaction (that is, *lack* of specific support for the regime) is independently associated with increased conventional activity. In Britain and the United States, but not elsewhere, one's loyalty to the opposition rather than to the Government party (that is, *lack* of specific support for the authorities) also increases conventional participation. This is another reflection of the much clearer divide between Government and Opposition present in these countries, especially Britain, than elsewhere. In particular, Britain and the United States were governed at the time of the surveys by the major party of the Right and therefore the supporters of the major Left party were in a higher state of mobilisation. This was especially true in Britain, where the political temperature was rising sharply during the 1973 miners' strike and the oil embargo which led, weeks after the survey was completed, to the defeat of the Conservative administration in the General Election of February 1974. This is what was meant earlier by the short-term mobilising effects of a withdrawal of specific support for the authorities.

Overall though the message is clear: a positive evaluation of the whole political system, all other things accounted for, encourages higher levels of conventional political activity. In the short term, becoming dissatisfied with the performance of the system and being out of sympathy with the Government party will increase activity further. But being dissatisfied with the system's performance does not necessarily breach the underlying faith that this system, and not some other system, is the right one through which to secure political improvements. This feeling alone underwrites the process in which political parties can continue to recruit and retain their helpers.

6.2 PROTEST POTENTIAL

It may be obvious from the above that the theory of system support,

The General Model of Political Action 139

as its name suggests, was designed primarily to explain continued support for democratic party systems – the conventional political arena. Political scientists have trodden this path before and it was easy to know what to expect. In applying the theory to unconventional political participation – protest potential – everything becomes much less obvious. Take, for example, the critical measure of diffuse support for the regime – responsiveness. If the belief that the present system is the right one to have, that it responds to the demands people make upon it, is what sustains the party system, surely protest will arise from a withdrawal of this kind of support? If the system is no good anymore, surely that is the time to seek new ways of making one's views known, ways that the authorities cannot ignore as they do now? Possibly so, but we already know that the activists and reformists are prepared to use both methods of political activity. Do they support the system or do they not? It is difficult to predict. It is even more difficult when one considers the likely rôle of internal efficacy. The politically efficacious citizen makes a clear statement: 'I can understand what is going on and can do more about it than merely voting'. More indeed: he or she can get involved in party politics but can also choose to demonstrate, boycott, strike or occupy. Protesters are nothing if not efficacious. So does internal efficacy sustain *both* conventional and unconventional political action?

Expectations about the role of specific supports and their lack also contain intriguing ambiguities. Policy dissatisfaction – a lack of specific support for the regime – ought to present no problems. We have insisted throughout that protest in complex modern political systems arises from a value-driven need for people with new political demands and ideas to get these new issues onto the political agenda. The same applies to many of those who feel that even in areas that are currently in the centre of political debate, the system is failing to deliver. Thus, greater policy dissatisfaction should lead to higher protest potential. In contrast, the rôle of specific support for the authority – whether or not one supports the political party in power – is much more problematic. Leftists, for example, will say they support the major party of the Left when it is in power, but such support will tend to be highly conditional. Do they surrender their protest options *on principle* when a Socialist party forms a government? It does not seem very likely. Similarly, Rightist critics of a Socialist administration tend to be caught in a dilemma. They will mobilise against a Socialist government in conventional ways but things have to get pretty drastic before they will take to the streets. That would conflict with the ideas of social order that their political philosophy is pledged to defend. In some places, therefore, they will leave that option to the armed forces.

What then, do the data tell us about these problems? Starting as before with the effects of diffuse support, we find that the belief that the political system is responsive to demands has no relation at all to levels of protest potential; there is a neutral association in each country. This may seem strange; surely protest is a reaction to being ignored? If one believes that the system is deaf to the needs of ordinary citizens, the recourse to protest methods is an obvious one. For some people, this is undoubtedly true. The problem is that this kind of cynicism is fairly widespread nowadays and is certainly not confined to the ranks of the protesters. Among many, probably among the majority, a cynical view of the willingness of politicians and officials to involve themselves in the needs and demands of ordinary people simply increases their sense of apathy and uninterest in politicians and all their works. It is also likely that many of those who feel that the system is uncaring and remote are among the most disadvantaged in society who, as the survey has shown, have the fewest resources to involve themselves in the energetic and time-consuming business of political protest.

The second aspect of diffuse support – personal internal efficacy – shows the predicted impact upon protest potential. Those who believe they can understand the complexities of modern politics and have more channels of influence beyond the polling booth are, in every national sample, more likely to add protest methods to their political options. The impact of efficacy is greatest in Britain (where it outweighs all other kinds of evaluation), The Netherlands and Germany but less in the United States and Austria.

This finding adds considerable force to earlier speculations about why there is a positive association between protest potential and conventional political participation. It is not only a structural association, that complex political conflicts in modern societies attract both kinds of behaviour. It is also because they share the same source in diffuse support in the same individuals: the belief in one's ability to be a competent political actor. Note too that it is not merely the element of political comprehension implied in the efficacy measure that is producing this unity of effect. In this analysis, the effects of higher levels of ideological thinking have already been accounted for and remain, of themselves, a significant and independent contributor to higher levels of protest potential. Efficacy is an additional statement of self-belief and, as such, is a highly significant source of the whole range of political behaviour in modern Western democracies.

As everything that has gone before would lead one to expect, policy dissatisfaction – a lack of specific support for the regime – has a powerful and independent impact on levels of protest potential. The more people feel that the system is failing to do the things it is supposed to do, the more they are drawn to the use of protest methods. This is true independently of the effects of postmaterialism. Thus we find strong confirmation of the general model suggested earlier. Value choices become politicised. They have greater impact upon protest potential through the way people evaluate the political system – both in terms of its performance and in terms of the dominant policy priorities of the regime which they judge inappropriate. The previous chapter provided a strong hint of this when it was shown that postmaterialist values contributed most to policy dissatisfaction when combined with anti-Establishment sympathies.

The effects of specific support for the authorities, whether or not one supports the party in power, proved as problematic as seemed likely in the discussion above. It depended entirely upon which kind of party was in power at the time of the survey. In countries having conservative governments (Britain and the United States) opposition increased protest potential. In countries governed by the major party of the Left (Germany, Austria, and The Netherlands) opposition was associated with lower protest potential. This means that the powerful effect of the underlying Left-Right dimension in politics has seeped into the system-support model of political behaviour when applied to protest potential. When the measure of government or opposition support is taken out of the calculation and replaced by a measure of whether respondents voted for a Left or Right party in the last general election, the picture becomes suddenly clear. Independently of all other measures, it must be stressed again, to be Left is to favour protest, to be Right is to reject it. This additional feature of the evaluation model of political behaviour is included in Figure 6.3.

6.2.1 Summary

The kinds of judgements people make about their political system and the way it is presently working, their 'political evaluations', intervene to promote political action. A broad measure of support for the system itself, for the 'rules of the game' if you will, together with a sense of self-belief in one's ability to act politically will promote conventional political participation. Opposition to existing authorities will provide a further stimulus. Seeing oneself as a competent political actor also promotes protest potential but the crucial evaluative source of protest is unhappiness with the existing political agenda, feeling that the political system has the wrong priorities and that change is needed.

This urge to reorder national priorities does not necessarily contain a challenge to the entire political system. Protest tactics are used equally by those who still see value in the present system and those who do not. If further proof were needed, this shows decisively that the spread of protest potential and the use of even the more extreme protest methods that the scale includes, does not signal the imminent demise of the democratic party systems of Western Europe and the United States. It is a challenge to what parties do or, more usually, what they fail to do and not a bid to install a new kind of political regime. Among the cross-section of the five national publics who answered these survey questions, protest is protest and not revolution.

6.3 THE FINAL MODEL OF POLITICAL ACTION

This evidence that different political evaluations form the final linkage in the general model of conventional and unconventional political behaviour led to a reformulation of the general model shown in Figure 6.4. In terms of measurement, the only difference between Political Evaluations 'A' and 'B' is that 'A' includes the evaluation of the existing Government and 'B' (the antecedent of protest potential) does not. For protest potential, the contribution of Left voting is introduced instead. Left voting, as a sign of general sympathy for a Leftist point of view, was found to be an indispensable part of an explanation of protest potential even when the impact of postmaterialism and age were held constant. While it may be said that a leftist point of view implies a negative evaluation of political regimes supportive of the capitalist economies in each of the five countries, it is conceptually different from the other evaluations included in the model and so is retained in a separate rôle.

One further analysis was carried out in order to determine the size of the relative contributions made by each of the main elements to the general model of political action. In this analysis, all the evaluations were combined into a single evaluation measure. This was

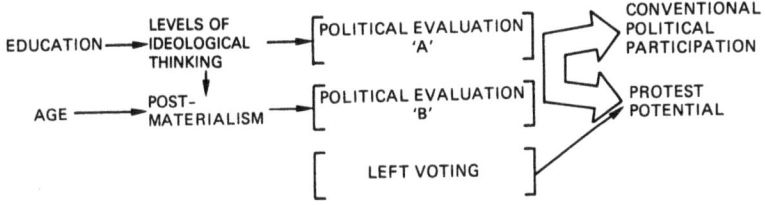

FIGURE 6.4 *The Revised Model of Political Action*

done in order to assess the overall contribution that judgement – what people feel – makes to the explanation of political behaviour. We know that what people feel makes a difference but, once background effects like age, education, values and ideology are accounted for, how *much* difference does political judgement really make?

The analysis showed that with respect to conventional political participation, judgement is very important indeed. In Germany, for example, the way people evaluate their political system and its performance outweighs all other factors in directing people into conventional political activity. Germans have a strong attachment to their political system. Those who participate in it do so from a strong sense of political competence. In other countries, political evaluations still play a very important rôle in promoting conventional participation, second only to the powerful effects of higher levels of ideological thinking. In The Netherlands the balance of influence is shared almost equally between judgement and ideological thinking. In Britain, the United States and Austria, ideological thinking is the stronger influence.

Age (that is, being *older*) and education retain some independent power to promote conventional political participation, except in Austria, but most of the predictive power of education, for example, is superseded by the higher levels of ideological thinking that education promotes. Postmaterialism has little rôle in this equation, except in Germany where postmaterialists are becoming more involved in the conventional political arena. It is no coincidence, therefore, that the Green Movement in Germany, unlike environmental movements elsewhere, penetrated the conventional party system by winning seats in many regional and state assemblies and in the national parliament in Bonn.

These considerations apart, the message is clear: people involve themselves in conventional political activity because they have the mental skills that allow them to see the political process as an ideological conflict. Such skills come hand-in-hand with the ability to make political judgements. They take sides in the political conflict but support the rules that govern its conduct. They tend also to be self-consciously aware of their skills. This gives them the self-confidence to be able to advertise their views to others in words and deeds. Their political judgements motivate them to do so.

The picture that unfolds with respect to protest potential is very different. Evaluations, the political judgements people make, play a relatively minor rôle compared to other factors. Not that evaluation is completely unimportant. Independently of other things, the same political self-confidence that promotes conventional activity also increases protest potential. So does a critical view of public policy and Government performance. But the greatest balance of influence is shared between four major factors: age (that is, being *younger*, of course), higher levels of ideological thinking, postmaterialism and voting for Left parties. Education is again relegated to a minor rôle since its influence is reinterpreted in the forms of ideological thinking and value choices. Education is, as the structure of the revised general model suggests, an important *source* of developments in mass political thinking rather than a direct cause of protest potential. In this sense, higher education may be acquitted of the direct rôle assigned to it by many observers of the spread of protest tactics in the 1960s and 1970s. Education is promoting the basic skills that allow young people to expand their political repertory. So it should, it is a function of their better understanding. It does not, of itself, provide the motivation. In the same way, sex education does not, of itself, motivate promiscuity. It just makes people better at it and, hopefully, more responsible too.

Weighing the influence of the four most important antecedents of protest potential: youth, values, ideology and Leftism, one finds some interesting cross-national differences. In Austria higher levels of ideological thinking are the decisive influence, while Leftism and values hardly enter the picture at all. This again is due to the much more restricted distribution of political action in Austria and the success of the then Socialist Government in meeting quite a lot of the demands of the Left. Even the most determined protesters can lose interest when the Government keeps doing the things they want. Thus, protest potential in Austria at that time was restricted to the political intelligentsia to a far greater extent than elsewhere.

In The Netherlands, Left voting emerged as a dominant influence, together with ideological thinking. This is surprising perhaps because The Netherlands has been characterised in earlier discussions as the true home of both protest and postmaterialism. However, voting for one of several Left parties in The Netherlands in the early 1970s was to express support for some highly active political groups who spent more of their time protesting on the streets of Amsterdam than they did haunting the corridors of power in The Hague. Support for this style of party would therefore be directly related to one's own choice of political action.

In fact, postmaterialism was not the dominant force behind protest potential in any of the five countries in the survey. Leftism (except in Austria), ideological thinking and, in Britain and the United States, even political evaluation slightly exceeded postmaterialism in the magnitude of their direct and independent influence on protest. This again tends to confirm what is suggested in the way the general model is drawn in Figure 6.4. Postmaterialism is a very basic antecedent of protest potential but it plays more of an intermediatory than a direct rôle. It has its maximum effect when associated with an active Leftist critique of the performance of the present system. So many of the really dramatic political protests seen in the last two decades, especially in Europe, tended to occur when the Left and the New Left agreed in their critique on an issue. Demonstrations in opposition to apartheid in South Africa are good examples of this.

In some ways, the most remarkable thing in this analysis is also the most obvious. The direct influence of age upon protest potential survives all the mediating effects of values, ideology, evaluations and Left affiliation combined. These latter four measures summarise people's answers to 54 questions in the survey interview. Yet the answer to the question 'How old are you?' still explains a large part of the protest potential measured in each country even when the answers obtained to the other 53 questions are accounted for in the analysis. In Germany and most especially in Britain and the United States, age remains the single most potent explanation of protest potential. Nor is it simply a matter of the oldest respondents resigning the political fray. The effect of age is linear. As one passes through one's 30s and into one's 40s (as your present author will testify) and on into the 50s and 60s, so political protest becomes more and more an intimidatingly energetic prospect.

This simple but important observation of the effects of age does not detract from what has gone before. The politicisation of ideology and values is still the major driving force behind the use of protest tactics.

Without these, probably little *political* protest would occur, even among the young. It does, however, make more understandable the Protester category in the Political Behaviour Repertory. Compared to the Activists and Reformists they are a-political. What they are is young.

6.4 SUMMARY

This chapter has led to an important conclusion about the nature of mass politics in Western nations. This conclusion also points up a paradox. Conventional political participation is the form of behaviour that is organised and sanctioned by existing élites and authorities. Yet its main source of motivation in individuals tends to be associated with issues – how people take sides. True, participants tend to be people who accept the rules of the game and understand politics well, but the spur to action seems a very individual one. They respond to what is happening in politics and act on a sense of self-confidence that they can do something about it by getting involved at the grass roots. In contrast political protest in its stronger forms is not sanctioned and organised by the existing authorities. On the contrary, authorities sometimes have a hard time coping with it and wish very much that people would not do it. Yet the main source of motivation in individuals tends to be associated more with their evaluation of the workings of the whole political and social system. So, whereas political protest seems, *when it occurs*, to have an ad hoc character, tied often to a single emotive issue, those who tend to get involved do so because they have an *enduring* commitment to social change.

This means that what we have been examining in this chapter is evidence of a real political process. The willingness to protest is not just a feeling that comes over people from time to time, possibly when they feel put upon by an unreasonable authority. It is an abiding political resource that is widespread in the community. It arises from mass attitudinal processes that are every bit as significant and enduring as those that support conventional political participation in the party system.

7 Generations and Families

This chapter is about political socialisation, the way in which each new generation acquires its political values and habits. We need to enter this field because the Political Action Study was always concerned with the explanation of political *change*. Already we have alluded to the importance of age and to changes in political values among the young in explaining what appear to be new forms of political behaviour. A constant theme of previous chapters has been that something new is going on and that it has something to do with real intergenerational change. The postwar generations of Western Europe and the United States have made new choices. They have new values, new demands and are set to tackle the world of politics in ways quite different from those favoured by earlier generations.

The main problem about discussing political change hitherto has been that cross-sectional survey data such as these do not give the analyst sufficient authority to speak directly about real political changes. Some helpful comparisons have been made with earlier studies but the main concerns, those that appear in the general model of political action, are represented by measures taken at only one point in time. Trend data, the same questions asked in successive surveys, are more helpful but even these do not allow one to say how changes in attitudes, for example, are linked to changes in behaviour in individual respondents. In the end, only longitudinal data give real authority to discuss how people's views change over time. That is to say, the same people are reinterviewed over a long period of their lives. Such studies are immensely difficult. For this and other good reasons, guessing about change on the basis of a single study is certainly allowed. There is, however, one research strategy that can add considerable value to well-informed guesswork: the study of families.

Such a strategy still does not inform one directly about political change. A family at one point in time is just that. It does, however, allow one to say a great deal more about how successfully one generation is transmitting its view of the political world to the next. The success or failure of that process is a strong indicator of the durability of existing political forms. The family is held to be the crucible of political continuity. Probably few parents sit their children down to explicit lectures on the political system but they do transmit a sense of the worth of the political system in its broadest sense. This is what was called in the previous chapter 'diffuse support for the regime'. Even critical writers recognise the force of these generalised feelings of support for the political system. Habermas calls it 'mass loyalty'. It tends to come as a package together with ethnic or religious identity, class consciousness, nationality, patriotism, respect for the institutions of authority (particularly if they are headed by a Royal Family), all adding up to a basic assumption that the system we have is one we ought to keep. This tends to be true even if one lives in a family where fierce partisan loyalties are expressed every day.

When the Political Action Study was planned in 1971, there was a widespread view among both popular and academic observers that something had gone wrong with this process. As the television brought news of yet another campus reduced to an embattled confusion, explanations were urgently sought as to the young protesters' motives. Some loose ideas concerning Oedipal rebellion were expressed. These tended to overlook the fact that huge numbers of young women were involved and that previous generations had remained quiet. Why now? Here Dr Spock and others were held culpable. Liberal and over-indulgent child raising in the postwar period had produced a generation too accustomed to unrestrained self-expression. There was a 'generation gap'.

Some of these explanations strayed into self-parody but they arose from a serious point. Families are different nowadays. They are smaller and more socially isolated than the extended family of prewar days. Styles of child-rearing had changed, patriarchy had receded, working mothers become usual, divorce more common. Education had expanded to extend the period of dependent childhood in the economic sense while family regimes had relaxed to shorten it in the social sense. The journey from childhood to full adult status now starts earlier and ends later. It would be strange if such important changes in the basic social unit of Western society had no social or political consequences at all. Such developments in cultural pursuits and consumer patterns were evident to all. New departures in political behaviour were, it was agreed, bound to follow.

To say that there is a generation gap between the political values of the young compared to those older is to formulate a very precise research hypothesis. If the lines of political socialisation have been interrupted in this way, then children will be found to have views different from those of their parents. This is what the Political Action

Study undertook to discover. The means to do so were simple. Whenever an interviewer found her respondent to be aged 16 to 20 years old, she randomly selected one of that person's parents for a second interview in that household. Likewise, if her respondent was the parent of one or more children aged 16 to 20, that child or a randomly selected child among more of that age, was selected for a second interview. In this way a sub-sample of *parent-child pairs* was added to each national data set. There were about 200 of these in each of the five countries, fewest in Britain (173), most in Germany (257). These are the data that will be used in this chapter.

Throughout, the younger members of each of these pairs will be called 'children'. Since they are aged 16 to 20, many are old enough to vote, to go to college, or even to have had this book assigned to them for their course in political science. They might well resent being called 'children'. The term is used here solely as a description of their relationship to their parents, and anyway it is a nicer word than 'offspring' or 'issue'. In the tables, 'offspring' is retained from the original volume for the sake of a statistical term and the need to be consistent about these things, as in '0→52%', for example.

Note carefully that we now have a new *unit of analysis*: the parent-child *pair*. Each piece of information is generated by two people, one a parent, the other a child, but it is *one* piece of information, not two. This, at least, is the case when the basic research question is in focus: do parents and children agree and, if not, what is the extent of disagreement and in which direction? We will, however, work up to this point step by step. Such caution is necessary because pair-data is not at all as easy to handle as it may appear. There are so many things to look at simultaneously. Basically these are of two kinds: *group* correspondence and *pair* correspondence. Measures of group correspondence are the extent to which parents, as a group, make replies that are similar to those made by children, also taken as a group. Here the information given by parents and by children are treated separately and not linked together, except, as we shall see below, where the proportions of agreeing and disagreeing pairs are considered. This information provides the broad limits of agreement and disagreement between the two generations. Measures of pair correspondence link the replies of individual parents to those given by their own child to provide a single piece of information describing how successfully or unsuccessfully parents have transmitted their views to their children. Three measures of both group and pair correspondence were used and all

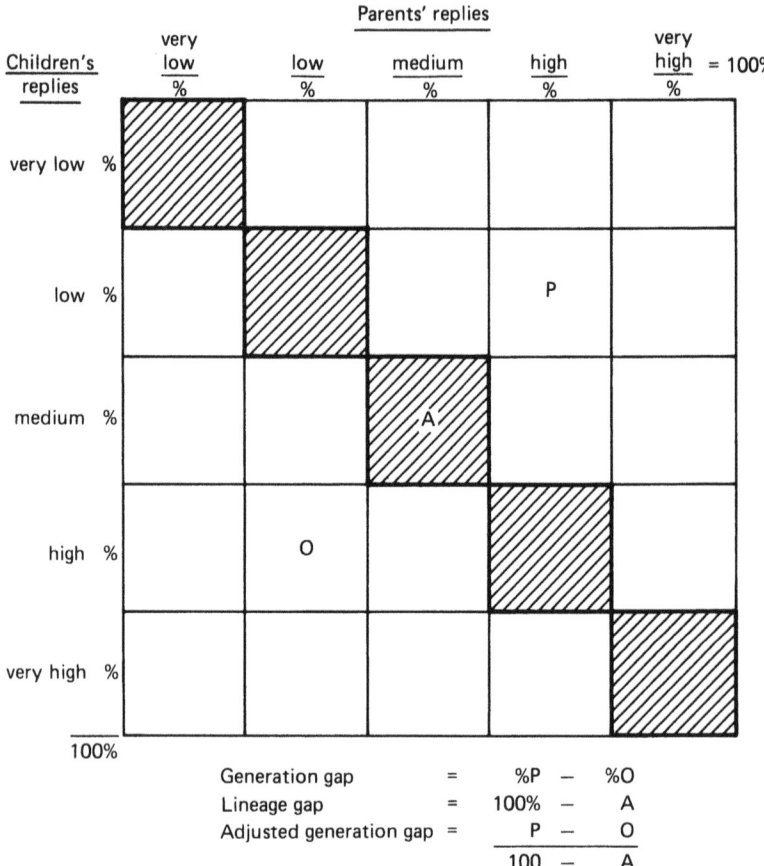

FIGURE 7.1 *Measures of Agreement and Disagreement between Parents and their Children*

will appear in the tables that follow. To understand these, the diagram in Figure 7.1 should be studied carefully.

Let us suppose that Figure 7.1 deals with a measure of political conservatism. It has five categories ranging from 'very low' to 'very high'. Each of the 25 cells represents the views of parents linked to the views of their children. The five shaded cells of the diagonal, therefore, contain all those paired cases where an individual parent gave the same reply as his or her child. All the other cells represent pairs who differed. The upper-right side of a diagonal ('P') are cells where parents are more conservative than their children. The lower-left side of the diagonal ('O') are cells where children are more conservative than their parents. This is all the information we need to construct our measures. These are as follows:

Group correspondence measures:

(1) The simple marginal distributions of parents compared to children, that is, the proportion of parents falling into each of the five 'conservatism' categories put alongside the same distribution for children.
(2) The average score of parents compared to the average score of children.
(3) The *generation gap*: this is calculated by the proportion of *all* parents who scored higher on the scale than their children ('P') from the proportion of all children who scored higher on the scale than their parents ('O'). Thus, if 40% of parents scored higher than their children and 15% of children scored higher than their parents, the generation gap will be shown as '25% → P'. That is to say, there is a net generation gap of 25% greater conservatism in the direction of the parents.

Pair correspondence measures:

(1) The *lineage gap*: this is calculated by subtracting the proportion of all *pairs* who agreed (namely, those lying on the shaded diagonal 'A') from 100%. Simply, what percentage of pairs failed to agree.
(2) The *adjusted generation gap*: this is calculated by dividing the generation gap by the lineage gap. This ratio represents the amount of disagreement that occurred within pairs given the total amount of disagreement among all pairs.
(3) *Pair correlations*: the lineage gap and the generation gaps are measures of *absolute* agreement in that they rely on the proportion of pairs who gave *exactly* the same answer. This may be unrealistic, especially when a measure has many categories to choose among. A correlation coefficient measures the extent to which parents who score above the average will have children who also score higher than others, even though their scores may not be identical to their parents'. It measures how accurately one can predict the *direction* of a child's score if you know the parent's score, and vice versa. Two coefficients will be shown called Tau and Gamma. Each ranges from + 1.0 to − 1.0 A plus-one (+ 1.0) coefficient means that knowledge of the

parent's score will always predict the child's. A minus-one (− 1.0) coefficient will do the same, except that a child will always have the opposite score, low rather than high, high rather than low. In terms of Figure 7.1, all cases will lie on the diagonal. A plus-one (+ 1.0) coefficient means all pairs occupy the top left to bottom right diagonal shown as shaded. The minus one (− 1.0) coefficient means all pairs will lie on the opposite, bottom left to top right diagonal. None of this ever happens, of course, but a high positive correlation of + 0.60, for example, means that many paired cases will lie on the diagonal while others will lie near it. Few pairs will be in the high-disagreement cells in the off-diagonal corners. The problem with these correlation measures is that the diagonal can *move*. Suppose all parents scored exactly one category higher on the conservatism scale than did their child. The correlation would be + 1.0 and so you can perfectly predict each child's score from knowledge of his or her parent's score. But no-one agreed. That is why we need to keep an eye on all these measures at once. In such a case the generation gap figure would have been '100% → P'. (Wouldn't it? Check for yourself.)

That concludes a necessary statistics lesson. Readers should be sure they understand these simple calculations or little of what follows will make much sense. The task now will be to take each of the important aspects of the general model of political action and search for those points in the chain that are being subjected to the greatest intergenerational strain. What aspects of political attitudes and behaviour do children appear to have inherited from their home backgrounds (that is, from their parents' views) and what aspects are they creating for themselves? At what points have the young departed? Two important aspects of the general model can be taken for granted: age, since children are invariably younger than their parents, and education. Half our sample of 16–20 year olds are not yet of university age, so it is pointless trying to compare their education to their parents'. Let us start, then, with the point of greatest potential weakness – postmaterialism.

Postmaterialism: What can we expect? Chapter 4 showed clearly that pure postmaterialist value choices, while still a minority interest in all age groups, occurred far more commonly among the young. The ratio of postmaterialists to materialists increased dramatically among successively younger age groups. The sheer scale of these differences was held to be evidence for real intergenerational change. This idea was supported by several helpful clues. The rate at which postmaterialist value choices had emerged among the young matched the rate of relative economic improvement in each country – the contrast between Britain and Germany being especially telling. Some inquiries into family background also suggested real intergenerational change. For example, postmaterialists whose fathers had supported Right-wing parties were apt to break with family voting traditions and vote Left.

However persuasive these ideas may be, they remain in the realm of well-informed guesswork. What now needs to be shown is that there is real intergenerational discontinuity, that parents and their offspring have different value priorities. All the necessary evidence is set out in Table 7.1 following the formula described above.

Consider first the case of Germany. The message from the marginal distributions is clear enough: 49% of children are found on the postmaterialist side of the five-point scale compared to only 10% of the parents. The average values are 3.3 versus 2.2. Parents and children are occupying different sides of the mid-point of the scale. In terms of purest postmaterialist choices, young Germans are *11 times* more likely to choose these priorities than are their parents. And this, it should be borne in mind, is a comparison between people who are 16–20 years old and their parents who, for the most part, will only be in their 40s. The economic and social transformation of postwar Germany has clearly wrought a corresponding change in political value priorities. (Writing this in Berlin, your author is surrounded by the evidence. The Alternative Movement permeates every aspect of this city.) The remaining evidence below the distributions bears out the case for real intergenerational change in Germany. The lineage gap is 75% (that is, only 25% of pairs are in agreement). The generation gap is '52% → 0' (that is, 62% of the children were more postmaterialist than their parents while only 10% of the parents were more postmaterialist than their children. So, 62% − 10% = 52%). This leaves a massive adjusted generation gap of .69 (that is, 52 ÷ 75 = 0.693). Relative disagreement is as great as absolute disagreement. The correlations are positive but tiny (Tau = .12, Gamma = .15). This means that there is a slight tendency for parents who scored relatively higher or lower on the scale to have children who (possibly from different *points* on the scale) score correspondingly higher or lower but it is almost negligible. These correlations were worked out

TABLE 7.1 Postmaterialism

	The Netherlands		Britain		United States		Germany		Austria	
	Parents	Offspring	Parents	Offspring	Parents	Offspring	Parents	Offspring	Parents	Offspring
Postmaterialism:										
Low 1	4%[a]	3%	4%	6%	13%	6%	26%	10%	21%	9%
2	32	10	24	21	32	19	42	19	37	32
3	26	21	36	28	28	22	22	22	12	19
4	27	32	26	36	19	33	8	26	27	28
High 5	12	33	10	9	9	20	2	23	3	13
$\bar{X}$	3.1	3.8	3.2	3.2	2.8	3.4	2.2	3.3	2.7	3.1
N	(211)	(214)	(168)	(168)	(236)	(239)	(253)	(249)	(202)	(205)
Pair Relationships:[b]										
tau-b	.08		−.03		.13		.12		.15	
gamma	.09		−.03		.16		.15		.17	
lineage gap	64%		63%		70%		75%		57%	
generation gap	31%—O		3%—O		26%—O		52%—O		28%—O	
adj. ""	.48		.05		.37		.69		.49	
N	(207)		(164)		(231)		(246)		(197)	

a. Percentages are based on a collapsing of the original ten-point scale.
b. Correlations are based on the original ten-point index. Gap figures are based on treating cells directly adjacent to main diagonal as part of main diagonal in the 10 × 10 matrix.

on the original ten-point scale so this is especially good evidence of real value discontinuity between German parents and their children.

The Netherlands, the United States and Austria all approximate to the German case, though not quite as dramatically. Postmaterialists are still strikingly more common among children than among parents. The adjusted generation gaps are large: .48, .37 and .49 respectively. The relative disagreement measured by insignificant correlation coefficients is also great. In these countries, too, the emergence of significant minorities of postmaterialists among the young is associated with a rupture in the transmission of political values within the family.

Mysteriously, none of this is true in Britain. The distribution of materialists and postmaterialists is more or less the same among parents compared to children. They have the same average score of 3.2 on the five-point scale. There is almost no generation gap; the proportion of children who are more postmaterialist than their parents exceeds the proportion of parents who are more postmaterialist than their children by a mere 3%. Relative agreement, the correlation coefficients, is actually negative though as near to zero as makes no difference (-0.03). This does *not* mean, however, that British children adopt their parents' views. If this were so, the correlations would be high. The lineage gap is as high as it is elsewhere. That is to say, 63% of pairs disagree. This means that they disagree in large numbers but in random directions. There are about as many postmaterialist British parents with materialist children as there are materialist parents with postmaterialist children.

One could have predicted this result partly from Table 4.2 in chapter 4. For the British sample as a whole the ratio of materialists to postmaterialists among the 16–24 year olds is 21%:13%. Among those more than 20 years older, the 40 to 59 year old Britons, it averages 27%:10%. These are broadly similar figures between the younger and older British generations but in other countries it is dramatically different. In Germany, for example, the corresponding figures are 32%:15% among younger Germans compared to 60%:4% among the older.

What was suggested by the aggregate data is now confirmed by the study of families. Britain's relatively slow economic advance since the war, starting from a relatively high base, has made little impression on the balance of political value choices across generations. There is plenty of intergenerational disagreement but not systematically in the postmaterialist direction among the young compared to the previous generation. Elsewhere, outstandingly so in Germany but less dramatically (as one might expect) in the United States, fast economic growth and the equally fast fading of the horrors of war have wrought a transformation in value priorities that seems to reflect real change between *adjacent* generations: parents and children. It is still open to us to believe that as these children grow up they will repent of their postmaterialism and end up after all just like their parents but it is hardly likely. Postmaterialism seems likely to claim a long-held place in the general model of political action. It will continue to pose new political issues and attract ad hoc political groupings to press their cause. The means to force those new issues onto the national agenda, meeting entrenched materialist interests head-on, will be biased in favour of political protest. The model says that the efficiency of this process will be enhanced by higher levels of ideological thinking. We will now see how this very different element in the general model is also transmitted intergenerationally.

Levels of Ideological Thinking: Unlike postmaterialism, we are now dealing with a cognitive dimension – with thinking rather than feeling, with mental skills and not partisan sentiment. This means that it is something that parents, generally speaking, ought to be better at than their children. Qualitative improvements in education ought perhaps to give children some advantages but these are likely to be outweighed by their parents' greater experience of the world, their monopoly of the morning paper, and so on. On the other hand, because we are dealing with mental skills in politics, politically knowledgeable parents ought to have politically knowledgeable children just as parents who have other mental skills, say in literature or music, will tend to encourage their children to acquire them too. Conversely, the homes of children who have politically illiterate or uninterested parents will be silent on all political matters and they will have least chance of picking up any basic political information at home either directly from their parents or from secondary sources. Conversation with visitors will avoid politics and when a current affairs programme appears on television another channel will be selected.

The data selected to test these simple ideas is shown in Table 7.2 in exactly the same format as before. The measure used is solely the 'active use' measure described in chapter 3, and not the combined 'levels of ideological thinking in politics' because too many children

TABLE 7.2 Understanding of Left-Right Continuum

	The Netherlands		Britain		United States		Germany		Austria	
	Parents	Offspring	Parents	Offspring	Parents	Offspring	Parents	Offspring	Parents	Offspring
Understanding:										
Low 1	6%[a]	11%	18%	34%	30%	29%	7%	11%	26%	31%
2	23	20	17	22	14	18	9	13	14	29
3	4	2	12	12	18	18	2	4	6	8
4	20	14	35	18	2	2	30	22	21	18
5	19	14	9	6	11	6	22	21	15	9
High 6	27	38	9	8	26	27	32	30	18	14
$\bar{X}$	4.0	4.1	3.3	2.6	3.3	3.2	4.5	4.2	3.4	3.0
N	(233)	(233)	(173)	(173)	(244)	(244)	(257)	(257)	(212)	(212)
Pair Relationships:[b]										
tau-b	.22		.17		.21		.19		.20	
gamma	.28		.21		.26		.24		.24	
lineage gap	45%		56%		50%		40%		48%	
generation gap[c]	4%–O		24%–P		4%–P		6%–P		13%–P	
adj. "	.09		.43		.08		.15		.27	
N	(223)		(173)		(244)		(257)		(212)	

a. Percentages are based on a collapsing of the original eight-point scale. All missing data cases are in the "low" category.
b. Correlations are based on the original eight-point scale. Gap figures are based on treating cells directly adjacent to main diagonal as part of main diagonal in the 8 × 8 matrix.
c. The percentage entry shows the difference between the proportion on one side of the diagonal and that on the other side in the parent-offspring matrices. P = parents, O = offspring.

had trouble really deciding what they liked and disliked about the two major political parties.

The evidence in favour of the view that mental skills in politics are smoothly transmitted between generations is, to say the least of it, uncertain. Overall, the distribution of the 'active use of ideological thinking in politics' is similar among parents compared to children and the generation gap is small except in Britain where children, as a group, lag behind parents. This is not because British parents are so knowledgeable. Quite the reverse, it is because the British children are so politically dim. For example, only 14% of British children are ideologues or near-ideologues compared to 51% of the German children and 52% of the Dutch. The apparently dismal British response has something to do with the strength of the Labour/Conservative dichotomy which, for British parents as well as children, actually defines the Left/Right continuum at an ideologically low level. Even so, the proportion who are simply unable to recognise it at all is very high. The same is true in the United States but the American distribution is bi-modal. Either they, parents and children alike, recognise Left-Right ideologically or, in similar numbers, they do not recognise it at all. Austria tends toward the British example, though with a larger minority of ideologues among both parents and children.

In terms of pair correspondence, continuity is relatively weak. In each country, no more than half of the pairs are found sharing the same level of ideological thinking and, because the generation gaps (except in Britain) are small, variation occurs in both directions. There are plenty of children who know more than their parents. It would be of value to know who they learned it from. In Germany it was almost certainly from their schools. Even in relative terms, correspondence is weak. More knowledgeable parents tend to have more knowledgeable children but it is an uncertain bet to try to predict very accurately if an individual child, at any level, scores higher than other children just because his or her parent scores higher than other parents.

The level of ideological thinking is the one element in the model that fuels both conventional and unconventional political action equally. It is, as the original authors of *Political Action* say, 'a bit unsettling' to find that so basic a factor as mental skills in politics, one that has important consequences for the formation of political judgements and the behaviour such judgements imply, should be so imperfectly transmitted within families. It is possible that more alignment will occur when these children grow older (half are only 16 or 17) and come to view the political world as people who have, after all, grown up not unlike their parents and who will talk to them as one adult to another about grown up things like politics. As someone once said: 'It is strange, you know, as I get older my father gets smarter'. Even so, a large minority of children who have acquired some mental skills in politics, in this case the ability to recognise the Left-Right continuum in more than a basic way, have managed this for themselves. It is less surprising, then, that many of them have also acquired new political values at the same time. Autonomy of thought implies autonomy of choice. The next logical step is to see how political partisanship, judgement and evaluation emerge within families.

Political Partisanship: Since we have just discussed understanding of the Left-Right continuum, the obvious place to start an investigation into political partisanship within families is parents' and children's self-placement on this dimension. A working hypothesis is easily come by: children are more 'Left-wing' than their parents. To test this idea, Table 7.3 first excludes all those who failed completely to understand the idea of 'Left' and 'Right'. The data are then presented as before.

The 'young Leftists' hypothesis does not fare well. Only in The Netherlands and Germany do children place themselves to the left of their parents in any systematic way. Even here, differences are not great: 37% of children in Germany, for example, place themselves to the left of centre, compared to 21% of parents and in both generations a 'centre-ist' stance is the most common. The Dutch case is particularly interesting. Here the generation gap is larger: '32% → P' compared to 21% in Germany and less than 10% elsewhere. Yet The Netherlands has the highest rate of *relative* agreement. That is to say, although Dutch children place themselves to the left of their parents, Left-wing children tend quite strongly to have parents who are more Left-wing than other parents. This tends also to be true in Austria and Britain but here there is no generation gap. There is the same *amount* of absolute disagreement, indicated by large lineage gaps in all countries, but except in The Netherlands and Germany it tends to be in random directions. In the United States there is not even any relative agreement between generations. Both American generations cluster in the centre of the scale and those children that venture in

TABLE 7.3 Placement on Left-Right Continuum

	The Netherlands		Britain		United States		Germany		Austria	
	Parents	Offspring	Parents	Offspring	Parents	Offspring	Parents	Offspring	Parents	Offspring
Left-right Placement:										
Left 1	8%	12%	12%	6%	3%	8%	2%	5%	6%	6%
2	18	36	21	22	12	22	19	32	17	19
3	32	32	38	47	54	42	45	43	40	42
4	30	17	21	24	20	22	28	16	29	22
Right 5	12	4	8	1	10	5	7	4	9	11
$\bar{X}$	3.2	2.7	2.9	2.9	3.2	2.9	3.2	2.8	3.2	3.2
N	(210)	(198)	(142)	(115)	(172)	(173)	(240)	(229)	(157)	(147)
Pair Relationships:[a]										
tau-b	.31		.24		.05		.17		.29	
gamma	.35		.28		.06		.20		.33	
lineage gap	57%		51%		56%		50%		47%	
generation gap	32%–P		2%–P		9%–P		21%–P		5%–P	
adj. "	.56		.04		.16		.42		.11	
N	(189)		(102)		(134)		(221)		(124)	

a. Correlations are based on the original ten-point scale. Gap figures are based on treating cells directly adjacent to main diagonal as part of main diagonal in the 10 × 10 matrix.

either direction do so without reference to their parents' views in any way. The overall weakness of parents' transmission of their broad political stance to their children is particularly surprising given that the analysis excluded the quite substantial numbers who failed to recognise the Left-Right dimension at all. The children in this analysis all shared with their parents at least a basic recognition of what Left and Right in politics means. Having learned this much one would imagine that they would have taken up at least a similar relative position as their parents as appears to be the case in The Netherlands. One possibility is that politically aware Left-wing children claim to be more Left-wing than their parents, while Right-wing children claim to be more Right-wing than their parents. Adolescents are said to be given to extremism of both kinds. The numbers, however, are rather too small to allow such detailed analysis.

Another possibility is that the adolescent generation has simply not settled down yet in their orientation to the real political world. They have their basic values sorted out quite well, as Table 7.1 showed, but the business of party politics and conflicts between political interest groups will seem to many of them rather remote. Many of them will not yet have had the chance to vote in an election. The survey found strong evidence for such a lack of political attachment. For example, only about half of the adolescents in the four European countries said that there was *any* political party to which they '. . . usually felt closest' though in the United States this figure was higher (77%). Among the parents, party attachment was far more common, ranging from a (surprisingly low) figure in Germany of 68% up to 91% in The Netherlands. The strength of this party attachment is also much greater among parents than their children. Even those children who choose to support a particular party are, in all countries, far less likely than their parents to say they feel 'close' or 'very close' to their chosen party.

Among those of the adolescent generation who have made up their minds which party to support, a rather different picture of agreement with parents emerges. They tend strongly to support the same party or at least to promise their vote in the same 'Left' or 'Right' direction as their parents. This is less true of the Dutch, who have so many parties to choose among, and in The Netherlands alone do children tend more than their parents to choose a Leftist party to support. Elsewhere, even in Germany where children are generally more 'Left-wing' than their parents, there is very little difference between the two generations in their choice of a Left or Non-Left political party. There is no generation gap and the level of agreement is extraordinarily high. The Gamma correlation coefficient is .83 in Germany, .86, in the United States, in Britain .91 and a near-perfect .98 in Austria.

Thus, when adolescents do make up their minds which party to support, they follow, initially at least, the broad voting tendency of their parents very faithfully. In Austria, only 9% of pairs disagree on the direction of their party choice; in Britain only 17%.

This level of agreement is enough to bring a smile to the face of the average socio-biologist. It is certainly strong evidence for the preservation of party cleavages by transmission within the family. It is all the more remarkable when one recalls evidence from other surveys (cf. Butler and Stokes in Britain) that mothers and fathers in the same family tend often to vote in opposite directions so children cannot follow both preferences simultaneously. On the other hand, only about half of children had chosen a party at all. Perhaps those that did are those who tend to live in homes where party preference is uniform and so are doubly encouraged to follow its direction.

7.1 POLITICAL EVALUATIONS

7.1.1 Diffuse Support for the Regime

It has been argued that the political value that one generation is most likely to pass on to the next, apart from party preference, is an overall sense of the worth of the system. For democracies to endure, each succeeding generation must accept the rules of the game. The party system and its instruments of national and local administration should be seen as appropriate and as responsive to the broad needs of citizens. If they are not, mass allegiance to the regime declines, participation in conventional politics falls away and arguments in favour of some other system are heard sympathetically. The story of the Weimar Republic in the early 1930s in Germany can be described in these terms. It is easy to forget that the Nazis were democratically elected. Changes in the fundamental character of the regime do not always require a revolution. All it takes is for enough people to feel disengaged, remote and ignored by the system and the resulting anomie and confusion will open the political arena to those seeking a new regime of government.

What then is the present health of this transmission process in the nations of the Political Action Study? Table 7.4 submits the 'system responsiveness' measure to our now-familiar cross-generational analysis. This measure, remember, asks people to say how much they believe that public officials and politicians care about the views of ordinary people, stay in touch with popular opinion and seek their views as well as their votes. The marginal distributions of these feelings, comparing one generation with the other, speak optimistically for the health of the system. In the four European countries, the adolescent generation tends to see the system as *more* responsive than do the parents. Even in Austria, where the young tend towards a more sceptical view than elsewhere, the Austrian adolescents still take a more benign view of their system compared to the strangely gloomy view taken by Austrian parents. (This, incidentally, casts some doubt on the view taken earlier that lower levels of protest potential in Austria were partly a function of the success of the Government at that time. This, however, is a measure of diffuse support and not specific support.) In the United States, on the other hand, the adolescent view is marginally *less* sanguine than the parents'. This, however, is due to the exceptionally high marks awarded to their system by the American parents; 42% of American parents scored high on the system responsiveness scale compared to only 18% in Austria and between about a quarter and a third elsewhere.

In terms of pair correspondence, however, the picture is more confusing. Lineage gaps are large; clear majorities of parent-child pairs occupy different points on the scale. Except in Austria, the generation gaps that are realised within the frame of lineage disagreement are quite small, European children having a slight edge on their parents, American parents a slight edge on their children. This means that most of the absolute differences within pairs (that is, *not* having exactly the same score on the four-point scale) occur equally in both directions. This is especially true in Britain. It is in Britain, however, that almost the greatest relative agreement is found. British children take a more benign view of the political system relative to other British children if they have parents who take a similar view relative to other parents. In Germany this relationship is slightly stronger, in The Netherlands and Austria slightly weaker. In the United States it is non-existent. Though American parents, in contrast to European parents, take an aggregate lead over the adolescent generation in praising the responsiveness of the system, they fail to imbue their *own* children with the same view. Equally, those fewer American parents who take a sceptical view of the system are as likely as not to

TABLE 7.4 System Responsiveness

	The Netherlands		Britain		United States		Germany		Austria	
	Parents	Offspring	Parents	Offspring	Parents	Offspring	Parents	Offspring	Parents	Offspring
Responsiveness:										
Low 1	18%[a]	13%	27%	23%	14%	18%	34%	26%	57%	36%
2	28	19	34	33	26	19	21	26	18	23
3	21	26	16	21	17	28	14	15	7	17
High 4	33	42	23	23	42	35	31	33	18	24
$\bar{X}$	2.7	3.0	2.3	2.4	2.9	2.8	2.4	2.6	1.9	2.3
N	(209)	(200)	(171)	(156)	(242)	(239)	(254)	(250)	(203)	(197)
Pair Relationships:										
tau-b	.21		.25		.06		.28		.14	
gamma	.29		.33		.09		.38		.20	
lineage gap	66%		66%		59%		60%		66%	
generation gap	16%—O		4%—O		10%—P		9%—O		24%—O	
adj. "	.24		.07		.16		.15		.36	
N	(190)		(154)		(236)		(247)		(192)	

a. All figures are based on a four-fold bracketing of the original mean index scores.

have children who claim to find the system responsive.
Probably there are quite a number of different influences crowding in on these data to produce an inconsistent pattern. In Europe, for example, the greater system responsiveness seen by the young may well be part of a naive view of politics as a democratic exchange between leaders and led. It is a simplification that encourages an acceptance of the system that later experience may disabuse. Young people rely less on the State directly for a whole range of welfare supports that are more urgently sought by adults and often denied. Many parents may give their children a benign and simplified view of the system that, secretly, they do not really share. Adults often believe that the State is threadbare and unresponsive, also that there is no God and no Santa Claus, but there are things that those of tender years ought to believe and they tell their children it is so. The American data, on the other hand, are, to repeat a phrase, a bit unsettling. There really ought to be greater correspondence within families on something so basic as diffuse support for the regime, in relative terms at least. But the system responsiveness index *is* a complex measure, containing a lot of ideas about the behaviour of public officials and elected representatives that are likely to be unfamiliar to the youngest respondents in the survey. Is there an even more basic idea that might carry the freight of diffuse support from one generation to the next?

Two questions were asked that have not been discussed in this volume so far, these are:

(1) Generally speaking, would you say that this country is run for a few big interests looking out for themselves or is it run for the benefit of all the people?
(2) How much do you trust the government to do what is right? Almost never, only some of the time, most of the time, just about always?

Replies to each tend to be closely correlated; that is to say, those who feel the country is run for a few big interests tend also to say they rarely trust the government, while those who say the country is run for the benefit of all are far more trusting. The two scores are combined into a three-category Political Trust Index (high, medium, and low) and this is shown in the same generational analysis format in Table 7.5.

First, some fascinating cross-national differences are apparent.

TABLE 7.5 Political Trust

	The Netherlands		Britain		United States		Germany		Austria	
	Parents	Offspring	Parents	Offspring	Parents	Offspring	Parents	Offspring	Parents	Offspring
Trust:										
Low 1	33%[a]	25%	48%	47%	49%	45%	22%	24%	16%	10%
2	30	38	32	29	28	33	26	30	33	38
High 3	36	37	20	23	23	22	52	46	51	52
$\bar{X}$	2.0	2.1	1.7	1.8	1.7	1.8	2.3	2.2	2.3	2.4
N	(190)	(195)	(154)	(137)	(233)	(227)	(220)	(216)	(186)	(192)
Pair Relationships:										
tau-b	.30		.43		.07		.27		.29	
gamma	.45		.62		.12		.42		.47	
lineage gap	53%		40%		59%		48%		49%	
generation gap	8%–O		2%–P		3%–O		4%–P		8%–O	
adj. "	.14		.04		.06		.07		.16	
N	(171)		(127)		(218)		(194)		(171)	

a. All figures are based on a three-fold bracketing of the original mean index scores.

Trend data have shown that in the United States, political trust has been declining steadily since the mid-1960s. By 1974, as the data show, nearly half of American parents and children share the same uniformly cynical view of official probity. The then incumbent, Richard Nixon, did little to reverse this trend. In Britain, identical figures are found again among parents and children alike. The Anglo-Saxon cousinhood is expressed in a cynical view of politics. The German-speaking cousinhood between Germany and Austria is expressed quite differently. They are each as trusting as the Anglo-Saxons are cynical and again there are no differences between the two generations. The Austrian case is particularly interesting because they recorded the lowest system responsiveness score above but now record the highest levels of political trust. It is a strange stance to take. They feel that officials and politicians ignore them but can be trusted to do what is right and care for a common collective good. It is a uniquely Austrian idea and it rehabilitates earlier ideas about political passivity in Austria being a function of public contentment.

Second, we find much better evidence for intergenerational transmission. Lineage gaps are lower. In Britain, for example, it is only 40% (that is, 60% of pairs agree) and agreement is high in all four European countries. Generation gaps are small everywhere indicating that departures from agreement tend to be in self-cancelling directions. In Europe, too, relative agreement is high, especially in Britain. Parents who are relatively more trusting or cynical have children who tend in the same direction even if they do not agree in absolute terms on the appropriate level of trust or cynicism. Here, at least, some basic element of diffuse support (or its lack) is being picked up in the home. It is, after all, the kind of level at which politics will be discussed in many homes. Grumbling about official mendacity, deploring (or enjoying) the latest political scandal or even expressing pleasant surprise that 'they have done something right for a change' has always been popular meal-time conservation. Another reason for the much higher level of generational correspondence is that, unlike responsiveness, the Trust Index is much closer linked to party choice. Since the direction of party choice is so successfully transmitted in many of the families in this study, the trust of cynicism that attends it will be transmitted at the same time. That is why the most clearly divided society, Britain, shows the highest levels of agreement between parents and children. It arises partly out of a shared view of the then Conservative administration which was having, in late 1973 and early 1974, rather a bad time of it.

The Political Trust Index, while making the European picture clearer, has only deepened the American mystery. Political partisanship is no less common and no less successfully transmitted in the United States than in Europe. Yet the lineage gap in trust is much higher and is unaccompanied either by a generation gap of any size (that is, they disagree in absolute terms in different directions) or by any significant relative agreement (that is, you cannot predict an American child's level of trust from its parent's). These, however, were fairly extraordinary times in the United States. Political cynicism had spread well beyond the confines of the party system. Nixon fell during fieldwork. Both generations had different reasons for feeling cynical. Many parents who supported the Vietnam War had children who did not. Many parents were dismayed at events in Washington that their children ignored. Diffuse support for the regime was coming under stress from different directions. Our data appear confused, perhaps, because people felt confused.

Although not strictly 'diffuse support' in the Eastonian scheme, internal political efficacy is very much the other side of the coin of political trust and, more especially, to system responsiveness. It is a key measure in the evaluation segment in the general model of political action because it strongly promotes both conventional and unconventional political action. If political efficacy wanes so does participation. The system goes unsupported. It is also very much a psychological dimension. It is a judgement about oneself as a potential political actor, that one *is* the kind of person who can influence the course of politics and not just by voting either. As such, self-belief of this kind ought to be strongly rooted in styles of upbringing, just as other forms of self-confidence are held to arise from the kind of encouragement one has received at home. In Table 7.6 the political efficacy measure is put through intergenerational analysis.

Again, cross-national differences are interesting. The Austrians fall back into their strikingly passive posture. Small wonder they accept that their system is unresponsive; few of them ever make demands upon it. Austrian adolescents are less efficacious even than parents elsewhere. Austrian parents, by a huge margin, resign all feelings of personal efficacy in politics. They seem caught in a benign time-warp. Their political passivity looks in 1975 very much like the German case many years before. Happily for the Austrians, their passive trust has proved better placed. In contrast, the Americans, parents and children alike, lead the field in efficacy, a result that accords with every other study of this kind. Though their trust in

TABLE 7.6 Political Efficacy

	The Netherlands		Britain		United States		Germany		Austria	
	Parents	Offspring	Parents	Offspring	Parents	Offspring	Parents	Offspring	Parents	Offspring
Efficacy:										
Low 1	25%[a]	18%	19%	27%	15%	17%	44%	31%	66%	46%
2	25	26	37	28	22	20	22	20	21	19
3	28	20	22	22	22	20	10	18	9	18
High 4	22	37	22	23	41	43	24	32	5	18
$\bar{X}$	2.5	2.8	2.5	2.4	2.9	2.9	2.1	2.5	1.5	2.1
N	(222)	(215)	(171)	(166)	(243)	(242)	(256)	(255)	(207)	(202)
Pair Relationships:										
tau-b	.20		.06		.13		.24		.08	
gamma	.27		.08		.18		.33		.14	
lineage gap	67%		59%		67%		62%		63%	
generation gap	17%—O		1%—P		1%—O		18%—O		30%—O	
adj."	.26		.02		.01		.28		.47	
N	(214)		(164)		(241)		(254)		(199)	

a. All figures are based on a four-fold bracketing of the original mean index scores.

political practitioners have taken many hard knocks they are, as they might say, still in there pitching, believing in their individual capacity to influence events. The other three countries lie between these extremes, having about equal numbers of efficacious and inefficacious people.

Evidence for the transmission of this apparently deep-rooted aspect of political psychology from parents to children is once more highly equivocal. In Britain and the United States there is hardly any. Lineage gaps are large, there is no generation gap so absolute discrepancy occurs in both directions. Nor is there any significant relative agreement. While about a third of parents and children have the same level of efficacy, others depart in random directions. In mainland Europe there is more agreement, especially in The Netherlands and more strikingly still in Germany. The adolescent Germans have a clear edge in efficacy over the parent generation and there is a moderate level of relative association too. This echoes earlier assertions that young Germans are actively taught to preserve their civil rights by using them. The Austrian adolescents also depart from their parents' total passivity and show the largest generation gap, though they still have a long way to go. In contrast to Germany, however, there is no relative association between Austrian parents' and children's levels of efficacy. This means that those young Austrians who are acquiring a sense of political efficacy are doing so independently. It suggests real intergenerational discontinuity but not one of great magnitude – not yet, at least.

Diffuse support, then, is imperfectly transmitted from parents to children except when it touches on the more enduring aspects of political partisanship. It cannot be said that support for the system, either as an evaluation of the system itself or as an evaluation of one's own ability to influence events is something that one gets from one's upbringing or not at all. Other factors are likely to be important. The school is an obvious source. Secondary socialisation into work and perhaps also into trades union membership is another. The communications media, above all television, are probably the most important of all. The extension of social and economic freedom in adolescence has clearly provided quite a lot of breathing space which many young people have used to advantage. Many are influenced by their parents, certainly, but the data show that many others make up their own minds about the political system they are about to inherit. It provides room for intergenerational change as well as continuity.

7.1.2 Specific Support

Hitherto this investigation into political socialisation has been guided by well established theory and some commonsense expectations. Not all of these were fully confirmed but we knew where we were going. Now we enter dark and pathless woods, the question of policy dissatisfaction. The measure is highly complex, combining importance, government responsibility and evaluation over ten issues. Any of these issues might appeal to different generations in different ways. Policy dissatisfaction was shown to have richly complex antecedents, arising from 'old' and 'new' political ideologies and partisanship. The older and younger generations may well be led to equal feelings of dissatisfaction through quite different paths.

Leaving aside, for the moment, the question of evaluation (how good or bad government performance is seen to be) Table 7.7 considers cross-generational differences in the overall issue agenda (how important these issues are *and* how much responsibility for them is assigned to government). In Europe, parents rather than children are more inclined to see these ten issues as important and to say that the Government ought to take responsibility for them. This is particularly true in The Netherlands, least so in Germany where the adolescent generation are more likely than adolescents elsewhere to promote the rôle of government. Again, the political education of German youth shines through the data. Although the lineage gaps are quite high, there being only a minority of pairs who agree precisely on their allocation of government responsibility, relative levels of agreement are quite strong, especially so in Germany and Austria. A concern for the provision of important services through the State is a value that is strongly transmitted in German-speaking homes. Given that parents lead in the aggregate, it seems likely that importance and responsibility ratings in Europe will rise among the adolescent generation as the adult concerns that the agenda largely represents become more important to them as they grow older. This is much stronger evidence than before of political socialisation at work.

The United States, however, provides once more a contrary example. Here it is the adolescent generation who take the lead in assigning responsibility to the Government. This difference is due largely to the strikingly low importance and responsibility ratings given by American parents. Big Government is viewed with much suspicion. Nor is there much relative agreement between the generations. Thus, those

TABLE 7.7 Overall Issue Agenda

	The Netherlands		Britain		United States		Germany		Austria	
	Parents	Offspring	Parents	Offspring	Parents	Offspring	Parents	Offspring	Parents	Offspring
Agenda Score:										
Low 1	14%[a]	26%	22%	28%	50%	36%	21%	24%	26%	36%
2	26	32	29	29	19	27	24	24	24	25
3	28	26	22	27	20	21	26	24	25	19
High 4	32	16	27	16	11	16	29	28	24	20
$\bar{X}$	2.8	2.3	2.5	2.3	1.9	2.2	2.6	2.6	2.5	2.2
N	(218)	(219)	(173)	(168)	(242)	(242)	(253)	(254)	(208)	(207)
Pair Relationships:										
tau-b	.23		.17		.08		.30		.34	
gamma	.31		.23		.11		.40		.44	
lineage gap	69%		73%		69%		60%		59%	
generation gap	27%–P		9%–P		16%–O		3%–P		14%–P	
adj. "	.39		.12		.23		.05		.24	
N	(217)		(168)		(241)		(250)		(205)	

a. All figures are based on a four-fold bracketing of the original mean index scores.

American adolescents who do favour higher levels of government intervention are not, unlike their European peers, picking up this view from their parents. More likely they are echoing civics lessons remembered from school or college. It is hard to guess whether their view will endure. More likely it will not and in view of the support lately given by younger voters to Ronald Reagan in his presidency, probably it did not endure.

Combining now the evaluation scores with the overall issue agenda (Table 7.8) we find a fascinating reversal of the cross-national and cross-generational picture. American parents are *more* dissatisfied with performance than are American adolescents and in Europe the opposite is true: European children are, as expected, more dissatisfied than their parents. This reversal occurs in the context of quite wide cross-national differences. The Austrian authorities continue to bask in high specific support from parents and only a little less support from children. The German authorities receive heavy flak from both generations but especially so from the adolescent generation. So while German-speaking homes instill a norm of government responsibility into their children quite successfully and both adolescent generations turn out more thoughtfully critical of government performance than their parents, the Austrians are broadly supportive and the Germans highly critical. German *parents* are three times more likely to take a wholly critical view than are Austrian *children*; German children four times more likely. Such aggregate differences between two adjacent language-sharing and really quite similar countries are hard to explain. Particularly so since Social Democrats ruled both countries at the time of the survey.

Britain and The Netherlands take a view of their governments' performance that is neither as critical as the Germans' nor as benign as the Austrians'. Here, too, the adolescent generation leads the critique even though, as in Germany and Austria, they assigned both priority and government responsibility to fewer issues. They want less than their parents but are more prone to feel that they are not getting it. Despite this difference between generations, the degree of relative agreement is still quite strong. This is especially true in Britain where children who are more critical than other children tend quite strongly to have parents who are more critical than other parents.

None of this, once more, is true in the United States. Here the parents want less from government, much less. Yet they are more prone than their children to believe that these relatively modest demands are unmet. Probably the issues of crime control, medical

TABLE 7.8 Overall Policy Dissatisfaction

	The Netherlands		Britain		United States		Germany		Austria	
	Parents	Offspring	Parents	Offspring	Parents	Offspring	Parents	Offspring	Parents	Offspring
Dissatisfaction Score:										
Low 1	27%[a]	15%	27%	18%	20%	24%	14%	11%	40%	30%
2	23	21	20	24	22	22	20	18	23	29
3	23	35	28	31	29	33	34	32	29	30
High 4	26	28	25	27	28	21	31	40	8	11
$\bar{X}$	2.5	2.8	2.5	2.7	2.6	2.5	2.8	3.0	2.0	2.2
N	(218)	(201)	(169)	(158)	(234)	(236)	(249)	(245)	(205)	(200)
Pair Relationships:										
tau-b	.13		.25		.02		.20		.17	
gamma	.17		.34		.07		.28		.24	
lineage gap	71%		66%		69%		61%		67%	
generation gap	12%—O		13%—O		8%—P		12%—O		12%—O	
adj. "	.17		.20		.12		.20		.18	
N	(191)		(155)		(228)		(238)		(198)	

a. All figures are based on a four-fold bracketing of the original mean index scores.

care and job security were taking a heavy toll of public confidence among the middle-aged generation. Their children, on the other hand, are far more prone to say that the Government ought to intervene in important social issues but are no more critical of government performance than are their European peers. One really does wonder what is going on in American homes. Do they ever discuss the issues of the day? The correlation coefficients suggest not. An American child's level of policy dissatisfaction is quite unpredictable from knowledge of his or her parents' dissatisfaction. Perhaps if foreign and defence issues had featured strongly on the issue-agenda some better-linked critique might have emerged among the American youth. So much was going on at the time that the two generations seem pulled in quite conflicting directions on policy issues without somehow being either in conflict or in agreement. They seem to be leading different political lives.

The case should not be overstated. There *is* continuity in the way that the two generations evaluate political objects, even if the evidence is a little patchy. The dividend of political socialisation is often paid later in life than adolescence. It is a matter of common observation that some adolescents experiment with political ideas but later return to a set of views not unlike those of their parents, particularly when they too become parents. On the other hand, the very clear evidence discussed earlier of a real change in basic political values among the adolescent generation must also be at work in these data. The analysis of policy dissatisfaction in chapter 5 showed that youth and postmaterialism were important antecedents of policy dissatisfaction but more especially so when linked to an identification with anti-Establishment political groups and with opposition to Establishment groups. Is this where the discontinuity lies?

The answer, as so often in social science, is 'yes' and 'no'. A careful inspection of the comparative 'sympathy scores' (the 0 to 100 scale described in chapter 4) shows that, yes, the adolescent generation is far more favourable toward 'student protesters', 'revolutionary groups', 'women's liberation' and far less favourable towards 'the police', 'the clergy', and so on than are parents. There are some interesting cross-national exceptions. For example, in The Netherlands parents are greatly more sympathetic toward student protesters than parents elsewhere by a huge margin (an average score of 51 compared to between 23 and 21 elsewhere). What divides Dutch parents and children is their attitude toward the clergy (67 vs. 49) and there are similar gaps between parents and children in Germany and, a little less so, in Britain. There is also a tendency in all countries, but most noticeably in Britain, for the adolescent generation to have less sympathy than parents for *both* the main political parties. Thus a Left-leaning youth has, in many cases, developed a highly conditional view of the major party of the Left: a plague on both your houses.

Overall, the adolescents in each country occupy a very different position on the combined Establishment-anti-Establishment dimension compared to parents. Expressed in standardised units (which in practice vary from about +3 down to −3) the differences are these:

	Parents	*Offspring*
The Netherlands	.39	− .38
Britain	.34	− .42
United States	.46	− .45
Germany	.44	− .44
Austria	.30	− .33

On average, the two generations stand about one standard deviation apart, either side of neutral. These are very large differences; bearing in mind that the majority of each generation will be found one unit either side of their respective averages. Thus only a minority of cases will overlap. Here we appear to have found differences in basic values between generations that are expressed in political evaluations in ways that, we know already, lead to dissatisfaction and then to political action, especially to protest potential. Even the United States falls into line with the European pattern.

There is, however, an important qualification to make. The 'no' part of the answer is that, unlike the case of postmaterialism which showed real intergenerational discontinuity, there remain quite high levels of *relative* agreement between parents and children. Overall, the intergenerational correlations are positive and significant, ranging from .19 in Britain up to .33 in Germany. Even the United States is on the higher side: .29. This means that children who are more anti-Establishment than other children tend to have parents who are more anti-Establishment than other parents. It is particularly interesting to note that sympathy for the more solidly-identified Establishment *institutions*, like the clergy, shows the highest rate of relative agreement despite showing the highest rates of absolute *dis*agreement. Take the case of Germany: parents award an average sympathy score of 51 to 'The Clergy', their children only 39. Yet the correlation between the parents' and children's scores is + .50. Those

German children who retain sympathy for the clergy have religious parents, those that lose it have secular parents. Pious parents tend to have mildly less religious children, agnostic parents tend to have atheist children, and so on.

In summary, then, children evaluate the political world in ways that bear the stamp of parental influence. The more solid and enduring objects, like political parties and established institutions carry the greatest amount of parental influence. The more abstract ideas, particularly value-priorities, carry the least. Children use their parents' views as a standard from which to deviate. Areas that carry the greater moral charge invite greater experimentation among the young. How then do these threads of continuity and discontinuity translate into difference in political behaviour? At this point we reach the sharp end of the general model of political action: conventional and unconventional political behaviour.

7.2 CONVENTIONAL POLITICAL PARTICIPATION

The general model tells us to expect that parents will have somewhat higher levels of conventional political participation than the adolescent generation. Commonsense agrees: it is when people establish themselves in their communities that they tend to get drawn into the institutionalised business of their local community and party politics. The model also says that better education, belief in the responsiveness of the system and greater efficacy will boost conventional activity rather more than will simply getting older. The data in this chapter suggest that the younger generation has more faith in the system and in themselves as political actors than do their parents. So are adolescents impelled by ideas and their parents by habit?

The data in Table 7.9 reflect these competing influences and do so in the context of considerable cross-national differences. In Britain, the United States and Austria, parents have a clear lead over children in their rates of conventional political activity. In Austria and especially Britain, this is due to the very low levels of activity among the young. The British parents have quite high participation rates so the generation gap in that country is huge. The Austrian case is also interesting because the Austrian children were shown earlier to have much higher levels of internal efficacy than their parents. It has yet to pay a dividend of greater participation but it is likely that it will. In the United States, the generation gap arises from remarkably high

TABLE 7.9 Conventional Political Participation

	The Netherlands		Britain		United States		Germany		Austria	
	Parents	Offspring	Parents	Offspring	Parents	Offspring	Parents	Offspring	Parents	Offspring
Participation:										
Low 1	30%[a]	34%	20%	51%	13%	24%	24%	34%	35%	49%
2	18	14	24	23	13	20	31	20	21	25
3	31	31	36	18	21	29	13	14	22	13
High 4	21	21	20	8	53	28	32	32	22	13
$\bar{X}$	2.4	2.4	2.6	1.8	3.1	2.6	2.5	2.4	2.3	1.9
N	(223)	(222)	(172)	(173)	(244)	(241)	(257)	(257)	(212)	(211)
Pair Relationships:										
tau-b	.26		.18		.14		.16		.10	
gamma	.35		.26		.20		.22		.14	
lineage gap	64%		73%		67%		65%		72%	
generation gap	0%		44%–P		30%–P		6%–P		25%–P	
adj. "	.01		.61		.45		.09		.35	
N	(222)		(172)		(241)		(257)		(211)	

a. All figures are based on a four-fold bracketing of the original eight-category scale.

levels of activity, typical of community life there, among the parents. American adolescents have the second highest rates of activity, quite close to the highly active German adolescents, but are still nowhere near the American parents' levels, half of whom appear at the highest point on the four-point scale.

In Germany and The Netherlands no generation gap appears: parents and children are equally active in conventional politics. High levels of internal efficacy instilled into particularly the German adolescent generation have clearly launched the young into early political activity. There are 'pull' factors at work here too. In The Netherlands, for example, entry into the party arena was made easy for young people by the rapid growth of radical parties like 'D–66' that set out quite deliberately to scoop up newly-fledged electors.

In three countries, The Netherlands, Germany and the United States, the adolescent generation has made a determined entry into conventional political activity. In the former two they match their parents' activity rates and, given the upward swing of activity that accompanies maturity elsewhere, they look destined to exceed parental levels as they too grow older. This will certainly be the case of the parent-led American adolescents. In Britain and Austria they have a lot of catching up to do but, given their higher levels of personal efficacy, there is no reason to suppose they will not. In these five countries, therefore, the party system may expect, sooner in some cases, later in others, to attract new recruits to the hustings.

The impression given is one of a fairly smooth socialisation process. Politically conscious and active parents appear to encourage early party choice in their children and, among these, activity follows. This impression is jolted, however, by the rather low correlations reported in Table 7.9. All are positive but only in The Netherlands do relatively active parents seem to have relatively active children and even there the relationship is not overwhelming. Elsewhere it is weak. This is particularly surprising given that we are dealing with a behavioural measure: what do you do? Yet the association between parents' and children's activity levels is no higher than that for some of the much 'softer' attitudinal measures. Since party choice is so successfully transmitted it is hard to see how so many children who accept their parents' *conventional* political choice and whose parents are active in supporting the party's cause, can avoid getting involved at similar rates. All the adolescents in these samples live at home. At election times they must have to hide in their rooms. Conversely, quite large numbers of adolescents are advancing into conventional politics unprompted by parental example. This must be especially true in Germany where, for example, 65% of pairs have different levels of activity with a mere 6% generation gap toward parents. The correlation is only .16 so both in absolute and relative terms, new recruitment to party work is quite strikingly independent of parental example.

7.3 PROTEST POTENTIAL

The independent effect of youth and the additional impetus provided by new élite-challenging values among the young described by the general model, lead to the obvious expectation that the adolescent generations will have far higher levels of protest potential than the parents. They do, as shown clearly in Table 7.10.

The cross-national comparisons are faithful to the patterns set in the general analysis. Among parents, the Dutch stand out as particularly protest prone. Among children, the Austrians and, a little more surprisingly, the British hold back from more committed levels of protest potential compared to the German, American and especially the Dutch adolescents. (The total sample analysis [see Figure 1.1] showed British youth on a par with German.)

In each country though, even in Britain and Austria, the adolescent generation has a very clear lead. The lineage gaps are not huge so the adjusted generation gaps become very large indeed. For example, in Germany 67% of pairs have different levels of protest potential and the generation gap is '44% → 0' so the adjusted generation gap is .66. This means that the great majority of all discrepancies are realised by adolescents exceeding their own parents' levels of protest potential.

Even though the general model insists that the passing years will exact a toll of the very high levels of protest potential among the present adolescent generation, the magnitude of the generation gap speaks of real intergenerational change. It supports the same contention of the general population analysis, particularly so as it is accompanied (in the European countries at least) by higher levels of efficacy and greater policy dissatisfaction among the youth. Behind these factors is the basic driving force of real intergenerational value change in all countries coupled with high levels of ideological thinking among the young.

There is one important qualification to add to this conclusion. The

TABLE 7.10 Protest Potential

	The Netherlands		Britain		United States		Germany		Austria	
	Parents	Offspring	Parents	Offspring	Parents	Offspring	Parents	Offspring	Parents	Offspring
Protest:										
Low 1	29%[a]	13%	42%	27%	30%	12%	43%	18%	59%	35%
2	30	20	28	28	30	27	28	24	29	37
3	23	36	25	31	34	36	24	33	11	20
High 4	18	31	5	15	6	26	4	25	1	7
$\bar{X}$	2.3	2.8	1.9	2.3	2.2	2.8	1.9	2.6	1.5	2.0
N	(213)	(217)	(171)	(163)	(235)	(232)	(249)	(244)	(161)	(167)
Pair Relationships:										
tau-b	.10		.17		.19		.29		.20	
gamma	.14		.24		.26		.40		.31	
lineage gap	72%		68%		68%		67%		60%	
generation gap	33%–O		22%–O		36%–O		44%–O		30%–O	
adj. "	.45		.33		.53		.66		.50	
N	(208)		(161)		(223)		(240)		(139)	

a. All figures are based on a four-fold bracketing of the original eight-category scale.

relative association between parents' and children's levels of protest potential is quite high. The correlation is low in the protest-prone Netherlands where 'deviant' parents are apparently more common. Elsewhere it ranges from .24 and .26 in Britain and the United States to .31 in Austria and to .40 in Germany. These figures are higher than those observed for conventional participation. This means that the *tendency* towards protest is slightly *more* transmissible from parents to children than is the tendency to become involved in the institutionalised paths of conventional politics, even though generation gaps run in opposite directions.

This finding, together with the strong relative agreement between generations speak in favour of what American commentators described as the 'red diaper' theory of protest in the 1960s. It was found by a number of academic observers, notably Flacks, Kenniston and others, that radical students were not in Oedipal rebellion against crusty Republican parents. On the contrary, their parents were Liberals. Few of our young potential protesters will be fully-paid up student radicals passé 1968. They had rather missed that boat. But a shadow of that kind of liberal-to-radical generation shift certainly haunts the data. It gives rise to an interesting question. Many of the parent generation who were once protesters will now be backsliding down the protest potential scale pleading advancing years and premature infirmity or whatever other excuse seems plausible to avoid being outmarched by the young. Yet they may still *approve* of protest tactics and it is thus approval where it exists, that encourages the young of the family to go out and get involved. When the analysis in Table 7.10 is repeated for the 'approval of protest' scale alone we do find much higher levels of approval among parents compared to their levels of behavioural intentions toward protest. The lineage generation gaps are smaller though generation gaps are still heavily in favour of youth. In terms of lineage similarity, actually a majority of pairs agree on their broad level of approval of protest tactics. The levels of relative agreement, on the other hand, are not strikingly high. Only in Britain and The Netherlands is approval more transmissible than intention. Elsewhere the opposite is true. Much the same pattern is observable when the 'effectiveness of protest' measure is used. Generation gaps are smaller still. Lineage gaps are larger and relative agreement remains at similar levels. Example, it seems, is easily as important as encouragement even if parental example is weaker in aggregate terms than the adolescent response.

7.4 SUMMARY: POLITICAL SOCIALISATION AND POLITICAL CHANGE

The analysis of parent-child pairs cannot inform us directly about *how* political views and behaviour are transmitted intergenerationally. It tells us what has happened. In our search among this evidence for signs of what might be real intergenerational change, we have been at pains to point out differences as well as similarities. More of these differences have been of an aggregate than a relational kind. Children take different views, often veering in a 'liberal' direction but, to varying degrees, they *are* influenced by their parents.

Suppose, for example, we had found that the large generation gaps in levels of protest potential were unaccompanied by any correlation between parents' and children's views? Or suppose *negative* correlations were found for protest potential and for values and judgements too? Worse still, suppose negative correlations had accompanied the parents' aggregate lead in conventional participation: that is to say that parents supported the party system and the democratic regime and the children withdrew from, or actively opposed it? This would be real intergenerational conflict on an irreparable scale – a sheering of political goals and behaviour between one generation and the next.

It is not an exaggeration to say that such a picture was highly acceptable to many observers in the 1967–70 period. This view, in some ways, was taken by the Study Group as a null hypothesis. The data are clear. It is not so. Parents remain positive referents for their children even if they do shift away from parents' position on many issues. The one unsolved puzzle that the data leave is this: those aspects of political thought that theorists hold to be more durable and therefore most transmissible across generations (political values, system support of various kinds, and so on) were found to show the weakest correspondence between generations, especially in political values. Conversely, some of those aspects that theorists hold ephemeral, especially something as allegedly transient as protest, showed much higher levels of correspondence between parents and their children. It seems fair to speculate, therefore, that the more passive aspects of system support are giving way to a greater emphasis on political involvement. Political value change stresses greater participation, efficacy is higher among the young, policy dissatisfaction is greater. It is an altogether more conditional view of politics, that it is too important to leave to politicians alone.

8 In Conclusion: The Future of Political Action in Western Democracies

It is the melancholy fate of people who do survey studies such as these to be told that they laboured long and hard only to find out what everyone knew already. Since its first appearance in 1979, the Political Action Study appears to have escaped much of this fate. Readers persisting this far will have seen sufficient innovation in method and analysis to be able to conclude that the study uncovered a new and different picture of mass political participation compared with that commonly found in earlier texts. Those reaching this conclusion will find themselves in broad agreement with professional reviewers. Not that these were uncritical, of course, but a consensus said that the study showed something new. Let us review the main points in a way that will set the findings of the study into the context of modern political change:

(1) What we have called the political action repertory, the range of things people can and will do in politics, expanded in the 1970s and has gone on expanding in the 1980s. Large segments of especially the younger population of these five nations came to accept the idea of political protest as a necessary and legitimate form of political behaviour. Some added protest tactics to the more conventional political actions whose practice they had inherited from older generations. Others, notably many young women, came to accept political protest without, *at the time of asking*, adopting conventional party politics too. As the original volume put it: 'What really appears to have happened – what is really significant – is that what was the extremism of the 1960s is becoming the legitimacy of the 1970s . . . this very diffusion far from diluting the idea of protest, may surely have increased its potency to contribute to political change. The governments of our five nations. . . . now have to contend

with a polity full of young well educated men and women who do not accept that their political efficacy is bounded by officially sanctioned channels of representative democracy'. Gazing toward the future, the original authors focused on the spread of protest tactics and said: 'We interpret this increase in potential for protest to be a lasting characteristic of mass publics and not just a sudden surge in political involvement bound to fade away as time goes by'.

Some time has now gone by and there still seems little to contradict this prediction. The emergence of 'alternative' political movements has gathered strength and pace all over the Western world. The activists have been active and their blend of conventional and unconventional political action grows ever more inventive and resourceful. This trend to dualist politics culminated and was symbolised by the entry of the Green Parties into the German parliament.

Perhaps the best example of the reality of protest potential came from the other side of the world. While Europe was being disturbed by the events of the 1960s and 1970s their expatriot cousins in New Zealand got on quietly with their farming and contrasted their domestic tranquility and relative racial harmony with the turmoil elsewhere. Then in 1981 the South African rugby football team proposed to visit New Zealand. Now the New Zealander's love of rugby football (similar to American football, which in fact it inspired, except that no-one wears protective clothing or helmets) is second only to the pride taken in its multiracial basis. White New Zealand players even adopted a Maori war dance for their prematch warm-up. The prospect of a tour by a racially-segregated South African team seemed offensive to many New Zealanders, white and Maori alike. So great was the offence taken in many sectors of New Zealand society that *within weeks* a vigorous and occasionally violent protest movement emerged that bore all the features of earlier European or American behaviour of the same kind. Protest potential is a political reality. It has become an enduring part of modern political life in all democratic countries and in a fair number of undemocratic ones too.

(2) This enlarged political action repertory is firmly embedded in social structure. At source, it has arisen from the expansion

and improvement of mass education. This fact alone will underwrite its enduring quality. What some have called the educational revolution of postwar Europe and the United States coincided with a vast expansion of communication media, especially television. Well-informed and critical young minds were able to translate this flood of political and social information in ways that were relevant to their lives and to what they thought they wanted from the future. The world of politics was no longer the remote and inaccessible world of career politicians and retired generals. It seemed open to participation to many ordinary young people who were increasingly well-equipped to participate. This they did and still do, often in ways of their own invention and choosing.

(3) The impact of education was indirect. Schools and colleges do not teach people how to demonstrate. But nor do they teach only facts. If they are successful they teach people how to learn. In chapter 3 we showed clearly how the spread of such mental skills among people had given rise to an ideological appreciation of politics that was more widespread than earlier texts had insisted. This is not to say that whole populations became students of political science. Large numbers of people remain unable to recognise the basic dimensions of politics. But a substantial portion of each national sample could do so and significant minorities showed themselves able to handle abstract political concepts with relative ease. These mental skills are strongly associated with political action. They are unlikely to decay.

(4) As characteristics of whole populations, *levels* of ideological thinking are ideologically neutral. Simply possessing the mental skills to be able to place political information into some abstract framework does not, of itself, suggest one style of political participation over another. Nor does it determine the attraction of a particular cause. The expansion of people's political action repertory toward a protest orientation had, in the early and mid-1970s, an indispensable connection with the ideological Left and their demands for social equality. This combination of mental skills and an equalitarian political outlook is highly characteristic of those who would add protest tactics to their political armoury.

However obvious this finding may seem to contemporary minds, it may reflect no more than the prevailing mood of the times. Such a survey undertaken in the 1930s would certainly have found the young ideologically-conscious Right also scoring high on the protest potential scale. The evidence shows that the real determining factor is which ideological grouping is supporting the status quo and which is seeking social change. In the late 1960s and 1970s this difference described, respectively, the political Right and Left. It was not always so in the past and it may be different in the future.

(5) The single most important element that ties the expansion of the political action repertoire to real social change in postwar Europe and the United States is postmaterialism. There are real intergenerational changes in basic political values. There is no need to rehearse once more the arguments linking value change to increasing levels of material affluence, except perhaps to stress again that material concerns, the 'bread and butter' issues of politics, will continue to be important while postmaterialist concerns will become relatively more important. Subsequent work by Inglehart has indicated that the economic recession that started in the late 1970s has somewhat checked the spread of postmaterialist values but has not reversed the trend.

The real significance of the persistence of postmaterialism among the young is that it provides a new basis for political conflict. It is linked to traditional Leftism through a shared concern for social equality but goes well beyond the classic concerns of industrial class conflict.

Increasingly, postmaterialists find themselves contesting their place on the national issue agenda as much with their former allies in the trades union movement as they do with the traditional custodians of the status quo. The story of the environmental movement exemplifies this. Steel unions are unmoved by the dangers of acid rain while their members are threatened by unemployment. This means that most of the postmaterialist practitioners of the New Politics will continue to operate on the periphery of the usual channels of political bargaining. They will need to use their own very considerable personal resources to maintain their leverage on the political system. They will continue to use protest tactics simply because they need to.

(6) Having shown how the enlargement of people's political action repertory is linked to social structure and social change, chapters 5 and 6 developed a general model to show how basic factors like mental skills and postmaterialism shape political action through a process of political judgement. They become politicised. Postmaterialism, for example, leads to policy dissatisfaction largely through an identification with élite-challenging groups and this dissatisfaction leads to protest. But perhaps the most important general conclusion to be drawn from the complexities of the general model is that the main props of democratic participation in politics remain intact. It bears repeating that conventional and unconventional political action are positively related. They share common antecedents, particularly in higher levels of ideological thinking and a personal sense of political efficacy. Particularly significant is that protest potential does not arise from a rejection of the overall political regime. There is no apparent crisis of legitimacy that threatens to collapse from within the whole conduct of liberal democracy. As another study has shown, a high protest potential is associated with pro-democratic attitudes. They quarrel with what the system does or fails to do but few among them seek to overturn the regime. Indeed, when one thinks about it, the kinds of behaviour that make up the protest potential scale – boycotts, demonstrations, rent or tax strikes, unofficial strikes, occupations and street blockades – are not really the tools of revolution. Revolutions are made by soldiers, not by well educated political activists seeking social change by a mixture of conventional and unconventional political action. Moreover, almost everyone questioned in these five national samples made clear their basic opposition to the use of political violence against people or property.

On the other hand, it would be quite wrong to conclude from this review that things will necessarily go on much as before. The social forces that brought about the enlargement of people's political action repertory are still moving rapidly. The economic recession of the early 1980s has only hastened the shrinkage of the industrial proletarian communities that formed the constituency of the traditional Left. New manufacturing ventures are capital and not labour intensive. Mass unemployment makes political organisation difficult. The tertiary sector of the economy is rapidly ascendent both in size and in status. More and more people who have jobs have post-industrial kinds of jobs, far away from the centres of production. True, economic recovery in the service sector is still labour intensive, to the extent that some observers feel free to talk about the emergence of a new servant class. Servants or workers, it remains employment of a kind that makes labour organisation very difficult and provides no social basis, no common social identity, for mass political mobilisation within a class-based party system.

Meanwhile, the proportion of the population who have had some higher education expands annually. People lead more and more privatised lives, own their homes, and grow used to self-determination. All this is steadily eroding the traditional class and community basis for political mobilisation that has determined political life in Western democracies for the last 150 years or so. What then is the real significance of the new political action repertory for the conduct of post-industrial politics now and into the 21st century?

8.1 INSTRUMENTAL AND EXPRESSIVE POLITICS

Samuel P. Huntingdon first raised doubts about the value of increased mass participation of the kind later uncovered by the Political Action Study. He asked: 'Post-industrial politics: how benign will it be?' The form of his enquiry rather begged the question of what benign politics exactly were or might be. It would be hard to defend the notion that the existing political system had reached a state of grace. But he cast a jaundiced eye upon the developments of the 1960s. He saw the development of 'single-issue politics' as a particularly potent threat. The use of protest tactics to coerce authorities in one narrow field of policy led to a kind of political hedonism, particularly so in the United States. It contrasted unattractively with the kind of give and take that is necessary among those active in conventional political parties which deal with a broad platform of policies. It leads to a concentration of moral righteousness among groups of activists that brooks no distraction or modification. The traditional urge for political compromise fades away and is replaced by determined extremism. Ironically, Huntingdon went on, this implies that the enriched and diversified political life of the post-industrial future, when enduring class and community cleavages are replaced by urgent issue cleavages, will have to be regulated by more direct and authoritarian means than at present. If he is right about this, then it is an unattractive prospect.

The burden of Huntingdon's argument is that there will be an ascendancy of expressive politics over instrumental politics. Expressive politics is characterised by a readiness to be mobilised in the cause of an issue in a free-wheeling, hedonistic (that is to say, self-interested) and spontaneous way. Instrumental politics is far more programatic. It mobilises people within the framework of a broad ideological stance. It has binding threads of consistency typical of people who are 'in politics'. The key to this distinction is political motivation and interest. Expressive politics is political action without political motivation. Instrumental politics is political action that is politically motivated. Let us make one more journey back to the data to see what light may be shed on this important question.

Figure 8.1, in contrast to some of the detailed analysis that has gone before, attempts an audaciously simple generalisation. Political action is defined only by whether or not one is a member of the inactive category among the five political action types. Thus, the conformists, reformists, activists and protesters are all taken together as people who are active. Political motivation is defined equally simply by whether people said they were 'not much' or 'not at all' interested in politics (= no motivation) or said they were 'somewhat' or 'very much' interested in politics (= some motivation). Although it is an apparently superficial question to ask, it should be remembered that political interest is strongly associated with more complex indicators of political motivation, like levels of ideological thought and so on.

In this way, four political types are defined:

(1) *Political Apathy*: inactive and having no interest in politics;
(2) *Political Detachment*: inactive but having some interest in politics;
(3) *Expressive Political Action*: political activity without political interest;
(4) *Instrumental Political Action*: political activity with political interest.

Table 8.1 shows how these four types are distributed in each of the five national samples. Political apathy, at least in the form these measures define it, is not widespread. Complete inactivity and un-

		Inactives	
		Yes	No
Subjective Political Interest	Not at all interested Not much interested	Political Apathy	Expressive Political Action
	Somewhat interested Very much interested	Political Detachment	Instrumental Political Action

FIGURE 8.1 *Four Styles of Political Orientation*

interest in politics is confined to fewer than one-in-four. Political detachment is even rarer; between one-in-ten and one-in-twenty. Thus the majority tend towards some kind of political action even though in many cases this is limited to the weakest forms. The majority divides itself into the expressive and instrumental types and it is intriguing to see that in all countries instrumental types dominate the expressive. This is only marginally true in Britain but elsewhere instrumental types outnumber the expressive by about two or three to one.

It is this ratio of expressive to instrumental types of participation that is the most intriguing point in assessing the implications of the political action repertoire for political change. One must be cautious. These are approximate, rule-of-thumb measures and there exist no similar measures from past studies that would assist comparisons over time. It is possible to say only that an expressive style of political action has established itself among sizeable minorities of people. Between a fifth and a third of the population of these five advanced industrial countries tend towards political participation but are not really interested in politics. Whatever demands they express by their participation, their exchanges with the authorities they confront are unlikely to be very rational. On the other hand, they are still heavily outnumbered by those who retain the more familiar instrumental approach to political participation, those whose urge to participate is accompanied by a broad interest in politics. If they are to be equalled or supplanted by expressive types in any post-industrial political future, then this process of change still has a long way to go.

Even though the instrumental approach to political action still holds sway over the expressive, Huntingdon's thesis would still carry force if expressive politics were concentrated among the most active. If the younger reformists, the activists and, especially, the protesters were to be found moving toward an expressive orientation while its older reformists and conformists were found clinging to an

TABLE 8.1 The Balance between Styles of Political Involvement

Political Style	The Netherlands	Britain	United States	Germany	Austria
Political Apathy	13%	23%	8%	16%	25%
Political Detachment	5	7	5	11	10
Expressive Political Action	29	32	22	19	18
Instrumental Political Action	53	38	65	54	47
Total	100	100	100	100	100
(N=)	(1136)	(1378)	(1605)	(2203)	(1264)

instrumental view, then what Huntingdon called the 'darker side of post-industrial politics' would be seen already casting a long shadow into the future. In Table 8.2 this last and most important point is examined.

In Table 8.2 a simple ratio is calculated by dividing the percentage of instrumental by the percentage of expressive types. These are given for each of the four active categories of the political action repertory in each country. For example, among conformists in The Netherlands, 77.7% are interested in politics (instrumental types) while the remaining 22.3% are not (expressive types). This yields a ratio of instrumental *over* expressive types of 3.44.

The first point to note is that in every political action group in every country, the instrumental approach to political activity is ascendent. No group is plunging decisively into hedonistic, a-political action. Most significantly, though, it is the reformists and the activists who contain overwhelming numbers of instrumental rather than expressive types. It is clear therefore that their use of direct action techniques is politically rational. It is entirely in keeping with central ideas of modern democratic participation. They add protest methods to their traditional political activities within a framework of broad engagement in mainstream political life. Taken together, they are a majority among all those who would use direct action. The main point the political action study set out to test seems strongly sup-

TABLE 8.2 *Ratio of Instrumental over Expressive Political Styles*

Political Action Repertory Types	The Netherlands	Britain	United States	Germany	Austria
Conformists	3.44	1.64	3.94	3.82	3.27
Reformists	5.25	2.51	5.77	6.93	7.04
Activists	7.00	3.08	7.94	7.00	8.83
Protesters	0.53	0.29	0.69	1.20	0.81
All Four Types	1.83	1.19	3.00	2.84	2.61

ported. The use of direct action is not a disorderly atavism from former, less democratic times. It is a legitimate part of modern political life. It is accepted most by those most involved in politics.

Standing aside from this general conclusion are the protesters. They are the jokers in the pack. They contain more instrumental than expressive types but only very marginally more. Their willingness to be mobilised in direct action and their rejection of conventional politics is accompanied by a large measure of uninterest in politics. It is they who represent the marginal and hedonistic element that Huntingdon foretold. They are not a large grouping but they are large enough to matter. How and when they are mobilised will depend often on who gets to them first.

8.2 CONCLUSION

The Political Action Study uncovered the basis for political mobilisation in Western democracies. Large segments of the populations of these five advanced industrial societies have expanded their repertory of political behaviour to embrace the likely use of direct action techniques. The majority who do so are young. If the evidence of the intergenerational analysis in chapter 7 is reliable, they embrace this new mix of political actions partly in response to the way they have been socialised into better-provided communities, stimulated by better education. Far from being anarchic or destructive, their new political action repertory serves rational ambitions more often than not. It arises from many of the same democratic sources that support the conventional political behaviours favoured by earlier generations. But it arises equally from a well-informed critique of modern society that embraces new values and an enduring dissatisfaction with the policy priorities of present administrations.

For those who worry about the future of twentieth-century democracy, and there are many who are gloomy about it, this conclusion is both welcome and unwelcome. It depends how one sees it. For the moment at least, direct action politics remain part of a widening spectrum of political activity. The demands that are made by the unconventional practitioners of the New Politics are not what Trotsky called transitional demands made solely as a prelude to revolution. They are for the most part demands sought for their own sake. But those that seek them mean them to be taken seriously. For their own part, they act seriously. When they can, they press political demands through conventional as well as unconventional means. The new young political élites are versatile rational activists. They deploy well-learned political skills and can relate what they do to enduring ideas about social change. By any definition of participatory democracy, this seems a welcome development. It does mean, however, that élite-challenging politics has become incorporated into the very centre of the political arena. It has penetrated every corner of modern political life. It raises some fundamental questions about just how governable modern industrial societies will become. Much will depend upon the extent to which their new political repertory is maintained by the present young cohorts and is adopted, or even widened still further, by those who follow.

Bibliography

Almond, Gabriel and Sidney Verba, *The Civic Culture* (Princetown: Princetown University Press, 1963).
Barnes, Samuel H. and Max Kaase, *Political Action* (Beverley Hills and London: Sage Publications, 1979).
Butler, David and Donald Stokes, *Political Change in Britain* (New York: St Martins, 1969).
Campbell, Angus, Phillip E. Converse, Warren Miller and Donald Stokes, *The American Voter* (New York: John Wiley, 1960).
Campbell, Angus, Phillip E. Converse and Williard L. Rodgers, *The Quality of American Life* (New York: Russell Sage, 1976).
Cantril, Hadley, *The Patterns of Human Concerns* (New Brunswick, N.J.: Rutgers University Press, 1965).
Converse, Phillip E., 'The Nature of Belief Systems in Mass Publics' in David E. Apter (ed.), *Ideology and Discontent* (New York: Free Press, 1964).
Converse, Phillip E. and Roy Pierce, 'Die Mai-Unnuhen im Frankreich – Ausmass und Konsequenzen' in Klaus Allerbeck and Leopold Rosenmayr (eds), *Aufstand der Jurgen?* (Munich: Jurenta-Verlag, 1971) pp. 108ff.
Dahl, Robert, *Polyarchy* (New Haven: Yale University Press, 1971).
Dahrendorf, Ralph, *Class and Class Conflict in an Industrial Society* (London: Routledge & Keegan Paul, 1959).
Davies, James, 'Toward a Theory of Revolution', *American Sociological Review*, No. 27. February 1962.
Easton, David, *A Systems Analysis of Political Life* (New York: John Wiley, 1966).
Flacks, Robert, *Youth and Social Change* (Chicago: Markam, 1971).
Grofman, Irving and Edward N. Muller, 'The Strange Case of Relative Gratification and Potential for Political Violence: the V-curve Hypothesis', *American Political Science Review*, No. 67, June 1973. pp. 514ff.
Habermas, Jurgen, *Legitimationsprobleme im Spaetkapitalismus* (Frankfurt: Suhrkamp-Verlag, 1973).
Huntingdon, Samuel P., 'Postindustrial Politics: How Benign Will It Be?', *Comparative Politics*, Vol. 6, January 1974, pp. 163–91.
Inglehart, Ronald, *The Silent Revolution* (Princetown: Princetown University Press, 1977).
Kaase, Max, 'Mass Participation' in M. Kent Jennings and Jan Van Deth (eds), *Continuities in Political Action: A Longitudinal Study of Political Orientations in Three Western Democracies* (Berlin: de Gruyter, 1989).
Kenniston, Kenneth, *Young Radicals* (New York: Harcourt Brace Jovanovich, 1968).
Lijphart, Arend, *The Politics of Accommodation: Pluralism and Democracy in The Netherlands* (Berkeley: University of California, 1975).

Lipsett, Seymour Martin, *Political Man* (Anchor Book Edition, New York: Doubleday, 1963).
MacFarlane, L.J. *Political Disobedience* (London: Macmillan, 1971).
Maslow, Abraham, *Motivation and Personality* (New York: Harpers, 1954).
Marsh, Alan, *Protest and Political Consciousness* (Beverley Hills and London: Sage Publications, 1977).
Marsh, Alan, 'Explorations in Unorthodox Political Behaviour: A Scale to Measure Protest Potential', *European Journal of Political Research*, No. 2, 1974, pp. 107–29.
Marsh, Alan, 'Environmental Issues in Contemporary European Politics' in Gordon T. Goodman, Lars A. Kristoferson and Jack M. Hollander (eds), *The European Transition From Oil* (London: Academic Press, 1981).
Miller, Arthur, 'Political Issues and Trust in Government, 1964–70', *American Political Science Review*, Vol. 68, September 1974, pp. 951ff.
Miller, Warren E. and Teresa Levintin, *Leadership and Change* (Cambridge: Winthrop, 1976).
Muller, Edward N., 'A Test of a Partial Theory of Potential for Political Violence', *American Political Science Review*, Vol. 66, September 1972, pp. 928ff.
Runciman, G., *Relative Deprivation and Social Justice* (London: Penguin, 1966).
Tilley, Charles, 'Collective Violence in European Perspective' in Hugh David Graham and Ted Robert Gurr (eds), *Violence in America* (New York: Signet, 1969).
Trieman, Donald, 'Problems of Concept and Measurement in the Comparative Study of Occupational Mobility', *Social Science Research*, No. 4, 1975, pp. 183ff.
Verba, Sidney and Norman Nie, *Participation in America* (New York: Harper & Row, 1972).

Index

active use of an ideological mode of thought in politics 61–5
activists
 definition of 30, 50
 and baseline model 50
age 36–6, 145
Almond, Gabriel 3, 56, 57

Barnes, Samuel H. xvii, 195
baseline model, the
 definition of 5
 analysis of 35–54
 'best possible' level of achievement 111–12
Butler, David 162

Campaign for Nuclear Disarmament (CND), in Britain 3
Campbell, Angus 57, 76, 114
Cantril, Hadley 111
Cantril, Self-anchoring Scale 111–13
Christian Democrats, in Germany 63–98
church 58
 and clergy 98, 99, 175
civil servants 98, 99
class consciousness 124
Civil Rights Movement, in USA 3, 110
cohorts 88–9
coefficient of reliability 12
cognitive skills model, the 5–6
Cohn-Bendit, Daniel 109
Communist Trades Unions, in France 87
Communist Party, in France 87
conformists 30
 definition of 30
 and baseline model 40
consociational democracy, in The Netherlands 128
conventional political participation
 definition of 1, 9
 measurement 9–15
Converse, Phillip 57, 72

Dahl, Robert 86
Dahrendorf, Ralph 5, 50
Davies, James 115, 124

de Gaulle, Charles 137
de Graaf, Cees xvii
de Toqueville, Alexis 115
Democrats 63, 68
diffuse support 132, 134 136–7, 162–70
dissatisfaction model, the 7–8
Dylan, Bob 28

Easton 8, 132
education 41–7, 72–5
elections 10, 15
elites 58, 59
elitist theory of democracy 2, 5–6, 72
environmentalist movement 29, 121
equality
 economic 83
 racial 83
 sexual 83
establishment/antiestablishment
 dimension of 101
 index of 101, 125, 130
expressive political action 140–3

Farah, Barbara G xvii
Flacks, Robert 182
formative affluence 91

general strike, in Britain 86–7
generation gap 148
government/opposition vote 125
great depression 59
green parties 185
Grofman, Irving 110, 115
Guttman scaling 12

Habermas, Jurgen 148
Heunks, Felix xvii
Huntingdon, Samuel P. 190

ideological concepts in politics 57, 68–71
 levels of 68–71
 index of 68
 and education 69–73
inactives
 definition of 30
 and baseline model 39
income 54–5

Index

incumbency 130
Inglehart, Ronald 7, 88, 89
instrumental political action 190-3
issue agenda 118-24, 172-3
interest in politics 76, 190-1
intergenerational value change 99
internal efficacy, index of 135

J-curve 115
Jennings, M. Kent 27
just deserts, measure of 112

Kaase, Max 15, 72
Kenniston, Kenneth 182
Klingemann, Hans D xvii, 61

left-right dimension 66, 125
left-right self anchoring scale 66, 80
levels of constraint in beliefs 81
Levels of ideological thought in politics 68-72
Levintin, Theresa 101
life cycle 99
Lijphart, Arend 128
lineage gap 151
Lipsett, Seymour Martin 2

MacFarlane, L.J. 19
Marsh, Alan 15, 17, 91
Maslow, Abraham 7, 60
mass communications 186
Marx, Karl 6, 115
medical care 120, 122
Miller, Warren 101
Muller, Edward 110, 115

Nazi Party 162
New Left 3, 6, 89, 187
New Liberalism 101
New Politics 88-9, 187
Nie, Norman 5, 33
Nixon, Richard 133

occupational prestige score 54, 124
Oedipal rebellion 148
Old Left 89
optimism, measures of 116

parent-child pairs 149
partisanship 126-7
peace movement 29
personal satisfaction, measures of 111-15

perception of privilege and underprivilege 126
Pierce, Roy 72
police 98-9
policy dissatisfaction, index of 118-24
political apathy 190-1
political action
  general model 89, 131-46
  measuring 9-28
  typolology 28-31
  social background to 33-55
  and the baseline model 33-55
political action repertory
  construction of 28-30
political authorities 132-4
political detachment 190-1
political importance of social equality 80-2
political regimes
political parties
  Christian Democratic 63
  Christlich Demokratische 63
  Union/Christlich Sozial Union 63
  Conservative Party 63, 167
  Communist Party 63
  Democratic Party 63
  Labour Party 63
  Partij van de Arbeid 63
  Republican Party 63
  Radical Party 63
  Socialist Party 63
  Socialist Party (Austria) 63
  Sozialdemokratische Partei 63
political socialisation 147-8
political trust, index of 165
postindustrial society 189-91
postmaterialist values 7, 86-108
potential for political violence, scale of 115
protest potential
  measurement of 15-24
  legitimacy of 24
  effectiveness of 24-5
  intentions towards 25-8
protesters
  definition of 30
  and the baseline model 50-3

recognition and understanding of an ideological mode of thought in politics 65-6
recognition of inequity, index of 126
reformists
  definition of 30

and the baseline model 49–50
relative deprivation 8, 110
revolutionary groups 98–9
Rosenmayr, Leopold xvii
Runciman, G. 110

sample xvii
sex 33–4
social class 54–5
social equality 80
Social Democrats, in Germany 69
Stokes, Donald 162
students 98–9
student revolution, in France 87
student sample, in Britain 104
socioeconomic status 54, 96–7
specific support, definition of 170–7
Spock, Dr 148
Stouthard, Phillip xvii
Subjective Political Competence 56
Suffragette Movement, in Britain 3
system responsiveness 113–7, 164–5

systems theory of politics 132

thermometer scale 98
Tilley, Charles 4
Treiman, Donald 54, 55, 124
Trotsky, Leon 194

unconventional political
 participation 1, 9, 36

V-curve 115
value model, the 6–7
value priorities 86–108
Verba, Sydney 5, 11, 33, 137
Vietnam War 3

Weimar Republic 162
Women's Movement 98
world war two 36, 89

zuilen 128

GPSR Compliance
The European Union's (EU) General Product Safety Regulation (GPSR) is a set of rules that requires consumer products to be safe and our obligations to ensure this.

If you have any concerns about our products, you can contact us on

ProductSafety@springernature.com

In case Publisher is established outside the EU, the EU authorized representative is:

Springer Nature Customer Service Center GmbH
Europaplatz 3
69115 Heidelberg, Germany

www.ingramcontent.com/pod-product-compliance
Ingram Content Group UK Ltd.
Pitfield, Milton Keynes, MK11 3LW, UK
UKHW041951230426
12048UKWH00008B/261